What people are saying...

1000 Tips for Teenagers is a collabo̶ with wisdom. It is a book for youth, but it also is a wonderfully insightful read for people of all ages. There is something for everyone as the topics covered within its pages range from deeply personal to day-to-day practical. Being a teenager can be confusing and complicated. During this time, 1000 Tips for Teenagers can be like a trusted companion. Anyone who cares about the teen in their life would do well to give them this book. It may just hold the wisdom, support and guidance your teen is looking for.

Linda Kiernan
Certified Passion Test Facilitator, Certified Life Coach, CH, BA
www.LindaKiernan.ca

This is NOT a book to read cover to cover. If you are looking for some long drawn out wordy book, this is NOT for YOU. Looking for some inspiration? Some guidance when dealing with all of life's curve balls perhaps? Open this book ANY WHERE and find what you need. Over and over again you'll find gems and jewels to live YOUR life. This book is not just for teens! Everyone young and old can benefit from this book. Compiled by the awesome Martin Presse and Kelly Falardeau best-selling author of "Self-Esteem Doesn't Come In A Bottle" she's at it again this time focusing on teens. Inspiring them to be themselves, love who they are, and to see life as an amazing journey. This time by reaching out to her friends and family asking them "What would you tell your teenager self if you could go back?" So open the book, be inspired, and know that YOU are not alone!

Aime Hutton
www.awakeninggoddess.com
www.wondergirlscamp.com

There is nothing tougher than being a teenager growing up in today's world, with the exception being a teenager without guidance from those who have been there and lived through it successfully. This tip book is focused solely on bringing light into the often dark places that our teenagers face. Without question it has in it the richest words of wisdom I have ever read. Kelly and Martin know that kids will listen because it's coming from the hearts of successful people all around the world.

Kellie Frazier founder of Connecting LLC
www.connecting101.org

Just finished reading "1000 Tips for Teenagers" - wow! I wish I had this when I was growing through my turbulent teens. There are some very good ideas, tips, and solid advice and inspiration which will help you, as a teen, or as a parent of a teen, navigate these important formative years. Bravo to my friends Kelly Falardeau and Martin Presse for drawing this wisdom together. This book needs to be in every household where there are teens in residence!

Bob 'Idea Man' Hooey,
2011 Spirit of CAPS recipient,
author of Speaking for Success
and 30 other success publications

This is one of the most inspiring and inspirational books for teens that I have read. Each section is filled with "easy to read" quotations that anyone can follow and invite into their lives. This will definitely help and motivate any teen, whatever their situation. My teens thought it was great and even I learned a few things. EMPOWERING.

Deborah Ward
Nova Scotia Burn Support- President
Canadian Burn Survivor Community - Secretary/Treasurer

1000 Tips for Teenagers

Co-Authored by
Best-Selling Author Kelly Falardeau,
Martin Presse
& 120 Other Great Friends

Cover done by Candace Lauman-Robichaud
Cover photography by Hillary, Simply Focused Photography
hill.ary.142@facebook.com
Thank you to our cover models: Jen Merriweather, Victoria Fehr, Brianne Doyle, Jena Lynne, Josi Lynnem, Cody Falardeau and Alex Falardeau
Edited by Jennifer Cockton, Tara Fitzgerald and Martin Presse

Kelly Falardeau and Martin Presse are available to speak at your events.
Email them at: 1000TipsForTeenagers@gmail.com or www.KellyFalardeau.com or www.MartinPresse.com

Dedication

This book is dedicated to my awesome kids,
Alexanna, Cody and Parker:

I wrote this book because you may not want to listen to my advice, but you may want to listen to all the other people in this book who will also have great advice for you and help you grow through your teenage years. Life is too short to be miserable; find ways to be happy in your lives and don't wait until you're an adult to be happy; be happy now, in the moment and discover your passion in your lives. Life is for the living and I will always love you three no matter what.

~ Love your Mom – Kelly Falardeau

My dedication goes out to the many who struggle each day to find their voice, their character and their spirit. You are not alone, you will find the answers.

Martin Presse

Note from Co-Author Kelly Falardeau

Last June, I had the great honour of being able to speak to 150 grade seven students and I allowed them to text me their questions so I could speak about what they wanted to hear. In that hour, I got 100 text messages and the first question was, "Have you ever contemplated suicide?" In fact, I got five questions about suicide. Wow!

I was shocked and at first didn't know how to answer it, but I decided that I must tell them how I prayed at night when I was a teenager. I used to pray by saying, "Dear God, please don't make me wake up in the morning, but if I have to, could you at least make me scar-less and pretty like all the other girls? Thank you, amen."

After that speech, I discovered my "why" in life. My "why" is that I don't ever want to see my own child or a friend's child commit suicide because I didn't help them and that's why this book is so important to me. This "why" is what gets me up every morning and gives me my fuel to work on our project and help the teens in this world, I want teens to know that even though suicide is at an all-time high, life is worth living and we haven't given up on them.

What is your "why" in life? Discover your "why" and whenever you are trying to choose between laying on the couch and doing nothing or getting up and being productive, you will choose being productive. I know because I do it every day when I wake up in the morning. I think to myself, would you like to lay on the couch and do nothing or would you like to get up, share your story and keep another teenager from committing suicide?

Kelly Falardeau

Introduction by Co-Author Martin Presse

Hi, I'm Martin Presse and this is Kelly Falardeau. We are the two people who created this book. We met while doing a radio interview. We immediately hit it off and decided to meet soon after the interview. We talked over dinner about growing up and how tough it can be for teenagers. We both felt that whatever challenges we faced, teenagers today have it far worse. We never had to deal with cyber bullying. For the most part any bullying ended on the playground. Kids today have to deal with it 24/7.

We initially decided to write a book called "Still Beautiful/Still Cool." Kelly would write about maintaining self-esteem from the girl's perspective and I would write it from the male perspective. The book is done but will be released in Jan 2013. We became so excited about that book that we decided to write a second book giving teenagers simple survival tips.

Initially we wanted to come up with one hundred, but the more we talked about the "tips" book the more other people wanted to become involved. Kelly came up with the idea of creating "1000 Tips for Teenagers" after seeing the massive flood of tips from friends and family.

We decided to focus on the tips book and create a whole program geared towards helping teens survive the difficult years. Along with that we wanted to help parents as well. Kelly and I have teens so we both know how turbulent those years can be. Our goal is simple. We want to help parents and teens maintain a high level of self-esteem. Kids with healthy and positive self-images have the tools to stand up for themselves and for those who can't stand up themselves. No longer will teenagers feel alone and misunderstood.

We hope you enjoy the book. The book will also be available on kindle and we have also created an App called "1000tips4teens." Parents and teens can browse the App together, play games, watch video and get to know the authors.

Martin Presse

Foreword

I was so excited when Kelly told me about the books for teenagers that she was co-authoring with Martin Presse. She began by describing the first book in the series, *Still Beautiful/Still Cool*. It had such powerful message and I wanted to know more. Then Kelly told me about the idea behind the spin-off book, *1000 Tips for Teenagers,* and I was hooked. I couldn't wait to get involved.

I found myself wondering, however, about how Kelly and Martin were going to come up with 1000 tips for teenagers all by themselves? It seemed like an insurmountable task. That was before I knew that the plan was to reach out to 100 amazing people who would each contribute 10 amazing tips. All of a sudden, the plan made perfect sense because after all, when you break what seems like an insurmountable challenge into smaller more manageable steps, that challenge becomes a plan.

I have two teenage children of my own and I know how overwhelming the teen years can be for young adults. I have witnessed firsthand how "insurmountable" some of their challenges can seem. What I love about *1000 Tips for Teenagers* is that not only does it inspire teens to dream big and reach for the stars, it also encourages them to break down their over-sized dreams and challenges into smaller, more manageable steps – to turn the challenge into a plan - just like Kelly and Martin did with their dream of writing this book.

When Kelly told me about all of the incredible people who wanted to write for the book and empower teens, perhaps I should have been surprised but I wasn't. There are so many who want to inspire the world to be a better place. So many people whom we can reach out to when we need a shoulder, when we need a lift, or when all we need is just one really amazing tip! I hope that the teenagers who read this book realize that they are not alone. They will never be alone. There is always someone to reach out to.

Please read this book with an open mind and encourage the teenagers in your life to do the same. Remember that one person's ideas may not resonate with you, but another's will. That is the beauty of this book. It is overflowing with something for everyone.

So feel free to flip through the pages, reaching out for the tips that feel like they were written just for you and when you're done reading, why not ask your teens which tips touched their hearts and why? Now that's the beginning of a great conversation.

These stories were written right from the hearts of 120 people who believe if even one of their tips helps a teenager, they have done their job and made a difference. The greatest gift that you can give in return is not only to read them but to share them and make them part of your life.

Toni Newman
Professional Catalyst
www.ToniNewman.com

A special "Thank You" to the following people who contributed their 10 tips for teenagers:

Kelly Falardeau
Martin Presse
Aime Hutton
Allison Orthner
Alvin Law
Amanda Welliver
Andre Lachance
Angela Schaefers
Angela Sladen de Rox
Annette Stanwick
Barb Scully
Bri Westhaver
Candace Lauman-Robichaud
Carly Turner
Carmen Jubinville
Carrie Kohan
Catherine Oshanek
Chad Hymas
Charmaine Hammond
Chet Gray Root
Cindy Rutter
Cynthia Segal
Dana Gamble
Dana Tremblay
David L McMillan
Deb Cautley
Denise Ouellette
Diane Shortridge
Dianna Bowes
Donna Reid
Dr Carmen Lynne
Dr Robyn Odegaard
Elizabeth Clark
Emily Adams

Fawna Bews
Gail Bamford
Gail Blackburn
Gemma Stone
Gina Parris
Greg Gazin
Helene Shaw
Iryna Synychak
Jack M Zufelt
Jaclyn Olsen
James 'Rambo' Smith
Jana Beeman
Janeen Norman
Jason Olandesca
Jennifer Belanger
Jennifer Cockton
Jeri Tourand
Jill Ethier
Jodi Dawson
Joe Calloway
Joe Kovach
John Su
John Westhaver
Juliette Miles
Kari Dunlop
Karli Butler
Kellie Frazier
Kelly Romanchuk
Kevin Metz
Kim Berges
Kim Berube
Kimberly Langford
Kimberly Schick-Puddicombe
Klarque Garrison

Erika Chell
Lani R Donaldson
Lauren E Miller
Leanne Power
Lily Chatterjee
Linda Kiernan
Lisa Larter
Lisa Litwinski
Lisa McCarthy
Liz Raymond
Lynda Fraser
Lynnet McKenzie
Malcolm
Mariana Konsolos
Mark Ivancic
Marla Martenson
Michael McDonnell
Michele Ashley
Mitch Reynolds
Nadine Shenher
Nancy Battye
Nancy Paul
Patricia Ogilvie
Paul Edwards
Rachel Olsen
Rebecca Brae
Malcolm Dayton

Laina P Orlando
Regina AH Ariel
Renee HolBrook
Rhonda Elko
Rita Jaskolla
Romeo Marquez Jr
Shannon Berry
Sharon Thom
Sheena Johnson
Sheila Unique
Shelley Goldbeck
Shelley Hladysh Suzuki
Sheri Fink
Sherisse Janvier
Steve Sapato
Suzanne Mazzarella
Suzy Manning
Tanner Michael Hartmann
Ted Rubin
Tish Lethbridge
Toni Newman
Traci Sparling
Tracy Meyn
Trisha Savoia
Troy Payne
Wendy Darling
Lisa Litwinski

10 TIPS FOR GREAT SELF-ESTEEM

#1. True self-esteem doesn't come from ANY kind of a bottle. You may get a little temporary liquid courage from a bottle of alcohol or pills, but it won't give you any lasting self-esteem. And that's the same as make-up, anti-aging cream or injecting chemicals into your face. None of those things will give you true self-esteem. Learn where your true self-esteem comes from – your heart and soul, not in any kind of bottle.

#2. The ultimate secret to great self-esteem is to learn how to make yourself feel great. It's as simple as that. Learn how to treat yourself great, you will feel great. Treat yourself like crap and you will feel like crap.

#3. The universe will provide you with what you want in your life, but you have to ask for it and then you have to recognize the signs that it's giving it to you. The universe does not send you a text message and say "Hey, I'm going to give you whatever you asked for on this day." It doesn't work that way, it gives you subtle little clues and it's up to you to take advantage of them and act on them.

#4. Do not allow other people's insecurities or comments to bring you down. If I was to let it get me down every time someone stared at me, I'd be in a hole forever. Despite the fact that at one time I was considered the ugly scar-faced girl, it didn't mean that when people were staring at me they automatically thought I was ugly. They could have been thinking how cute I was. I'll never know what everyone is thinking and it's none of my business. It only matters what my opinion is of me.

#5. Find your passion in life and do what brings you joy not pain. For example, if you hate piano lessons and would rather ride horses, do it. Find a way, even a small way. When you do what you love and bring joy to your life, you'll be great at it. When you do what you hate, you can't get good at it because you don't want to. Find your passion and do what you love.

#6. Take the "T" out of can't. Quit saying, "I can't do that." How do you do that when it seems like the only option is to quit? If there is something you really want to do, don't say "I can't do that," because when you do, your mind will agree with you and say "yes, you're right, I can't do it." It's only natural you won't be able to achieve your goal because you've already convinced yourself you can't do it before you even tried. If you really want to do it, you need to take the T out of can't and say to yourself, "How can I do that...?" When you say that to yourself, you open up your mind to the possibility of doing it and your mind will come up with the solution on HOW to do it.

When you ask yourself a question your conscious mind will generally want to find an answer. If you just give yourself a statement that says "I can't do that", you're right, you can't and your mind won't even try to find a way to do it. Your mind will just agree with you. Simple as that. So, to take the "T" out of can't, just ask yourself, "how can I do..." and fill in the blank.

For example, when I decided I wanted to write a book with 1000 tips for teens, I could have had two different thoughts. I could have thought "I can't write a book of 1000 tips for teens, that would be impossible, I don't know 1000 tips" or "How can I write a book of 1000 tips for teens?" Obviously I thought the latter question because the book is written.

When I asked "How?" the answer came quickly, "How about asking 100 people to write 10 tips each and then you'll get your 1000 tips written for you." And that's what I did, I started asking people for their tips and voila we had a book written. So don't say to yourself "I can't do that", instead ask, "How can I do that?" and the answer will come to you eventually.

#7. I'm going to hit you hard with this one, suicide. I have some strong feelings about it. If you succeed at committing suicide, death in this lifetime is FINAL. It's not like the movies, there's no coming back to redo your life. There is no more texting your BFF, no more sleepovers, no more hugging your favorite pet, no more Justin Bieber or One Direction concerts, no more facebook or Twitter or going shopping with your BFF. There's pain. There's sadness. There's broken hearts, lots of them. There's a funeral with all your real friends and friends you didn't know you had with tears in their eyes and sadness in their hearts because they didn't help you and didn't see it coming. There's parents wondering what they did wrong and wishing they could have one more chance to do it all again to recognize the signs and redo what they did wrong. Do you want to cause that kind of pain to yourself and others?

Don't take attempting suicide lightly because you just may go too far and actually succeed. Reach out for help if you're thinking about suicide. People do want to help, but YOU HAVE TO ASK for it. I know, because I was there. As a teenager I used to pray at night to my God and say, "Dear God, please don't make me wake up in the morning, but if I have to could you at least please make me scar-less so I can be pretty like all the other girls in school. Thank you. Amen." Look where I am now, I went from the ugly scar-faced girl to Best-Selling Author and Top 10 Most Influential Speaker and a recipient of the Queen Elizabeth II Diamond Jubilee medal all because I didn't quit life when I first got burnt as a two-year-old.

#8. Find ways to empower your friends and people you don't know instead of pick on them. Give out more compliments. It's so much more fun to make people feel great than to cut them down with mean comments.

#9. Discover the beauty in your heart and soul because it matters more than your outer beauty. The truth is, when I finally accepted I was beautiful no matter what anyone else thought, I started getting told I was beautiful, sexy, gorgeous, everything I wanted to be called and I have a very imperfect body. I have scars covering 75% of my body. When I stopped looking in the mirror and seeing all my ugly scars and started to see all my little parts that I loved about me, like my big beautiful green eyes, my cute little nose, my cute burnt ear, my laugh, my sense of humour and my hot ass (yes, there's a cute love story to go along with that and it's in my first book *No Risk No Rewards*) I started to see that I was truly a beautiful person. I didn't need to look like Angelina Jollie in order to be beautiful, I just needed to accept me and love my little parts (check out a special program that Kellie Frazier and I produced called www.LoveYourLittleParts.com to learn more about how you can do that too). When you look in the mirror QUIT calling yourself ugly. Find great names you want to call yourself and quit beating yourself up. You're beautiful just the way you are.

#10. Life is just beginning for you and you've only just begun. When you are a teenager, you think your parents are old and you will never get as old as they are. Think again my friend. You will get that age and you need to know that just because that guy or girl doesn't like you now, it doesn't mean he won't like you later, he just might be too scared to show you.

I never had boyfriends in school and it wasn't because they didn't like me, it was because they were too scared of stepping out. I didn't know that as a kid. I didn't find out until I was an adult. I thought it was because I was the ugly scar-faced girl that I didn't have boyfriends, but it wasn't that at all. The guys were scared of being judged by their friends. They didn't know how to handle the criticism they might get if they liked the girl who was "different." You will meet many people in your life, you don't need to find someone in school to settle down with right away. You have plenty of time to find your soul mate.

I didn't have my first boyfriend until I was 18. How did I know the guys were scared? Because I found out when I was 45 that one of my friends who knew me since I was only three, admitted to me that he had always loved me, even through high school. He was my first kiss at 18, but he was too scared to take that step with me because he didn't know what his friends would think.

I ended up marrying another man and had three beautiful kids with him. So even if your label is the ugly scar-faced girl when you're a teenager, yes you can still fall in love, get married and have kids. Although I am now happily unmarried, I believe I am still going to find my true love and don't regret going through my marriage.

Kelly Falardeau, international speaker and best-selling author of *No Risk No Rewards* and *Self-Esteem Doesn't Come in a Bottle* and a recipient of the Queen Elizabeth II Diamond Jubilee Medal. She is also a burn survivor since the age of two. www.KellyFalardeau.com

10 TIPS FOR TEENAGERS BY CO-AUTHOR MARTIN PRESSE

#1. Change your internal dialogue. Tell yourself how great you are 100's of times a day.

#2. Never be afraid to walk away. There is tremendous power in making that decision.

#3. Today is just one day. It will never define who you are for an eternity.

#4. Whatever you are going through will pass. It might take a day, a week or a year, but know this for sure, it will pass.

#5. Who you are at 15, 16, 17 or even 18 is not who you will be at 25. You will be stronger. Life will do that do you.

#6. Treat yourself...you deserve it.

#7. Exercise. Your lungs and your heart will thank you later

#8. Your goals are all yours. Do not ever let anybody define what you can and cannot achieve.

#9. Life is like a deck of cards. Each day you will be dealt a new hand, you may not like it but wait till tomorrow, you will be dealt a new hand. It's what you do with the hand you're dealt that matters most.

#10. Each person you meet has a story to tell. Somewhere in that story is their essence. Somewhere in your story is your essence. Find it and you will find who you really are.

Martin Presse
2008 World Championship of Speaking Finalist
Comedy Stage Hypnotist
Author of "The Booya Guide to Great Public Speaking"
www.MartinPresse.com

10 TIPS ON CONNECTING TO OTHERS

#1. Be open. Being mature means to be bold and direct, but it also means being open. Expand your heart and mind to learning new things. Say 'YES' to opportunities.

#2. Listen. This is one of the most important skills you can ever acquire. It means to truly hear what another person is saying without opening your mouth. Make eye contact. These are gifts you give to others - including strangers.

#3. Expose. There are no secrets in life - have you noticed? There is nothing hidden that doesn't come out into the open eventually. Expose what you need to so you can start with a clean slate.

#4. Show compassion. There is nothing more honoring to someone than being compassionate toward them. It is not pity. Compassion is love.

#5.Understand. When you went through a tough time, wouldn't it have been nice to find one other person who understood what you were going through?

#6. Be brave. This is living with courage. Step up when you are asked to and know something good will come out of it.

#7. Give yourself time. Be patient with yourself. Nothing worth living for happens overnight. If you can do this, you will also be patient with others.

#8. Celebrate. When you feel goodness come to the surface of your spirit, celebrate it. Smile, clap, sing, dance - your celebration becomes an inspiration to others.

#9. Genuinely care. One thing this world lacks right now are people who care.

#10. Connect. If you can do all the above, you will have great relationships for the rest of your life. That is true success.

Kellie Frazier is an author, speaker and trainer who has written and published hundreds of articles, was featured on CBS/CNN Radio, Motivational Radio, and authored books such as Raising Fearless Teens, "Connecting Faith, Hope and Love", and "It's About Time YOU Showed UP," while contributing to other books such as "Careers from the Kitchen Table." Kellie is truly inspired by men and women who navigate life with logic and compassion and who believe that LOVE truly is what matters most. www.connecting101.org

10 TIPS TO BE YOUR REAL SELF
(because your real self rocks!)

#1. There is only one you in all of space and time.

#2. You are here for a reason. You have a purpose. The world needs you!

#3. All chords are needed for the song of Life. If you don't play your chord, that piece of music is missing from the world.

#4. Your heart will only be fully happy when you are fully your true self.

#5. When you are NOT Real, the love others give you will be for the image you portray. Only love for your Real self feels real.

#6. Your Real self is also your most beautiful, powerful, and brilliant self.

#7. You came here to this planet to be YOU! You came here to experience and express exactly who you really are.

#8. When you are Real, you become stronger, lighter, and brighter.

#9. When you are Real, you give others permission to also be Real.

#10. When you are Real, you become a true leader and the Hero of your own life. This fulfills the greatest desire of your own heart and the greatest desire of the world.

By **Lynnet McKenzie** www.OpeningToEcstasy.com

10 TIPS FOR HIGHLY SUCCESSFUL TEENS

Teenagers are awesome! Most have a zest for life, are anxious to learn new things and are fun to be around. Some struggle so I want to share some wisdom that I wish I had known when I was in my teens. "Learn wisdom in thy youth" (Alma 37:35) was a scripture that I did not know about and I paid a very severe and unpleasant price for it. I would not want any teenager to go through what I did. I trust that you will benefit from my experience, the knowledge and wisdom that I now share all around the world.

#1. How and what you think matters. It affects how you act and the level of happiness you can have. Thoughts are the cause all your actions. Do an action every day and soon it is a habit. Habits are what make up your character...who you are. Who you become and the kind of life you lead will be as a direct result of your character. Therefore, from this day forward decide to think good, positive and right thoughts about yourself and your future.

Positive thoughts include, I am capable of learning anything I really want to, I am a good person, making mistakes is a part of life so I am okay with me when I do, and I don't need to get an "A^s" to be smart or okay. I can do and be whatever I want with my whole heart. Decide every day to be a strong, powerful, good, moral person.

Seek advice from qualified people who know how to think properly about whatever it is you are interested in becoming or doing.

The following are examples of wrong or limiting or even deadly, thinking. Be careful not to allow yourself to be limited by wrong thinking.

If you put a buzzard in a pen that is 6 feet by 8 feet and is entirely open at the top, the bird, in spite of its ability to fly, will be an absolute prisoner. The reason is that a buzzard always begins a flight from the ground with a run of 10 to 12 feet. Without space to run, as is its habit, it will not even attempt to fly, but will remain a prisoner for life in a small jail with no top.

The ordinary bat that flies around at night, a remarkably nimble creature in the air, cannot take off from a level place. If it is placed on the floor or flat ground, all it can do is shuffle about helplessly until it reaches some slight elevation from which it can throw itself into the air. Then, at once, it takes off like a flash.

A bumblebee, if dropped into an open tumbler, will be there until it dies, unless it is taken out. It never sees the means of escape at the top, but persists in trying to find some way out through the sides near the bottom. It will seek a way where none exists, until it completely destroys itself.

#2. Treat others the way you would want to be treated. This is a variation of the Golden Rule which says "Do unto others what you would have others do unto you". Be the one who is kind, considerate, nice and helpful. A little teasing is okay but a steady dose of putdowns or mean statements are something that you should not participate in. Rise above that sort of behavior. If others are being thoughtless, mean or doing things that are not acceptable decide NOT to join in.

#3. Decide today, right now, that you are a valuable human being. As is. Period. Do not let your self-worth be determined by money or lack of it; how popular you are or are not; what your grades are, your physical appearance, talents or lack of them. You have value because you were born. Your brain can learn how to do and be just about anything your heart wants. The truth is that you can learn whatever you need to have a successful life's experience. By the way...I promise you that as you mature you will find that you have many talents. It will be fun discovering them. When I was a teen I never dreamed in a million years that I would be a best-selling author or that I would be traveling all over the world speaking to audiences on success!

#4. Never give up! We all make mistakes. We all get let down and have our feelings hurt. Every human being fails..... not just once but many times. It doesn't matter how many times we fall as long as we get up one more time than we fall down. Doing that is one of the things that makes a person a success in whatever they really want. Did you know......

➢ The world famous basketball player, Michael Jordan, was cut from his high school basketball team? He went home and locked himself in his bedroom and cried.

➤ In his first three years in the automotive business, Henry Ford, the creator of the Ford automobile, went bankrupt twice?

➤ Einstein was disappointed, but not defeated when his Ph.D dissertation was rejected saying it was irrelevant and fanciful?

➤ Walt Disney went bankrupt several times before he created Disneyland?

➤ Decca Recording Company turned down the "Beatles" because they did not like their sound.

Remember this....failure is an event.... not a person. You may fail at things but YOU are never a failure!

#5. Friends matter. Choose your friends carefully. They will greatly influence how you think and act. A true friend will encourage you to be your best self and you feel great around them. To have good friends be one yourself. (For the Strength of the Youth Booklet by The Church of Jesus Christ of Latter Day Saints) Be the kind of friend that others want to be with because you encourage them and they feel good around you.

#6. Respect your body. Do not put anything into it that could cause you to lose your ability to act and think clearly or become addicted. Your body is where your spirit lives so treat that "house" like it is a palace. Stay away from drugs, tobacco and alcohol.

#7. Media and entertainment. A lot of the media and entertainment is good and very fun. Some things are harmful. Stay away from anything that is vulgar, immoral or pornographic in any way. These things weaken you as a person and can destroy true happiness.

#8. Sexual purity. Physical intimacy is one of the biggest challenges teenagers deal with. There are a lot of reasons not to have premarital sex. Loss of self-esteem, unwanted children, STDs, lives turned upside down, adoptions, and abortions are some of the big ones. As a girl never use your body to be popular or liked by guys. You will always end up feeling bad. Sex between a husband and wife is beautiful. Decide today to wait until you are married and I promise you will be glad you did.

#9. Integrity. Be a person of high integrity. Always. Being a person of integrity and someone others can trust takes courage and commitment to always do what's right. Always be totally honest in everything you do and say. Do not lie, cheat, steal or shoplift. These things hurt you as well as others.

#10. You are never alone. This is very important for you to know and believe. I personally know that you have a Heavenly Father who loves you and will help you. He will guide you and support you. He can help you do things you don't think you can. He did all those things for me and I know He will do all that for you too. All you have to do is look up to Him in faith and pray for his help.

In many ways, people are like the buzzard, the bat, and the bumblebee I mentioned earlier. They struggle with their problems and frustrations, never realizing that all they have to do is look up in faith and ask God for help.

Jack M. Zufelt, "Mentor to Millions" Author of the #1 best-selling book, **The DNA of Success,** www.dnaofsuccess.com (FREE video there for you)

10 TIPS TO LEADING A GRATEFUL LIFE

On any given day STUFF can happen that makes you feel as though life sucks. Not so. You see the key to leading a glorious, inspired, big gulps of wonderful kind of life is to believe you ARE already doing it. Now I know it is easy to get sidetracked with all the challenges you can be faced with so I created these 10 tips to help you lead a grateful life.

#1. Wake up every day with a grateful heart. Before you are even out of bed, you should be giving thanks for waking up to lead another day.

#2. Treat your body well. This body is the only one you get. Nourishing, exercising and respecting it will allow you to accomplish what you were sent here to do.

#3. All you need to be on any given day is KIND. If you live by this and look for ways to practice kindness your world will be filled with wondrous moments of experiences you cannot even imagine.

#4. When old people talk, listen. Their stories led the world to you and are filled with the advice of having been there. This is especially important for your grandparents – listen with respect.

#5. Laugh out loud and often, but never at the expense of someone else.

#6. Find a cause that matters to you and volunteer.

#7. Dance, play lacrosse or the trumpet or music loud and often. The point is to find activities you love to spend your free time doing. Hang out with people that appreciate your talent and never, ever apologize for what you like.

#8. Although it doesn't feel like it sometimes, know that "This too shall pass". Write that out on a Post-it and put it on your mirror. It will help you appreciate the good times a little more and more importantly, it will lift your heart during those times when you think you simply cannot manage the sadness. Remember, this too shall pass.

#9. Approach every new situation or person with a sense of wonder as you don't know yet what they can and will teach you.

#10. Each and every night before you go to sleep, write down in a journal or repeat in your mind a few times – three things that took place that day for which you are grateful. Have this be your last thought before you drift off to sleep.

The point is to be grateful. Look for a new way every day that you can expand what you already do as a grateful person. As an individual, you have the choice to be in a good mood, or horribly upset and frustrated by where you are, so choose to be happy. Scientists have studied gratitude and have found that it can be something we control. Our happiness reduces stress and illness, improves sleep habits and most importantly draws people to you.

By making gratitude a part of your everyday life the world becomes a thing of wonder and grace rather than a scary, depressing planet where we just get by. So I challenge you to take a 30-day Gratitude Challenge. Start a journal and write out how you are feeling emotionally, physically and mentally. Over the course of the month document all those little elements of your day that were tiny blessings. At the end of the month, review where you were when you started and see how much better you feel. You may be surprised that such a simple shift makes room for such monumental change. So c'mon, BE grateful!

By **Dana Tremblay**. For more information and helpful tools useful for leading a grateful life visit www.gratitudeandsoulshine.com or on Facebook at http://www.facebook.com/GratitudeandSoulshine.

10 TIPS FOR STRESS RELIEF

#1. First tip is to remember that you are not alone on this journey. God is with you, whether or not you are aware of that truth or not. After having a life after death experience due to a certain chemo treatment a few years ago, I can personally assure you that God exists and is very much aware of everything that you feel stresses you out in life. If you have not started talking to God every day then I invite you to start today. There is nothing to be afraid of in this life because everything passes away except God. As I worked with youth for over 20 years I had many moments when I was asked, "how do I know God is with me?" I would simply say, "Ask Him to show you that He is with you, ask for the eyes to see, ears to hear and the heart to respond to all of the ways He will come to you in your day." Ask Him any questions you want and then guess what He might say back. This opens up the communication channel between you and God. A few years ago as I was going through advanced cancer, a good friend of mine died. Before she left this earth she said, "Lauren, I know how much you love robins so when I figure out how to come to you from the other side, look for me in the robins." A week after she passed on, I was driving in my car, missing my friend, I started to cry so hard I couldn't see the street. As I pulled over this bird flew straight at my windshield, so close that I thought it would run into it and then it flew straight up revealing its red chest (a robin). Just then, several other robins dived bombed my windshield, all of them robins. My friend figured it out. Remember you are not alone on your journey of life. You are surrounded continually by a great cloud of support and love. Knowing this will decrease your anxiety in life each day.

#2. OK so here is the deal, stress is the label you place on a biological response to a perceived threatening situation. When something outside you happens that you feel threatened by, your body reacts in 3 main ways: fight, flight or freeze mode. You are not in a physical jungle anymore as your ancestors were. They worried about being attacked by a wild animal. The jungle now exists in your head. That's right, in your mind, the thoughts you think create the stress or anxiety you feel in your body and ultimately your reality. Your thoughts form your choices and your choices you form your life. As I went through advanced cancer a few years ago, I had the choice every day of what I wanted to focus on. I could have focused on the fact that I lost all my hair, I was going through 2 years of chemo, 14 surgeries, 6 weeks of daily radiation and a lot of physical weakness. Whenever I made the choice to focus on what was working out for me verses what was not working out for me I noticed by body started to break down even more. When I started to focus on what was working out for me, my body started to heal. I could still see, hear, walk, laugh and love.

#3. Stay awake at the GATE of your thoughts. This is the place where you either sink your own ship or have the ability to ride the waves of life. Life unfolds all around you throughout each day, you start out in a place of observation and then you label what is happening around you as good or bad. As soon as you place that label, then your emotions respond. For example, you get up for school, have breakfast and do what you have learned to do to get your body to your first class of the day. Many times you are just going through the motions until something happens outside of you that bumps you off the observation course and you label that experience as threatening and negative. All of a sudden your mood drops and the dark clouds come in. Maybe a friend of yours had a bad morning and did not respond the way you expected them to. Way too often you jump to a negative conclusion that something must be wrong about you. What if you woke up tomorrow and you had the ability to take nothing anybody says or does personally? Next time this happens and you feel your heart start to race (the biological response to a threatening situation) say this, "the more upset I am about what they just said or did, the more I am able to remember that I am OK and I have the ability to choose my response. I am willing to love and accept myself even though they said that or did that and I choose to increase my confidence in my ability to come up with a creative solution."

#4. How does stress show up for you and how do you handle it? Do you run from threatening situations through avoidance or intentional silence? Perhaps you're a fighter and when someone says or does something that threatens your personal space you go into an attack response. Another response that you might use is to freeze. Have you ever said, "I just froze, I didn't know what to say back" or "I don't know what to do in this situation, I feel stuck." Did you know you have a very special part of your brain located by the brainstem called the RAS (Reticular Activating System)? The RAS is responsible for tuning into whatever you choose to focus in on. The cool thing is, you have the ability to choose what it will seek to find for you in your world. For example if you consciously make the choice to tune into positive relationships based on the belief that you are capable of awesome relationships with your peers then guess what, your RAS will start to seek and find awesome relationships by helping you tune into them. On the flip side, if you don't believe that you are capable of creating awesome relationships because maybe you have past situations that caused you to create a program in your system that says, "nothing ever works out for me in my friendships" then your RAS will tune into information that backs that belief up. Take some time to write down what you really want to see in your relationships, focusing on the positive and keep that list some where you can see it each day. Thanks to your RAS, whatever you choose to focus on GROWS BIGGER quickly and you are the gatekeeper of that focus. That's a lot of power you have so choose wisely what you focus on each day because your body is listening.

#5. Stress is simply a signal in your body (lack of focus, agitation, insomnia, migraines, back pain, mood swings,

depression) giving you the opportunity to identify and adjust your perception of any situation. I have worked with youth groups for 20 years and I was always amazed when groups came back from a mission trip helping people who virtually had no material possessions, warm water, safe housing or a guarantee that they would eat another meal, their entire perception of their life shifted. When asked what they gained from being in a 3rd world country many of them said, "It gave me instant perspective of what is truly important to me and I feel badly about how much I complain when these people are just looking for their next meal." Are you feeling frustrated about your life? Go down to your local soup kitchen and serve the homeless, you will find your perspective quickly changes and your sense of purpose lights up inside.

#6. Watch out for the drug of approval. Before you were 5-years-old you did not care much about what other people thought of you. You would dance when you felt like dancing, laugh when you wanted to laugh, asked for what you wanted without shrinking back, and went for whatever you felt like going for without worrying about what people would think. You also freely expressed how you felt. The drug of approval is like a little serpent that crawls its way into your life and robs you of your God given ability to simply be you. Remember this, you are not the opinions or responses of those people around you. Understanding this now this will save you a lot of heartache. Once you release your need for certain reactions from your peers you will return to that free experience of being you.

#7. The last 20 minutes before you fall asleep are very powerful moments. Whatever you focus on during those last few minutes of the day will drop into your subconscious mind and re-emerge the next day. At the end of your day write down 3 things you liked about yourself in that day. For example, "I like the way I _____ "and fill in the blank. Then write down how you were blessed by other people or God: "I loved the sunset tonight." Next ask yourself this question, "where would I have wanted to add more love for God, myself and others throughout my day? End with saying out-loud 3 things you are grateful for in that day. Sometimes you will feel like saying, "I'm not grateful for anything, I had a horrible day." When this is the case break it down to the little things that for many people are just a dream, "I am thankful for food, shelter and a warm shower." Remember, whatever YOU choose to focus on will grow BIGGER thanks to your RAS.

#8. Laugh each day even if it's fake. When you laugh you lower stress hormones in the body. Stress has been linked to all kinds of physical ailments such as heart disease. Make it a daily practice to laugh. Laughter boosts your immune system and oxygenates your cells creating a healthy atmosphere in your body. Next time you feel the dark cloud coming over your mood try making yourself laugh. When you think you have nothing to laugh about, act your way into laughing. Studies show even if you fake laugh you still get the positive benefits in your earth suit. You will usually crack yourself up in the process.

#9. Dance and Exercise your body every day. When you get up and move your body you help drain toxins. Try bouncing up and down on the balls of your feet while you use your fingertips to tap on your thymus. Your thymus is located two inches down below the U-shaped dip at the base of your neck. This will also help relax your body. When you sit at your computer for more than an hour get up and do this exercise, you will find when you return to work you get more done because you are able to concentrate better.

#10. Next time you feel anxious try an energy psychology like EFT, Emotional Freedom Technique, often referred to as acupuncture without the needles (founded by a Gary Craig, an engineer). To learn how to specifically do it, contact me and I will give you the directions.

Lauren E Miller, Founder of Stress Solutions University, International Speaker, Award Winning International Best Selling Author, has received national and international recognition including Redbook, Ladies Home Journal, Family Circle, Discovery, Lifetime, CNBC, MSNBC and the International Journal of Healing and Care. Utilizing Stress Solutions University.com, bi-monthly Live Stress Relief Hotseat Video Calls, workshops, conferences and 1:1 programs, Lauren equips people globally with mindset skills and physiological techniques to de-stress their lives, regain inner clarity and step into personal excellence.

For more information on Lauren E Miller please visit her websites: www.laurenEmiller.com
www.stresssolutionsuniversity.com
www.stresssolutionsuniversity.com/stressreliefhotseat

10 HAPPINESS TIPS FOR ERASING STINKIN' THINKIN'

What's stinkin' thinkin'? It's *YOUR* mind chatter that nags you about how you "can't" "won't" "shouldn't" and constantly reminds you about what you "stink at"!

However, it's only your thoughts!

Teens sometimes a false notion that if "he" asks you out or if "she" smiles back at you, then you can feel good about yourself. The truth is, "he" or "she" won't always be there for you no matter how much you want to believe that!

Happiness comes from the way you think. That's it!

The following list of how to control your own stinkin' thinkin' has had such amazing response I wanted to share them with you here.

This will take about two minutes to read and I promise you, if you have a desire to feel better, are teachable and can follow directions, even one of these will restore your energy, help you regain your focus and give you more confidence in your life! So here goes:

#1. Be mindful of who you hang around all day long. I know, I know, I hear you saying, "Ya but... we have to be in classes with them!" You will encounter obnoxious people every day! But you don't have to spend all day with them. When you become aware of how much time you spend with a negative person, (including your family) give more time for yourself. Oh yes and delete them from your social media profiles!

#2. Put up boundaries. Physical boundaries help determine who may touch us and under what circumstances. Mental boundaries give us freedom to have our own thoughts and opinions. Emotional boundaries help you to deal with your own emotions and disengage from the harmful, manipulative emotions of others. A boundary is as simple as knowing when to say YES and when to say NO. Then ask for help!

#3. Be a Duck! Remember you don't have to receive or even consider some of the hurtful negative things people say and do! You're laughing at "Be a Duck!" Did you know that a duck's feathers repel water? Water beads off the duck's back. This is a powerful strategy you want to learn to do when someone says bad things to you. *Let it roll off your back!*

In the case of bullying and abuse, you want to walk away and regroup your thinking. However, you might also want to say, *"Listen I have too much love for myself to permit you to speak to me that way, so when you want to behave like a sane person, we can continue our discussion."* Cut it off. Make a decision to end the downers! YOU are worth more! And ask for help!

#4. Learn to FOCUS quickly on the things that are positive, worthy of praise, and noteworthy. Happiness is something you can choose to be. Easier said than done? Actually it's quite simple. With only a few seconds of refocusing your attention on feeling just a little better or appreciating what's in front of you, you begin to change. Holding that focus for at least 17 seconds can begin to make better.

A scale from feelings, from best to worst would look something like this:

- Joy/love/appreciation
- enthusiasm/eagerness/happy
- hopefulness
- boredom
- pessimism
- frustration/impatience
- worry
- blame
- revenge
- anger
- jealousy
- fear/grief/depression/despair/powerlessness

The thing that matters most is that you consciously reach for a better feeling. So that means if you are angry, you do yourself a huge favour just by getting yourself to worrying or even bored! Sound silly? It works! Then learn to move up this scale a little at a time.

#5. Stand up straight! Posture represents positive body language. This is totally about thinking tall as much as it is standing tall. Stand up straight, shoulders back, breathe deeply from your chest, and look upwards. This posture sends a message to your brain: be alert, resourceful. Use this technique when you need a boost or a change in attitude.

#6. Manage your thoughts as they come up. Do you guard the thoughts you have about yourself as though you fear someone else could hear you thinking? Do you protect every thought and opinion, every hour, constantly keeping track to make sure nothing slips out in conversation? Are you literally afraid of speaking up because you believe someone will criticize or laugh at you?

This is a by-product of a "suspicious state of mind". Managing your thoughts is a lot different than being fearful of speaking out and thinking you will be found out. When you realize it's **SUPER EASY** to share your opinion, which is the "confident state of mind" you want to cultivate, you'll stop distrusting. You'll manage your opinions, but you won't slip into a hesitant way and live in fear and doubt.

Thus, another myth! Control. Control is a symptom of suspicion. Becoming aware of your thoughts is actually the opposite. An example is rather than fearing you will be picked on and deciding to hide, instead, you could challenge yourself to be brave at least once each day – no matter what! Nothing more needs to be said. What a wise decision – give it a try – challenge yourself – you're the only one who has your well-being in mind!

#7. Use affirmations to change limiting thoughts. Dr. Wayne Dyer's *Excuses Begone* lists some valuable affirmations. Here are a few that work very well for excuses. (Excuse listed first, then the positive affirmation)

⅄ It will be difficult – I have the ability to accomplish any task I set my mind to with ease and comfort.

⅄ I don't deserve it – I am a Divine creation, a piece of God.

Therefore, I cannot be undeserving.

⅄ I'm not smart enough – I am a creation of the Divine mind; all is perfect and I am a genius in my own right.

⅄ I'm too scared – I can accomplish anything I put my mind to, because I know that I am never alone.

#8. Create your ideal life! Sure, I hear you. You're too young! Actually, the sooner you identify what you truly want, the sooner it will appear in your life! Let me ask you this first. Is there always a reason for why you never quite believed you were excellent just the way you are?

Many of you might be laughing at this point and that's a good sign. Others might be feeling completely sick to their stomach and that's a good sign as well... as long as you do something with that emotion rising up in you.

You are excellent just as you are and you are entitled to feel great! That means you are also entitled to set out a life plan that includes your values, desires and best foot forward!

Let's uncover a few beliefs about your ideal life:

⅄ You'll want to identify what your beliefs are in these areas: Health & fitness. Intellectual life, Emotional life, My character, My love life, My social life, My career, My quality of life, My vision.

⅄ First, identify what your premise or beliefs are in each of the categories above that **limits** you from having the best in each.

⅄ Now write down a belief for each that **supports** you having the best in each.

Great effort! Here's how to change your beliefs to empowering ones:

⅄ Model the behaviours and beliefs of people you admire

⅄ Learn their belief systems

⅄ Analyze their actions, rituals, lifestyles

⅄ Read biographies and opinions of people who inspire you

⅄ Begin to do some the things that they do!

#9. The most powerful remedy to erase 'stinkin thinkin'

Forgive. Start with yourself and then others. Do not exclude anyone or any situation. I realize it's easier said than done but having experienced bullying and rejection personally in my life as a teen, I can say with full confidence, "you deserve to let it go." You deserve to be free. Do whatever it takes to get to the other side of that pain and keep short accounts.

#10. If you knew you could not fail, what would you do?

Be realistic. Write your ideal vision down: Your expectations of your teen experiences must be objective and not governed by your emotions. Be willing to go the extra mile, take the extra time and do whatever it takes to get input on what you can expect in your grade, home life, and work. Masterminds and mentoring help tremendously with this. Ask for help! And write down your vision. Revisit it every 3 months and see how much it changes... how much you've changed!

Remember you have the power to change your thoughts from stinkin' to supportive.

When you realize that by changing your mind and reaching for a better feeling thought, it is impossible for you to ever again be bullied, afraid or stay depressed. Impossible! **Your mind is the only place that freedom and change will ever occur. If you're serious about feeling better more often, test out one of these top tips.**

The power of your thoughts is everything. Give yourself permission now – it's your head, your thoughts, your life!

Patricia Ogilvie is a former junior high school teacher, certified business and life coach, Patricia Ogilvie has helped hundreds of people transform ideas, services and personal situations into successes. She guides you by teaching simple tools you can use over and over to unlock your power and potential for a vibrant lifestyle. She believes in you whether you want your business presence to excel, or get your personal lifestyle in order – let her help you. Contact Patricia at www.patriciaogilvie.com

10 TIPS FOR A GREAT ATTITUDE AND A BRIGHT FUTURE

Do you ever look at others and wonder how they can be so happy? Everything seems to be going their way and your life isn't that great. I have come up with ten suggestions that will help you have a great attitude and a bright future.

#1. SMILE. This is the number one rule for a reason. People who smile, even when upset or discouraged, inevitably find reasons to be happy. It takes far fewer muscles to smile than to frown. Why waste your energy feeling pessimistic and down-trodden? Putting on a smile is like putting on rose-colored glasses. Give in to laughter, give in to smiling, give in to happiness.

#2. SURROUND yourself with great people. You are only as good as the people you surround yourself with. The people around you have a big impact on you. They impact who you are, how much money you will make, and what you value. They also impact how you think. If you surround yourself with negative people you will be negative as well. You can't help it. Hearing negativity all day leads to negativity. The opposite is also true. Surround yourself with positive people and you will be more positive.

#3. TEACH others at all levels as much as you can, as often as you can. Sharing your knowledge with others always makes you feel like you are helping out and serving a purpose. You always have something to share and teach someone else.

#4. UNDERSTANDING is a hallmark characteristic of a powerful young teenager today. Be understanding of others and their situations. We all have bad days. You never know what someone else is going through and dealing with.

#5. DELEGATE appropriately. Don't feel like you need to take on the world and do everything on your own. Ask your friends, teachers, parents, and siblings to help. More than likely they are just waiting for you to ask. You would be surprised how many people love to help a loved one.

#6. SERVE. Find someone in need of something and help them achieve it. There is no greater joy than providing service. Mow the lawn for your dad, do the dishes for your mom. Go visit your Grandma or call up a friend that you haven't talked to in a while. Develop those relationships early on and cultivate them for a lifetime.

#7. FIND SOMETHING YOU LOVE TO DO. Find something that will help you wind down and de-stress at the end of the day. Whether it is exercise, sports, singing, painting, reading, etc. Find something you are good at and enjoy doing. You will be happier and feel better about yourself when you are able to better yourself in the things you love to do.

#8. MAKE THE BEST OF YOUR SITUATION. Know that there's always someone else who's worse off than you. You got a C on that Chemistry test? Well, someone else failed it. You broke your leg? Someone else doesn't have a leg. Remember that you have a LOT compared to someone else. Don't dwell on the could-haves, the should-haves, the wishes, and the wants. Dwell on what can be done now, in the present time and place. There's no joy in what almost was.

#9. READ POSITIVE AND INSPIRING BOOKS. One of the best ways to maintain a positive attitude is by reading positive books. These books serve to encourage you, inspire you, and teach you. Reading requires that you sit still and focus. By focusing on something positive you'll keep a positive mindset throughout the day.

#10. BE THANKFUL. Take some time and be thankful. Be thankful about what you have, who you are and what your life is like. Think through all of the things you can be thankful for. Even if you are in a tough time in life there are many things you can be thankful for. You need to look for them and recognize them. The very act of focusing on what you are thankful for will help you maintain your positive attitude.

Even if you only can do one of these at a time. Maybe do one a week until they become a habit. You will be happier in the long run. Always remember to give more than you take from others. If you do this with a positive attitude I can promise you that you will not only change your life, but all of the people you are surrounded by.

At the age of 27, **Chad Hymas'** life changed instantaneously when an accident left him a quadriplegic. Since that time Chad has been recognized by the state of Utah as the *Superior Civilian of the Year.* He is the president of his own communications company and an internet marketing company.

At 37 years of age Chad is the one of the youngest ever to receive the CPAE award and be inducted into the National Speaker Hall Of Fame. As a member of the National Speakers Association Chad spoke at over 220 events last year. He travels as many as 300,000 miles a year. Chad travels the world sharing his message with teenagers. He shares with them how he has been able to overcome his paralysis and live the happy productive life he was meant to lead.

Chad is married and he and his wife are the proud parents of three children. They currently reside in Rush Valley, Utah on a 200-acre wildlife preserve. Chad is a *world-class* wheelchair athlete enjoying basketball, wheelchair rugby, hang-gliding, and snow skiing. In July 2003 Chad set a ***World Record*** by wheeling a personal marathon of over 500 miles from Salt Lake City to Las Vegas. Chad is also the author of the regionally best-selling book *Doing What Must Be Done.*

PS- If you would like to get in touch with me, check out my website http://www.chadhymas.com. I would love to be updated on your progress!

10 TIPS ON LIFE

#1. Right and wrong is ONLY a matter of opinion.

#2. Your purpose in life ends when you're dead, so stop searching for it because you are already living it!

#3. The most important opinion is your own.

#4. Help yourself first so that you are able to help others.

#5. NOTHING is FREE!

#6. Negative people are a blessing in disguise.

#7. Follow your heart no matter what your mind says.

#8. Your intuition is NEVER wrong!

#9. The most important person in this world is you.

#10. Emotions are the lie that mask the truth.

John Su coins himself as "The Student of Life" and says his purpose in life is to be "The Chiropractor of Thought." John's top 3 values that he lives his life by are: growth, alignment and balance. His passions are practical education, Argentine tango and violin. John currently helps people invest in real estate, but his dream is to be a revolutionary designer for the Alberta educational system. www.ImperialInvestmentRealty.com www.InvestorSage.Wordpress.com

10 TIPS ON CREATING A LIFE YOU LOVE

#1. Prepare your future. The quality of your thoughts equals the quality of your life.

#2. Tell the story you want to live. Begin to focus on where you want to go and continue to tell that story. Eventually you will see it unfold as you direct it.

#3. Your inner world reflects your outer world. Your thoughts, words, and actions impact your life and in fact create it. This happens from the inside out. Thoughts lead to choice, choice leads to change, change leads to action and action leads to your destiny. You create your life based on who you are on the inside.

#4. Increase your confidence by knowing what you value. Peel away the layers of what society, parents, peers, media, and all outside forces have imposed on you. Evaluate what it is you value, the degree to which you are living your values and priorities and learn how that is dependent on the level of your self-confidence.

#5. Your life is your message. Words have impact but the real impact comes from the actions you take with the people you interact with. People you encounter get a feel for who you are at a level that is beyond words.

#6. Embrace your "unlovable" side. A lot of what keeps us from our full potential is the fact that we don't fully love and accept ourselves. Begin to explore and embrace your shadow side – the side that you tend to view as "not so good" and that you try to hide from everyone. Begin to understand that all your qualities serve a purpose and embrace all of who you are.

#7. Listening to your higher self. You are governed by two inner aspects, one leads you away from what you want (fear-based, ego-mind), and the other draws you to it (higher self). Many times these two battle it out, but by becoming aware of these two aspects you can decipher which one is trying to lead you. Become aware of the "should's" and "have to's" that you relent to out of the fear that if you don't you won't succeed. By acknowledging some of your fears you can release the hold they have on you and begin to live your life fearlessly from you Higher Self.

#8. Release judgement. Every relationship in your life plays an important role. How you respond to those relationships directly impacts you. By coming from a place of compassion and understanding you will learn how to release your judgement of others as well as the judgments you place on yourself.

#9. Creating balance in a busy world. Let's face it, we live in a fast-paced world. Often times this means that our own needs take a back seat. Self-care needs to take priority in order to be successful in life and create balance that leads to a peaceful, calm and meaningful life.

#10. Live from a place of integrity. Living a truly "successful" life means living a life of integrity. Who we are and who we continue to grow into is the true indicator of living a happy life. Living from a place of integrity means being authentic, real, sincere, and genuine regardless of what situations arise in your life.

Trisha Savoia is founder/owner of Absolute Awareness. Through her programs, writing, and speaking she uses her skills and experience as a mother, teacher, business woman & clinical hypnotherapist to teach people how to live their fullest lives and impact others while doing so. She helps you to peel away the layers to get to the core of who you are so that you live your life to a higher standard, attracting all that you desire and deserve. She teaches you how to balance life guilt-free and tap into your intuitive sense, which leads to living a life of greater ease, fulfilment, meaning, happiness, and abundance. You can find her at www.AbsoluteAwareness.ca.

10 THINGS ALL TEENAGERS CAN CONTROL

There are so many things in life that we simply cannot control, but what about the things we can control? We have the power of reasoning and choice, both of which give us so much control over our own life situations. The following is my reminder list of the 10 Things All Teenagers Can Control:

#1. Taking action. We all have days when we feel stuck and think there is no way to make forward progress, but we can always take action, even if it is just a small step in the direction you want to go. You also have control of what actions you take: you can take a stand for a cause you believe in and encourage others to do the same; you can refuse to put up with mistreatment in any situation; you can decide to act with integrity at all times.

#2. Attitude. You can't control someone else's attitude, but you can control your own. It is up to you whether you get angry at your friends who give you not-so-positive feedback, or if you choose to see ANY feedback as valuable and a chance to learn. Are you going to be the person who makes the best of a tough situation or are you going to have a defeatist attitude and just give up? You choose!

#3. Commitment. Commitment involves your heart, which only you can control. That means nobody else has the power to compromise the strength of your commitment or force you to dedication to something. When you intentionally give your time, energy, talents and love to particular projects, relationships and charities, you are in full control of those commitments and everyone benefits from your choices.

#4. Empathy. Will you try to first understand, or to be understood? Empathy starts with you and your interest in someone else and his or her experience. You can control the way you approach any interaction – with friends, family, significant others, teachers or anyone!

#5. Focus. You get to control what you pay attention to, where you put your focus. We forget sometimes with all the information available that we do not have to listen to everything. The same goes for the rest of your life – you get to set your priorities and set your focus as clearly as you want. What means the most to you? What do you care the most about? What is most relevant to your family, your friends, and the rest of your life? Those are the things that should be getting your focus.

#6. Friendship. This is about our personal decision to be a friend... because of course, we can only control our own half of a friendship. I learned from my father the value of true friendship, watching him offer his own time and assistance to neighbors with no expectation of return favors, and never "keeping score." When someone is in need, you control whether or not you will reach out to that person with an offer of help.

#7. Listening. You can control if you will listen to someone, then how you will listen. When you ask a question, do you pay close attention to the answer? And even if you haven't asked a question, do you still focus on what someone is saying, taking care to hear their words and the meaning behind them? There is a lot of chatter out there, so it is even more important to keep your listening skills fresh, both in written and spoken conversations.

#8. Hearing. Hearing, to me, is what you do when you take listening one level further and involve your heart and understanding. When you truly hear someone, you empathize with them, and seek to understand where they are coming from and even what they are feeling. You control whether you give that extra effort or not. Do you find yourself "blocking out" what someone is saying because you either don't agree with it, or can't be bothered to understand? Try really hearing someone, and chances are you will find them interesting, wise, and possibly even a great sounding board for you.

#9. Learning. Learning happens inside your own mind, and although others may influence it, you still control how open you are to taking in new information and making it a part of your life. You always have a chance to grow and learn, which gives you a way to stay excited about your life, your friends, and your future. They say life is an open book, so why not choose to learn from all of it??

#10. Love. You might think you cannot control love, but what you do with your heart cannot be decided by anyone else. Will you keep your heart shut, or will you open it so love can come in and go out? When you give love, it makes everything you do more significant and meaningful – for those you connect with AND for yourself. It can be as small as opening a door for someone overloaded with groceries, or as big as risking your life to serve your country. Or... simply being there, always, for a family member. Every act of love matters.

All of these have significant impact on the relationships in your life. You can't control each relationship, but you can decide to give relationships top priority in your life. Always remember... it really is All About Relationships!

Ted Rubin is a leading social marketing strategist and in March 2009 started using and evangelizing the term ROR, Return on Relationship™... a concept he believes is the cornerstone for building an engaged multi-million member database, many of whom are vocal advocates for the brand, like the one he built for e.l.f. Cosmetics (EyesLipsFace.com) as the Chief Marketing Officer between 2008 and 2010, and the one built for OpenSky where Ted, was the Chief Social Marketing Officer. His book, Return on Relationship™, is due to be released in September.

On May 1st, 2011 he accepted the position of Chief Social Marketing Officer at Collective, a company he has worked closely with since it was founded by John Andrews. Ted is also on the Advisory Boards of Blue Calypso, Chinoki, OpenSky, SheSpeaks, Zuberance, Taptank, and Crowdsourcing Week.

Many people in the social media world know Ted for his enthusiastic, energetic and undeniably personal connection to people. Ted is the most followed CMO on Twitter and has one of the deepest networks of any marketer in the social arena. ROR is the basis of his philosophy...It's All About Relationships! @TedRubin www.tedrubin.com returnonrelationshipbook.com

10 TIPS FOR DEALING WITH A CHILD WHO IS BULLYING

Here are some very important key KINDNESS/LOVE RESPOND tools for any situation in dealing with a child or anyone who is bullying:

#1. Respond in love always, everything else is fear.

#2. Show kindness when an act has happened. This is the time for extra love, understanding and learning.

#3. Listen and validate your child's feelings. You are always learning how to be a better parent. Listening to your children will help you know what they need.

#4. Ask questions only. When you child comes to you with a problem allow him/her to talk it out. Help your child come to a solution on his/her own by asking questions but not by providing answers.

#5. A child who is surrounded by parents with self-love, respect, understanding and kindness will learn how to do better and know better. They will shine their light onto others, be happy, contribute and know their life and the lives of others matter.

#6. Do all that you can to give yourself tools, wisdom, and understanding. Embrace the beautiful scars of your life, find your love born within and shine on! Your wisdom, strength, kindness, integrity, and self-love will guide your child's life and to happiness.

#7. "Time" to children is love. Know what is going on in their lives as much as possible. Be a soft place for your child to come too always. Communication, trust and respect are key.

#8. Children will always remember how they were left feeling! This is most important!

#9. If your child is the one being bullied, the tools of self-love, reverence, and kindness will make all the difference in his or her response!

#10. Wake up, be amazing and go back to bed! Ego responds and teaches fear. Love responds and heals the world.

Juliette Miles is a Transformational/Inspirational, Life Coach, Author and Speaker. She is the Creator of The Greater Omnipresent Domain and Embrace Your Beautiful Scars and Shine On to live your best life journey series.

Contact Juliette for coaching empowerment, self-love tools, journey to self-love series and change your "STORY" today. For you were born to be LOVE, BE AMAZING, and SHINE ON!! The Greater Omnipresent Domain, Inc. - The Greater Omnipresent Domain, Inc. www.JulietteMiles.com

10 TIPS FOR SURVING CHILD SEXUAL ABUSE AND HOW TO MOVE PAST THE ABUSE

#1. Love thyself! Love thyself! Love thyself!

#2. Go back in your mind's eye and see the abuse as an observer without experiencing the pain again... You are safe... See your abusers past and why they did what they did... See the situation from every angle.

#3. Come from a place of compassion and forgiveness. See why they are the way they are and ask for healing for all concerned.

#4. Volunteer! When you do something unselfishly for someone else you forget your worries and move past your own pain in order to help another.

#5. Visualize your outcome! Your past does not equal your future, so create your new chapter in life as if you have full authority to design whatever future you can imagine and then go for it! Believe and you WILL achieve!

#6. Journal! What you commit to paper will manifest if desired whole heartedly! Also let go of trauma and past pain by putting it on paper. You release your hold on it – freeing your heart and soul to go for what will benefit you.

#7. Do not judge others or gossip about them. More people than you could ever imagine have been abused physically, emotionally or sexually. So if someone does something or says something that creates drama or pain – see where it's coming from. They are merely trying to attract further criticism or pain in their life – don't participate in the cycle of abuse, but rather decide to take the position of compassion and inner humor of how amazing the universe truly is.

#8. Do something special for a loved one. Show them or tell them that you love them. And even if they don't react like you'd like them to... Realize it's not about them - it's about you and how you share your words and thoughts of love unconditionally.

#9. Do something for yourself. Treat yourself to a manicure or a massage or a night out to a professional hockey game – whatever makes YOU happy, treat yourself because you are THE best friend you could ever have.

#10. Believe in a Source Energy! Whether it's God, Buddha, Allah or Grandfather Spirit, believe you are NEVER alone! You are protected. Nothing is lost in spirit's eyes – including yourself! You are perfect exactly how you are! So love thyself and the universe will respond in kind!

By **Carrie Kohan**, National Child Advocate

10 TIPS ON REALITY

#1. Being born is a literal (not biblical) miracle. Considering all the stuff that takes place for conception, then the growth of a fetus into a baby, then the birthing process itself...that alone is truly miraculous. To expect yourself to be perfect is really pushing things!

#2. Pretty much anyone can have a baby (with respect to those who can't). So considering the fact your parents brought to their relationship their own baggage, not to mention a huge dose of genetics, how you turn out is really a gigantic poker game. Some get a winning hand and the others, well, don't. How you play the hand you are dealt, that's a different story.

#3. Kids don't come with a manual called "How to Raise a Child." Considering the fact most people's experience on child development is, like, none, the job of raising you is the toughest one there is. Like a job, and think of you co-workers at a fast food place, movie theater, etc., some people are really good at their job and some people suck. parenting is the same. Does that answer a few questions about someone you know?

#4. Life Is not fair!!!! One of the most commonly used expressions by teens is, "That's not fair!" Right! Did someone actually tell you it was? They lied! Just consider simple math and sports; two teams play, one wins, one loses. Fair has nothing to do with it! One tip to consider; if you learn to lose, you appreciate a win and you then see fairness is all about your reaction.

#5. You are not the most important person in the world! If someone told you that, they are either lying or they need a tighter grip on reality. Last count, there are over 7,000,000,000 (that's billion) people on the planet. Deciding who is most important is simply ludicrous but even more bizarre is way too many folks believe they actually count more than someone else. Is it me or is that the most egotistical thing ever? When you learn to control your ego, your life will change.

#6. (Very closely related to #5) Get over yourself!!! Since you are not the most important person alive, quit acting like you are. Does the term "Drama Queen" ring a bell? By the way that refers to both boys and girls. The things you react to in your teen years will be a mere blip for the rest of your life but that's adult-speak, isn't it? Trust me, if you lower the volume and take things less personal, your stress will drop too. Stuff happens so the sooner you learn to get over things, the easier life will get.

#7. Some people are very good looking...some people are ugly; fact of life! If you are blessed with the beauty gene, congratulations and while we're on the topic, just 'cause you're attractive doesn't give you a license to be mean and further-more, Snooki from Jersey Shores is a horrible role model! You have no doubt heard the line, "Beauty starts from the inside" and are probably rolling your eyes at the lame phrase right now. Pop Quiz! When you look at celebrities like Joan Rivers who have had so much plastic surgery they have no real skin left, does that make them look attractive or stupid? I know my answer, what's yours?

#8. School for most takes 13 years to complete. The first five or six seem pretty easy then the rest can be a bit of a challenge; It's Supposed To Be!!! Sorry if this is a surprise but growing through adolescence is what sets up our adult life. How many teams have lost every game in pre-season and then won the championship? More important, like in the book, "Tuesday's With Morrie" by Mitch Albom, there's a great line that talks about learning as much from what hurts us than what loves us...I agree.

#9. (In reference to #8) Once you graduate from high school and you really need to do that, all those people you thought would rule your life forever... don't. Sadly, some people get bullied and if you do, you believe this will happen for the rest of your life. Trust me...It Gets Better! But please pay attention; It Is Up To You To Make It That Way! My dad used to tell me, "Boy, there ain't no shiny limousine coming to pick you up and take you to your life! You need to walk, and since you have no arms, you'll probably walk twice as far. But have faith...you will get there!" Brilliant!

#10. (My favorite) IT IS WHAT IT IS! Do yourself a big favor and stop analyzing everything and just say, "It is what it is!" Really brilliant!

Alvin Law is an award winning speaker, best-selling author and awesome musician playing drums, piano and trombone. He was also born without arms! Alvin has spoken to over 1.5 million teens in his career and specializes in motivating people through reality. For someone who had few friends, never dated and had bleak employment prospects, today he is married to Darlene, is a dad to Vance (born 1985) and owns his own communications company (with his wife) that has taken him to six of seven continents around the world. Not bad for someone whose life could have been "Not Fair." He can be explored at www.alvinlaw.com

10 TIPS FOR TREATING PEOPLE WITH RESPECT

#1. Don't do anything that would bring harm upon your family name.

#2. Don't do anything that you wouldn't do if your mom or dad was there.

#3. Be an example and a leader with respect not a follower without respect.

#4. Do what you've been taught from your family and/or school.

#5. Don't touch or grab the other gender inappropriately.

#6. Be true to the family name you bear.

#7. Don't have excuses have respectful results.

#8. Use please and thank you.

#9. Help as many people you can each day.

#10. Share you smile it can only go for miles and it show how much respect you have.

By **Chet Gray Root,** A teenager with a ton of wisdom in him.

♥ ♥ ♥ ♥ ♥

10 TIPS FOR LEADING A HEALTHY LIFE

#1. Treat your body with respect. It's the only one you have, be kind to it. Treat your body the way you would treat your best friend, with kindness, love and affection.

#2. Make small changes. If you struggle with drinking enough water then start by increasing your intake every week until you are drinking enough. If you struggle with sugar, remove one thing from your diet at a time. Don't overwhelm yourself, otherwise the changes won't stick. Small, gradual changes will enable lasting healthy habits.

#3. Do what you love. Staying healthy requires physical activity; this doesn't mean you have to go to the gym every day if that's not enjoyable. Find a sport you love or a dance class, something where you are moving, sweating and having fun, this will make it sustainable.

#4. Eat protein at every meal. Protein will keep you fuller longer and is beneficial in maintaining healthy muscles. Proteins come in many forms including: poultry, seafood, red meat, lentils, eggs and dairy. Aim to eat small meals, every three to four hours, throughout the day.

#5. Drink water. Though it can seem "boring" to drink water, it is extremely important for both our mental and physical well-being. Water flushes the unwanted toxins through our body, it makes us think clearer and be more alert. You can also drink water in other forms such as herbal tea, but avoid any drink that has artificial sweeteners in them.

#6. Eat breakfast. Breakfast is the most important meal of your day; it will start your metabolism and is proven to make you more productive throughout the day. Eggs, oatmeal and Greek yogurt are all great options for a delicious morning meal.

#7. Create balance. No one can be perfect 100% of the time, nor would we want to be. It is normal to want to eat a piece of birthday cake, but choose your indulgences. Every week there could be a birthday, anniversary or special occasion. It is okay to indulge but plan ahead of time and don't beat yourself up for having that piece of cake.

#8. Communicate. Leading a healthy life can be fun, involve your friends, get excited and share your struggles. Even the fittest of people still struggle. Having a support network will lead to a lasting, healthy lifestyle.

#9. Love yourself. Whatever shape or size you are, you are human and beautiful. Love yourself for who you are, respect yourself for what you contribute. Tell yourself every single day you are worth the effort to get up that extra hour early to get your workout in before school or work.

#10. Be adventurous. Try new things all the time; push your limits because you never know how far you can take yourself. Live life outside of the box, you will be amazed at what you discover.

By **Bri Westhaver.** Growing up I was a chubby kid. When I entered high school and my family separated I used food to comfort my pain. I gained a significant amount of weight during school, the loneliness of being the fat kid made me want to eat more, which in turn made me more fat.

It was a never ending cycle. After hitting my breaking point of 360 pounds I decided to change my life. I successfully went from a size 28 to a healthy size 10 and lost 190 pounds. It was hard work, it took dedication and persistence. It takes my commitment every single day to never go backwards, but I would never undo anything I did.

Today I am a healthy body weight, I'm not skinny, but I'm healthy. I'm active, I sweat every day and I love my life. Change your life now, don't wait. I hope my tips help you to stay motivated to living a healthy lifestyle.

http://briannawesthaver.blogspot.com twitter: @briwesthaver

10 TIPS TO EXPERIENCE
HAPPINESS IN LIFE

#1. Life is a journey. It is never a straight path from A to Z. It will take twists and turns you never could have imagined all to provide you with a more abundant life than you ever could have envisioned for you. Enjoy the ride. Be open.

#2. Your life has a special purpose. Share your wisdom and talent with others. Your gift is what energizes you and makes you unique. Your gifts will open others hearts to live their lives with passion and purpose. Believe in you.

#3.In giving to others, you will receive. Life is about impacting the quality of others' lives. It is not about how much stuff you can accumulate for you. Looking for happiness in things leaves you with a gut wrenching emptiness. In helping others, your needs will be met. Be of service.

#4. Life gives subtle messages. Life is always choreographing your next move. More than likely, it is not what you had planned. Pay attention to the subtle messages. Trust the process. A power greater than you has a magnificent plan for your life. Listen carefully.

#5. Things happen for you, not to you. There is a gift in everything that happens in your life. Be open to the lessons that life events teach you. Avoid becoming a victim stuck in anger. Use the lessons you have experienced to teach others. Embrace life's gifts.

#6. Trust your intuition. Your intuition is your body's wisdom. If something does not feel right in your gut, do not engage. Stay out of ego that will argue against your intuition. Your intuition is always dead on. Honor your body knowing.

#7. The Universe mirrors your thoughts. Your thoughts are powerful. What you think about you create in your life. The only thing that will limit you is the power of your imagination. Imagination will take you anywhere. Choose your thoughts wisely. Imagine.

#8. Don't take you too seriously. Just when you think you have everything under control, life happens. It is how you react to what happens that creates stress. Breathe. Mistakes are our greatest teachers. Learn to laugh at you. Lighten up.

#9. Live fully every moment. Life is what happens in the moment. Life keeps moving and changing. Do not get stuck in the past or put all hope in the future. See beauty in the simple things in life in the everyday moments. Live now.

#10. Life is an inside job. Freedom is being your authentic self. You do not have to impress anyone. Live what brings you joy. Co-create with others to impact humanity. Listen to your heart. Your heart knows your purpose. Be Your Unique Self!

Suzy Manning is the CEO of SIZZZL, Powerful Women Who Ignite the World. She is a transitional coach, speaker, author, and radio show host helping women live and lead from their true authentic self. Her expertise is helping women in transition create a solid unshakable foundation within them to design lives and businesses from inspiration, inner wisdom, and a place of service. www.sizzzl.com

♥ ♥ ♥ ♥ ♥

10 THINGS I SHOULD HAVE DONE WITH MY MONEY AS A TEENAGER

Here are 10 quick tips about getting your financial life off to a screaming success. Any teenager can do these 10 things, as they don't cost too much and will help you plan for the future.

#1. Save 20% of what you make into a Tax Free Savings Account (TFSA). As a teenager, if you earn money from a part-time job or summer work, you have lots of extra disposable income. Without having to pay any bills, rent, mortgage, etc. all your earnings become surplus cash-flow. Be disciplined. Take 20% of that cash flow and stick it into a Tax Free Savings Account (TFSA).

#2. Start a small, cash value life insurance policy. Everyone needs to start think long term with their money, and the younger you start the better. The longest term financial products are life insurance contracts, simply because they run for the rest of your life. Start with a small permanent life insurance policy (like $50,000 of whole life or universal life insurance) and watch it grow and build up cash value. It will start slow at first, but the discipline of saving into such a policy early will reap huge rewards throughout your life.

#3. Research grants, bursaries and scholarships for post-secondary schools. You would be amazed at how few university and college students never look into getting a scholarship or a bursary. In fact there are thousands of student support programs in Canada, giving away millions of dollars in free money. If you don't ask you don't get. And not all bursaries are for academic achievement. Some support certain cultural or ethnic groups, sports, special interest groups, etc. for students going to post-secondary education.

#4. Have a part-time/summer job. I don't think it would surprise you if I told you that not everything you need to learn is taught in a classroom. Some of the most valuable life lessons are learnt from working in a part-time, after school job or finding a good summer job. Learning to work hard and earn a paycheque will teach you the value of money and you will respect how hard it is to earn money.

#5. Don't waste money on a car — yet. Cars can be an endless money pit. You should never go into debt at a young age to buy a car. But even if you get a used car, there is maintenance, insurance, gas, etc. It can cost well over $1,000 per month to be on the road at a young age, especially if you get into one accident or get one speeding ticket. You can really mess up your insurance rates for a long time. I suggest learning to love public transit until you can comfortably afford a car.

#6. Set a budget for your fun money. Almost all of your earned income at a young age would be considered "disposable income" unless you have earmarked another use for it. So, don't just dispose of your money on frivolous things like going to the movies 4 nights a week and drinking $5 coffees at Starbucks. Set a budget for how much of your money is for fun stuff, and stick to it. Once you run out of your weekly fun money, stop spending.

#7. Free activities are often the most fun. When I was a poor university student, the best time we had was going for the day to Cranberry Flats in Saskatoon, SK. It was a free provincial park on the river where we could swim and hang out on the sandbars of the river. Like the beach, but more land-locked. It was free. We packed our own lunches and drinks, and had a great time. There are endless things you can do in Canada that won't cost you any money. Just get out there and explore nature and your public parks, municipal recreation facilities, etc.

#8. Get your parents involved in your financial plans – they'll probably want to help. What is the #1 source of free money for teenagers? Your parents! But they hate it when you beg for cash just to go waste partying. If they were included in your savings plans, your education plans, looking for scholarships, etc., they would probably be ready to help. Maybe propose a matching scheme, where they match dollar for dollar the money you save for university or college. That's like a 100% return on your investment in the first year.

#9. Don't smoke! I'm not talking about the health risks. The cost of smoking will carve a hole in your wallet. Let's say a pack of cigarettes is $10, and you smoke 5 packs a week. That is $2,600 per year. Stop smoking – *you're richer than you think.*

#10. High school is not the end of your education. You've probably heard your parents and teachers tell you to get an education beyond high school. Why? It will enrich your life and make you a more rounded person. Yes, but from an economic standpoint, young Canadians with a post-secondary degree or diploma will on average earn a lot more money over their lifetimes than someone with only a high school diploma. An education equals a better standard of living and greater financial success.

Mitch Reynolds, MBA is the President of Life Guard Insurance, Canada's best online source for life and health insurance information. He has been in the insurance and investment industry since 2000, when he graduated from the University of Saskatchewan with his Masters of Business Administration. He has worked for Sun Life Financial, Clarica Financial, RBC Insurance, and ATB Investor Services before starting his own online life insurance brokerage. www.life-insurance-broker.ca

♥ ♥ ♥ ♥ ♥

10 TIPS FOR DRIVING SAFELY

These tips are being given here by Kelly Falardeau's friend and fellow burn survivor John Westhaver. When John was 18-years-old he was in a drunk driver accident with three of his buddies. John happened to be the only survivor of the car accident, but he also ended up with burns covering his body. He is now a motivational speaker talking about "Choices" to teenagers all over North America.

#1. Don't drive intoxicated. No alcohol, street drugs and/or prescription drugs.

#2. Put away the handheld devices. This means your cell phone, iPod, and any other device that requires you to take your hands off the wheel and your attention off the road. The text message will be on your phone when you get to your destination. Let the call go to voicemail. If you need to make or receive a call, a text message or an email, pull over and get to a safe place before doing so.

#3. Give yourself travel time. Give yourself plenty of time to arrive at your destination and extra time for unexpected traffic delays. GPS devices are great for calculating drive times.

#4. Know your route. If you are unfamiliar with the area, it may be easy to get lost which can cause added stress to your driving if you need to be somewhere by a specific time. GPS devices are great for this and most nowadays tell you the directions aloud while you are driving so you can focus on the road.

#5. Have a safe reliable Designated Sober Driver (DSD). Your DSD should be someone that will not leave you stranded somewhere. They should not become intoxicated by drugs or alcohol. They should also never put you in danger while they are driving. Not everyone likes to be the DSD, so share the duty and take turns. Be the DSD and take pride in knowing you are committed to getting your friends home safe and that they will do the same for you.

#6. Buckle up. Wearing your seatbelt will prevent you from being ejected out of the vehicle when involved in a crash. This could prevent serious injury or death.

#7. Drive the speed limit. Obey the posted speed limits, they are there for everyone's safety. Save the speeding and racing for the race track.

#8. Don't drive tired. Driving while tired is just as bad as driving impaired, so if you feel tired pull over and get out and walk around for 5-10 minutes, this will help circulate the blood in your butt and legs and the fresh air will wake you up. For long trips, give yourself 10 minutes to get out for every hour that you plan to drive.

#9. Don't drive with a hot head. This means if you are angry, mad, upset or emotional. Give yourself time to clear your head before driving.

#10. Don't give into peer pressure. Driving with your friends is probably one of the most fun things we can do, however sometimes our friends encourage us to speed, drive dangerous and push the limits. Be strong and don't give into this pressure. Live to drive another day.

By **John Westhaver**, Burn Survivor/Professional Speaker
www.jmmspeaking.com

♥ ♥ ♥ ♥ ♥

10 TIPS FOR SURVIVING YOUR TEENAGE YEARS LIVING ON YOUR OWN

I left home at the age of 15, not because of my parent's rules, sibling issues or defiance but due to sexual abuse that was happening at home. When I left, I was A-B Student going into grade 10 and I had a good group of friends but after moving across the country to a place where I knew no one, my life was very different. It was challenging to be on my own and I had to grow up really fast but 13 years later I am happy to say I made it through those years quite successfully. Today I am 28, very happily married and a mom of 2 kids.

#1. Think hard- Are you ready? Sometimes living on your own is not an option when your safety is at risk. But there are a million other reasons teenagers decide to live on their own. Make sure you have thought it through from every angle and do your research before you make the decision. It will change your life, your relationships with family and friends as well as the way you see yourself. If at all avoidable I would suggest trying an alternate route. Can you try working it out with your parents? Is there another relative you can try living with for awhile? What about a friend's family?

#2. Set your priorities! Life on your own is very different then living at home. Yes there is freedom but with that freedom comes tons of responsibilities. Every choice you make can and WILL affect you for the rest of your life. So make a list of priorities in your life right now. School, job, apartment etc.

#3. Get a job. If you are trying to go to school full time and work it is important you find an employer that is supportive to your needs. Discuss the option of taking longer or extra shifts on weekends, PD Days and holidays to make up for the hours you are at school. Full time hours in the summer. The more hours you can work on your off time, the less stress you will feel during the school year.

#4. Know what resources are available to you. There are tons of resources available for youth living on their own. Contact your local social services as well as community programs in your local phone book. These resources would/ could include Food Bank, free school supplies, transportation vouchers, medical benefits, and even social assistance.

#5. Counselling. Teenage years are stressful enough but if you add in the responsibilities of an adult it can be all too much. It is important to keep a good relationship with your doctor and if you are feeling stressed, overwhelmed or depressed ask for a referral to a counsellor. Having a good counsellor will make all the difference in the world.

#6. Start a savings account. There will always be a day when you will need every cent you can find. Get in the habit of saving some of your cheque every month. I know there may not be a lot left but every dollar counts.

#7. Learn to budget. Sadly money never goes as far as we all hope. Set a budget. Don't forget to include rent, utilities, phone, set up charges, down payment on apartment, transportation, clothing, food and spending money.

#8. Find a place to live. Ideally you have time to do the first 7 steps before you have to find a place. Finding a place to live can be tricky. First off you will need the first month's rent as well as a security deposit and you may need someone to co-sign on the lease since you are under the age of 18. Make sure to ask lots of questions and do not jump at the first place you see. How much is the rent? Are utilities included? (lights, heat, water) How far is it from school and work? Is it a safe area? Is there a lease? Is it furnished? Often it is a better choice to rent a room or a basement suite rather than an apartment since the costs are much lower and often include all utilities and cable.

#9. Choose your friends carefully. Having your own apartment can make you the "cool" kid in school really fast, but sadly it attracts the wrong "friends" Learn to say NO! Your apartment is not a party house. Remember you have a lot to lose.

#10. Food and sleep. Food was one of the hardest things I found living on my own. It is so important to say away from fast food options and to learn to shop and eat healthy. Packing your lunches and snacks through the day will help save you money as well as give you the energy you need to keep going. Teenagers require sleep; it is a scientific fact that teenagers require more rest then adults. To function at your best and have the endurance to tackle both school and work you will need a good quality sleep schedule.

BONUS TIP: Ask for help, even adults need help from time to time. Don't be afraid to go to your school counsellor, a friend or family if you need help.

Jennifer Belanger beat all odds, she is now a happily married mom of two boys. She is an entrepreneur at heart and believes in following your dreams! You can learn more about Jennifer at www.JenniferBelanger.com

10 TIPS FOR TEENS TO LOVE THEIR FUTURE

#1. Realize you can do anything! That's right anything. Don't let any circumstance or any person put you in a box on what you can accomplish in life. You were made for greatness.

#2. Your future is full of great opportunities. Now more than ever the opportunities that are in front of this new generation are incredible. Realize the land of opportunity is yours. There will be so many, so consider each one wisely.

#3. Recognize that you have specific gifts and talents. Have you ever noticed how we are all different and enjoy different things. Those specific things you love to do are your gifts and talents. That's what makes you unique. Don't worry about being like everyone else....be YOU!

#4. Look inside to see what you're passionate about. What are the things that make you excited? Happy? What can make you so mad or upset? These are the things you are passionate about. Most people work in jobs they hate for a lifetime but this is not you because you are reading this right now. Plan to work in a field that you are passionate about, because you are meant to profit from your passions.

#5. You are meant to change the world. You may have been told in the past that you are a problem but, "You are not a problem you are called to be an answer!" That's right you are an answer to a problem in the world. Your specific personality is coupled with your specific gifts and talents to go forth and change some area of society and therefore the world. I got involved in helping orphans with Global Care nine years ago. It's amazing how you can change the world one child at a time.

#6. You will have global friends. That's right. What an exciting future you have. The world is so small because of technology you will have friends from many different ethnic origins all over the world. You are not swashed in a small community, being tempted with peer pressure. You will have friends around the globe who will celebrate with you and you will celebrate with them.

#7. There's a book inside of you! That's right I'm not talking about reading a book, I'm talking about you writing a book. See I believe there is a book inside of everyone. Start thinking about what kind of book you could write, now. Confess, "I am going to be an author." I have 3 children who are all 13-years-old and each of them has written and published a book already. You will too!

#8. Realize you have the power to change. Nothing has to stay the same!! The reason why so many people hate their life is because they get sick of the same old same old. Day in and day out. The same problems and feeling like they never get a break. But your future will be fantastic because you realize by reading this you carry the greatest power that has ever been in a human....the power to change. That means any area of your life that you are unsatisfied with you have the power to change. People can change their relationships, their financial status, their interests, anything. How do you start this powerful power to change? By changing your attitude. Begin to see the good future in store for you by recognizing you have the POWER!

#9. Your life will inspire another generation therefore you will live forever. You will never be forgotten. Long after you are dead and gone people will still talk about the great things you did, the places you traveled and the people you helped. Your story will inspire your children, your grandchildren, your great grandchildren, and even your great-great-great-great-great-great grandchildren. Your life is worth something because it will influence so many.

#10. Realize that God loves you so he prepared a brilliant future for you. Each of us is created with a body a soul and a spirit. Your body is your BODY. Your soul is your mind, your will and emotions, and your spirit is your conscience inside of you that was created to know your creator. Often people think of God as some big old guy in the sky who is angry at the world. But this is not true, God is a Father to humanity and he looks at you as His child. He is a good Father so guess what he wants a great future for you. He sent His son Jesus to die on a cross to secure a brilliant future for you not just here on earth but for eternity. All you have to do is open the door and welcome that spiritual relationship into your life.

Well there you go, the 10 tips I have for you to Love your future. My hope is that these principles bring the wisdom to guide you into the good life. That you will develop and become all that you are meant to become, and that one day I'll be reading your story!!

Dr. Carmen Lynne is a passionate speaker who believes in training people to be released to fulfill their destiny. She is an international speaker who speaks on business, family, and personal development. She has published seven books and holds a yearly conference called the Increase Intensive. Dr. Carmen pushes herself to always live beyond just the four corners of her life by doing relief work consistently in Haiti and Mexico. She resides in Alberta Canada with her husband Steve and their seven children. To read other materials of Dr. Carmen's, please email: gcccanada@gmail.com

10 TIPS TO BEING YOURSELF

I have been really excited about our efforts to reach out to teens over these last few months. Our platforms allow us to talk to them about the power of entrepreneurship! I've taken the liberty and listed 10 ideas we convey to them regarding principles we believe will make them feel good about being "themselves".

#1. Carve out your individualisms, as hard as it may be during your ever so collected teen years. While there nothing at all wrong with being part of a group, team, organization, etc… now is a great time to carve out a few distinctions that will begin to make you unique!

#2. Be resilient. Almost everything your parents tell you that will happen if you go down the wrong path will indeed happen. The bad news is you're going to go down those paths anyways out of curiosity and the belief that your parents have no working knowledge about anything! The good news is other than criminal acts you'll survive and be better for it. Humans (and teens) become stronger and wiser from life's experiences so be resilient and know you're going to bounce back nicely.

#3. You are our future! As much as we adults like to rave about how teens can't tie their shoes or think and chew gum...you are our future. This means, we secretly worship you in our efforts to poor all of our life's lessons in you so you won't have to go through all the hurt and pain we did (see #2). So, relish in the fact that we don't think you are dumb. We know you will one day be Pres. of major companies, invent new technology, run our Country and take care of us in our twilight years.

#4. Yep! You are our future, but you are also our now! This generation of young "whipper snappers" can multi-task like no one I've ever seen. You wave through computer programs and iPhone with the ease of a trained professional. Know your strengths and hone in on your power. If you only take what you know and add a dash of good ole fashion "reading"!? (I know the forbidden word)... you could accomplish what no other generation has done before. I have the utmost confidence in you so I hope you see your greatness and lead us old people to a better day.

#5. Never stop dreaming! One of the great things about your teen years and that you believe you can do and be anything. The truth is...you're exactly right. No matter what anyone tells you never stop dreaming...

#6. You're actually learning more than you think. I hated all (and I do mean ALL) of those silly little chores my mother made me do growing up. I hate to fold my clothes, wash them, wash the dishes and the most excruciating of them all....clean my room!?? Funny thing is as an adult, it made me more independent. I could cook for myself, clean my own clothes and take care of my living space. Those traits allowed me to have a head start on my peers in college and then in life. So, if nothing else, at least you are learning while you are complaining!

#7. Stop wishing you were older! It's very easy to think as a teen you're in the worst age cycle of your life! You can't drink, smoke or stay up all night (at least not legally!). you can't wait until you're 21 or older. You believe life will really unveil itself to you once you reach that hollowed age! Well guess what? It's not all it is cracked up to be! You are in the best years of your life so enjoy them to the max. Soak it up and breathe. Don't be in a rush to move forward and leave high school. Believe me once they walk you through the doors and wish you a bon voyage, you can't come back and believe me you'll want to. You ever heard the saying "If I knew then what I know now?" Exactly!

#8. Don't worry, there's still time! You will undoubtedly make a whole bunch of asinine mistakes. You'll think while going through those mistakes that you life is ending and you'll never be able to resolve the errors of your wicked ways. Nonsense!!! As long as the mistake did not take your life and you can still breathe...there's hope. You still have time to move forward and do and be all the wonderful things you dreamed to become. You simply have to learn one trick! Learn from your mistake! If you learn, you grow and growth is goooooodddddd. Stop being so hard on yourself, trust me life will be hard enough. We all make mistakes; it's what you do next that really makes a difference.

#9. College is not for everyone and it's totally ok! I'm sure by now everyone is telling you go to college and be somebody and that's not the worst choice you could make. However, there's nothing wrong with getting started with life NOW! College is not for everyone. Gaining an education can come in many forms and some of the most effective and noteworthy entrepreneurs did not go to or finish college. You can still be a very successful businessman/woman without going away to waste a perfectly good 4 years of your life!

#10. The beautiful thing about being a teen is that you know everything! Yep, your parents are completely void of knowledge or common sense. The bad news is that you'll one day soon grow up and you'll not be a teenager any more. The good news is that you'll have kids who'll then think you're absolutely without any info worth taking two seconds to stop and listen to you! Enjoy the good times!!

By **Klarque Garrison** www.klarquegarrison.com

10 TIPS TO BE YOUR AUTHENTIC SELF

The authentic self, found at your absolute core, is the composite of all your skills, talents and wisdom. All of the things that are uniquely yours and need expression, instead of who you believe you are supposed to be and do. So here are ten ways to help you consciously discover your authentic self!

#1. Love, honor and respect. All who came before you and all who will come after. Include yourself in that as you are the one who is here now.

#2. Be creative. Build, paint, sculpt, draw, play music, carve, sew, scrapbook, weave, color, write, compose music, find interesting ways to solve problems (instead of one solution look for 3 or more). Regardless of how out there or realistic they seem. It may support the expansion your thought patterns there for creating more options and empowering choice.

#3. Get out into nature. We are nature and nature is us! If you choose to venture forth and learn about and surround yourself with natural things it will be simpler to listen to our authentic self. Wilderness treks, weeklong survival camps, planting herbs in pots, having plants in the house, running barefoot in the grass, sitting under a tree, having a picnic outside, working with horses, or anything else that comes to mind. Observe, interact take it in.

#4. Challenge your beliefs. For one day write down all the questions you may have thought, heard, said or felt. Those questions are there for a reason. See if you can answer them or find the answers for them. Everything you have been taught or told, everything you read, see on t.v. on billboards, etc. you can choose to continue to believe what you believe blindly or you can challenge them, question them.

#5. Express and release your emotions in a healthy way. Some days or experiences can seem over the top and sometimes out of control. Here are some ways to express your emotions in a healthy way first your intent to either release, bring up or express an emotion or emotions. Write, journal, paint, color, make music banging on some pots and pans or anything else that can be an instrument, work out, exercise.

#6. Experience. Do you like Sushi? How do you know? If someone told you planting a garden is horrifying and someone else told you it was divine, who would you believe? Each person has their own perspective so the only way to find yours is to have the experience. Some things you may not want to experience and that is a choice you will make for yourself. Even if you may not have the opportunity or means to do some things right now, you can choose to make goals for yourself.

#7. Listen to your self. As you come into your own as only you can, remember the only person you have to live with forever is you. Our intuition can be a powerful source of information if we recognize it for what it is. Listen to your body, your mind, your emotions, and your spirit. These all play an integral part in our whole being. The more you know about you, the more choosing what you want authentically, will be simpler.

#8. Speak your truth. Even when nobody seems to listen or believe you, your truth speaks volumes about who you are authentically. Did you ever see someone being bullied and not say anything or had the answer to a question in class and not raise your hand? By doing that you may have been allowing outside pressures to influence your actions, instead of creating your own. Nobody can know what is going on for you, if you refuse to say it.

#9. Regenerate and relax. By setting your intent to and then taking the time to regenerate and relax it gives us the space needed to regroup and start fresh again. Proper night time sleep, taking a "bathroom" break so that you can take a few deep breaths, meditation (with a tape or on your own) Spend time with yourself. The more you know about you the simpler it will be to connect with your authentic self.

#10. Nourish all aspects. What you choose to put into your body will determine what comes out. Food and hydration are key for our bodies. A wide variety of nutrient dense- whole natural foods can give your body what it needs to grow and nourish. For your minds learn a different language or to play a musical instrument, read books for information that get you to think out of the box, do mind puzzles. Feel your emotions create situations where you can feel supportive emotions. Spiritually get energy in healthy, natural, clean ways.

Rhonda Elko is a stay at home mom with two beautiful boys and a wonderful husband. She is certified in Intuitive and Energetic Development and currently working on her certification in PsychoEnergetic Therapies. She has always been intrigued by why things work the way they do. One thing she has learned on her journey thus far is that she needs to be doing things she authentically loves to fuel her to create what she wants her life to be. Gardening is one of those things; she can work hard for hours in the hot afternoon sun and feel rejuvenated and ready for anything the world brings her way. She enjoys working with clay and has now taken up a new hobby, soapstone carving. As she has been inspired and supported in her life, she feels it is her responsibility and passion to pass on that inspiration and support to others. I hope your journey in life is filled with love, honor and respect in a gentle kind way!

10 TIPS TO CONNECT TO YOUR INNER AWESOMENESS
Recognizing Your Interests, Skills and Talents

Do you know what you want to be when you grow up? If you don't, you're not alone. Many adults who have long left their teen years behind still don't know what they want to be when they "grow up" either!

Choosing a life path can feel like such a big and complicated decision with far too many options, but in its basic form it's really quite simple. It all starts with getting to know yourself.

The secret behind a happy, fulfilling life lies in choosing things that match up with who you are at your core. It's easy to get lost in this simple strategy due to the expectations of parents, teachers, friends and other people who influence your life. That is why a little time dedicated to self-reflection can have a big impact on your future.

With all the major decisions that are bound to come your way such as post-secondary, career and relationships, the better you know yourself and what matters to you, the better chance you have of making choices that are a good match with who you truly are.

As Oscar Wilde said, "*Be yourself, everyone else is taken.*" You be you. No one on this earth can be you as good as you can. Every single one of us has an inner awesomeness that is unique and special. The greatest contribution you can make is to fully realize your awesomeness and then share it with the rest of the world. The starting place is to consciously recognize your interests, skills and talents. Below are 10 questions that will get you started in the right direction.

#1. Think back to times when you felt really alive, excited and brimming with happiness. What were you doing? These moments are clues to passions, dreams and desires you were born with. Value and own their importance!

#2. What things do you simply love to do? The list could be endless, but here are a few: sports, reading, art, dance, music, debating, organizing things, fixing things or helping friends with problems. Keep a running list of these items and explore what kind of careers they could possibly add up to. For now, when you are feeling sad and blue, these are the things that will cheer you up.

#3. If you were absolutely free of any and all restrictions, what would you spend your time doing? Imagine there is nothing that can hold you back. There is no need to worry about money, time, what other people will think or even whether you think you are capable or not. Pretend you don't need to know "how" things will happen. Your job is to know "what" you want to happen. No restrictions, no limitations, the choices are yours. What would you do? Permission to dream. Dream big!

#4. Who do you admire and why? This person could be real or imagined, someone you know or someone famous. What qualities do they possess that you appreciate and value? These are clues to your inner awesomeness. The qualities you value in other people are qualities you value in yourself. If you spot it, you got it!

#5. What can your friends count on you for? Some examples: helping with problems, being a good listener, helping with schoolwork, making them laugh, cheering them up, keeping secrets, being a leader or trying something new. These unique qualities partially define who you are. They are of great value now and will be forever.

#6. What are you a natural at? This is a little tricky because the things we are naturally good at we take for granted. Write what comes to mind, and then you might want to ask your family and friends for their thoughts. When I was a teenager I could pick up practically any instrument and play it. I thought everyone could do this and took this talent for granted. I missed my chance at being a rock star!

#7. What things challenge you? Not always, but this could also be a clue to a future career. For example, someone who is really challenged at math and understands the struggle of learning it, can end up becoming a fantastic math teacher. The current day struggle might lead to future success. Then again, it could also be the thing that steers you away from math for the rest of your life! You decide.

#8. What things in this world really bother you? What causes get your attention? This could include things like homeless children, animal abuse, lack of schools in poor countries, scarcity of clean drinking water, hunger, pollution, war, illiteracy or injustices. If it matters to you that means it's connecting to a value you hold deep within.

#9. Ask a trusted friend, family member or teacher to think of a word that describes the very best quality they see in you. Sometimes other people see us more clearly than we see ourselves.

#10. What would you say at your retirement speech? I know this one is a bit of a stretch, but it can really bring to light some of the subconscious ideas, values and dreams that deeply matter to you. Imagine your retirement party and all the special friends and family members who are there to honour your years of work. In your speech, what would you say were your greatest accomplishments, what were you most proud of and what were the things for which you were most grateful. Give your imagination permission to think big!

Rock Your Way to Success

Realize your unique interests, skills and talents.

Own and value your awesomeness.

Choose in favour of things that are a match with who you are at your core.

Know with confidence you are doing the right thing for you, no matter what anyone else thinks.

Linda Kiernan is a Certified Passion Test Facilitator™ and Certified Life Coach, CH, BA. Beyond the titles, she is a courageous explorer of the inner frontier. What is courage? To her courage is the commitment to fully be yourself. It is the willingness to look within, the conviction to claim what you love and the gumption to act on your innermost desires, regardless of what anyone else thinks.

She loves a good question. She finds the most powerful shifts occur when she asks questions that lead clients to their own realizations. For example, put your hand over your heart, take a deep breath and ask yourself, "If I weren't afraid, what would I do?" www.LindaKiernan.ca www.iLoveBeingGrateful.com

10 TIPS TO STAY HEALTHY AND HAPPY

#1. Set goals: The best way to accomplish anything is to set SMART goals. SMART stands for Specific, Measureable, Attainable, Realistic, and Timed.

> **Specific**: Set a goal that is specific such as, "I will ride my bike four times per week for thirty minutes"; rather than, "I will ride my bike."

> **Measureable**: Make sure your goal is something you can measure such as, "I will be able to complete 15 push-ups on my toes within two weeks."

> **Attainable**: Ensure your goal is challenging yet attainable. For example if you set a goal of walking for five minutes, this will not challenge you; however, a goal of running for

at least 20 minutes three times per week is challenging enough to keep you motivated yet attainable.

Realistic: Often people set goals that are not realistic such as, "I will lose 20 pounds in one week," which only sets a person up for failure and disappointment. However, set realistic goals such as, "I will lose one pound per week by doing at least 30 minutes of cardiovascular exercise three times per week."

Timed: Setting a timeline will keep you focused on your goal. If you have a special day, such as graduation, that you want to feel great for mark it on your calendar and set small, weekly goals that will set you up for success before your special day.

#2. Know why your goals are important to you: If you understand WHY your goals are important to you it will be easier for you to stay focused and work hard to reach your goals.

#3. Get regular exercise: Exercise is an important part of being healthy. Exercise provides the body with many benefits, including: increased strength, muscle mass, and endurance, heart and lung health, enhanced self-esteem and self-confidence, calorie burning and weight control, and a sense of accomplishment. The recommended amount of exercise is 30 – 60 minutes of cardiovascular exercise, such as running, walking, cycling; four to six times per week. Resistance training with light weights two to four times per week and stretching and flexibility activities such as yoga every day.

#4. Eat healthy, whole foods: Fruits and vegetables are healing foods. A diet rich in fruits, vegetables, a moderate amount of healthy fats, and lean proteins will provide you with the nutrients you need to have enough energy to play sports, study, and spend time with your friends and family. In addition to eating healthy foods be sure to eat slowly and mindfully, watch your portion sizes, and stop eating when you are full.

#5. Drink plenty of water: Your body is over 70% water; therefore, staying hydrated is essential for your body to function at its optimal level. Drinking water purifies your body; riding it of toxins and will increase your energy levels. The recommended intake is two litres of water per day with an increase of half a litre to one litre if you are active.

#6. Sign up for an extracurricular activity: These activities will provide you with the opportunity to meet new people, be creative, active, and build self-confidence, and self-esteem.

#7. Talk about your problems and feelings: Talking is hard for some people; yet talking is the best way to work through a problem or feelings of sadness and anger to prevent depressions and anxiety. Recruit a buddy; someone you trust, whether it be a friend, family member, teacher, or teen help line that you can be honest with and divulge your thoughts and feelings.

#8. Get involved in your community: Volunteer at a local animal shelter, school, or food bank and help people in need. This will provide you with a sense of gratitude and appreciation for what you have in your life. If you want to go to a University to gain a degree volunteer work will look great on your application.

#9. Maintain a regular sleep pattern: Playing video games, instant messaging, talking on the phone, studying, and spending time with your family takes energy; therefore, getting seven to eight hours of sleep every night will increase energy levels and decrease anxiety.

#10. Believe in yourself: Get up every morning and look at yourself in the mirror and repeat these words three times: "I love myself and only deserve the best." This will start your day on a positive note, increase your self-esteem, and help keep you focused on whatever you put your mind to.

Rachel J. Olsen, BSc., MBA is passionate about inspiring others to accomplish their goals and finding true potential by making healthy lifestyle choices. She delivers life-altering information through wellness coaching, speaking, and personal training. Rachel is a certified raw vegan chef and nutritionist, an athlete, author, speaker, motivator, and a true example of how dedication, perseverance, and taking responsibility for one's own life can result in reaching optimal health and success. She owns Saldare Ltd. and holds a Master's in Business Administration degree, a Bachelor of Science with a major in Mind Sciences in Kinesiology, and numerous personal training and wellness certifications. www.saldare.ca

10 TIPS FOR EXPRESSING YOUR MAGNIFICENCE

As a mother, who has two teen sons at home and a grown daughter who was the quintessential teenage girl, I have lots of experience in sharing tips with teens, especially when they didn't ask for them! But to make this list more official, I consulted with my youngest son, currently 16, to glean the ten best tips, out of the hundreds of thousands awesome ones that I have offered to him. Here are the ten tips that have had the greatest impact on his life, so far.

#1. Be true to yourself: Develop an intimate relationship with the Source from which you come from. Although it is called by many names: God, Source, Spirit, Life, Universe, Allah, Buddha, Yoda, etc., your understanding of it must be uniquely yours, so politely, ditch your parents ideas, if theirs do not resonate with you.

#2. Be true to yourself: Only you know what is best for you. A sign of maturity is the ability to be open to hearing the wisdom others have to share, based on their life experience. Thank others for their perspective, and then pick and use what you like and let go of the rest. Unless you have your own unique beliefs and ideas, you will be looking at life through other people's perspectives.

#3. Be true to yourself: Remember that you are what you think you are and your thoughts always generate your feelings and emotions. If you want to feel good about yourself, you must think well of yourself. If on the other hand, you think poorly of yourself, and others, you will feel bad, sad or depressed. People, who believe in themselves, feel confident and experience success, but the reverse is also true.

#4. Be true to yourself: Become aware of how your body feels. Your body never lies, so when you feel good, you are thinking thoughts that are positive and true about you and others. When you feel bad, you are thinking thoughts that are negative about yourself and others. Commit to caring for your body, and it will always be there to take care of you. Know it, respect it, and trust it.

#5. Be true to yourself: Life is like a giant puzzle, where everything happens for a reason as a way of gathering all the pieces that fit together to complete your "life" puzzle. When you are faced with choices, consider how you want your completed Life to look, and then make your choices based on the impact and consequences of those choices. And because life is so good to us, we are always at choice on how our puzzle turns out.

#6. Be true to yourself: Don't take things personally. If you commit to choosing happiness over being right, you will experience every person, situation or thing, as an opportunity to choose again. Personally speaking, choosing to be happy is the bomb!

#7. Be true to yourself: Be you, because everyone else is already taken. Your uniqueness is a gift you bring to the world. Have FUN finding new ways to express your individuality, while at the same time, appreciating and respecting the individuality of others. And yes, this includes your parents and teachers! When you are true to your heart, you will always feel confident and happy. When you try to live up to someone else's idea, of who you should be, you will spend the rest of your life chasing their approval, and resenting them for *your* choice.

#8. Be true to yourself: We are all born curious, so commit to staying curious. Be sure to Google and Wikipedia your way through life. When we develop a love for learning, we experience life as an adventure. When we expand our knowledge, our thinking will not become outdated or repetitive. Have you ever been around a crotchety old person who doesn't get you? Don't become that person.

#9. Be true to yourself: You move in only two directions: towards your dreams or away from them. Learn to discern the difference between your two inner guiding voices: one says "I can" and the other says "I can't." True happiness comes from knowing which voice speaks truth and, which voice is just static noise that distracts us from achieving our dreams. Here's a hint, check in on how your body feels about what you are thinking, and remember truth will always feel good.

#10. Be true to yourself: Know you are magnificent because you were created whole, perfect and complete. If you want to create a magnificent life, then follow what excites you!

As a life coach, most of my clients are adults, yet I have had the pleasure of coaching quite a few amazing teenagers. What fascinates me about this contrast is that every single adult I coach dramatically improves their life, when they re-connect with their joyful, fun and spontaneous inner-teen. And every single teen I coach, feels dramatically better, when they stop trying to live up to adult standards, and just remembers to be a teen! Yes, we all have to grow up, but when we are true to ourselves, we discover a perfect balance. Here's an interesting fact: you will only be a teen for 6 years, so live it up!

Since teenagers know everything, I'm sure you picked up that I am really giving you just one tip: Be true to yourself. But just in case I still have your attention, here are a few more details worth repeating: Happiness is a choice, stay curious, and above all else, remember that life is a journey and only *you* can choose to make it a fun one!

You are magnificent...yes you are!

Inspired by her own awakening, **Laina Orlando** offers a modern interpretation of timeless wisdom and spiritual truth. Through simple, yet profound, techniques and tools, she guides those open to understanding the sacred journey, from conception to enlightenment. Our journey has one purpose: to assist us in becoming aware of how we came to forget who we truly are: a physical expression of The One Source of all that is—Love! Laina's mantra: "Life is fun and easy!" www.LainaOrlando.com

10 TIPS ON LIVING A FULFILLING LIFE

I just entered my 30s, and my teens are a distant memory, but the residue of that stage of life will always be in my heart. Many themes of teenage-hood are timeless, and there are also new challenges that have emerged as a result of our rapidly evolving world.

When I was a teen, I had something important to say, but it was always veiled in insecurity and timidity. Now that life has beaten me up a little more, I've toughened up and have learned how to speak up a little louder and more authentically. I'm not going to get all parental here. I'm not your mother, and, while we're on the subject of mothers, she's doing the best she can. Be kind to her.

Here's what I have to say.

#1. Life isn't meant to be perfect, and neither are you. There will always be moments of pain, sadness, disappointment, hurt, and struggle. It's part of the gig. If you tell yourself you'll be happy *when*...you lose the weight, you get the job, your parents are cooler, or you friends stop being cruel—you will continue to suffer. All that is real is this moment. Live in it and you'll suffer less and experience more joy.

#2. And, while we're on the topic of perfection, there's nothing wrong with you or your body. Really. Please believe me. That voice in your head that tells you nasty things is lying, and you don't have to believe it.

#3. We all have issues. The sooner you start dealing with them, the sooner you'll get to know your true self, figure out what's right for you, and start living a life you love. Learn how to heal the past, love the present, and light up the future. And, be honest with yourself about self-improvement. Growing into your true self is a beautiful thing, and it feels light and expansive. Shedding crap that's weighing you down feels good (though it's not always comfortable). This is the kind of self-improvement that is good for your soul. Watch out for the trap of self-improvement that is all about changing yourself in order to be "good enough." It originates from feeling unworthy, unacceptable, and inadequate. It's an un-fill-able hole, and you can waste your life trying to fill it. It feels desperate & draining, heavy & empty. It's easy to slip into this pit and hard to scramble out of it. Really, it's best just to avoid it all together.

#4. Discover what you love and do more of it. If you think you love drugs, or shopping, or sugar, consider the possibility that you might actually be loving the feeling of soothing pain or numbing heartache. Let yourself feel what you feel, and get some support if you need it. If you really love sleeping until 2:00 pm, or watching 12 hours of TV, or completing three-day marathons of Halo, consider the possibility that you're resisting that struggle that can accompany life. What you resist persists. Get out there. Do something that your heart and soul genuinely love.

#5. If you mess up, think of it as an opportunity to make something beautiful. The worst mistakes I've ever made turned out to be the greatest lessons I needed to learn. Don't try to always make the "right" choice. Take action in spite of uncertainty. Screw up and then open yourself up to the lesson. It's always there; if you look for it, you will find it. Major mistakes and subsequent self-reflection will teach you who you are, who you're not, and who you want to be.

#6. Life is not a competition. We're all in this together. Enough said.

#7. It's worth the time and effort to take a look inside your heart and know what deeply matters to you. Knowing this will allow you to make decisions that fill you up instead of suck you dry.

#8. The little things end up being the big things. Don't tell little white lies. Share your smile. Get in a little exercise every day. Don't sugar-coat your truth. And, while we're on the topic of sugar, if you cut it out of your life now, you'll be better off. Really. It's nasty stuff that messes up your mind and body.

#9. Log off. Of Twitter, of facebook, of your phone. Get comfy being with yourself. Connect with the healing vibes of nature; bury your hands in the grass and your feet in the sand. You have a limited capacity for connection. If you're plugged into technology, you're unplugged from yourself and nature.

#10. Tap into and hold onto your true self. It's who the world most needs you to be. This ride can be a rough one. Don't let the darkness extinguish your light.

Gemma Stone is a registered clinical psychologist who combines the science of psychology with the power of spirituality to help people heal the past, love the present, and light up the future. Head over to her digital home www.GemmaStone.org and sign up for the Guide to Living a Happy, Healthy, Successful Life.

♥ ♥ ♥ ♥ ♥

10 TIPS TO HANDLING FEELING LIKE A STRANGER IN YOUR OWN FAMILY

First of all I would like to tell you that you are not alone. In these days there are uncountable kids and teenagers in the same situation, somehow not understood or even feeling they are not wanted, because there is no point of interest that could be a match for a family life in peace and harmony. The idea of what that should look like is too different between parents and children. What can we do when we discover that reality as a young person? Run away? Hang on? Disappearing in self-denial and unworthiness? I can tell you that I am one of these beings too and as a 16 year old girl I came very close to wanting to end my life. Today I am grown up and I have been blessed with many miracles in my life and I will give you 10 reasons to understand why your life is like it is, who you are, what you have come to accomplish on earth and what you can do to find yourself as well as happiness and joy in life.

#1. Understanding why. Everything in existence is on its evolutionary way, so is planet earth and all life on it. There are several cycles of life running simultaneously and when all cycles are in total alignment with each other, mayor shifts occur. In these times we enter a new spiral of evolution. We got years, decades, centuries, millenniums, 5 millenniums, 10 millenniums, a quarter of a millenium. Different planets are moving around the sun. Time works similar and alignment happens when a decade, century, millennium, 5 millenniums and 25,000 years are coming together into one time frame. That is our situation now. All children born in that time frame are already coming with the new life frequencies. It is a different understanding, manifesting the new spiral of evolution on earth. Parents have been born at the end of the old spiral with a totally different structure and understanding of what life looks like. They have been educated to function in a stressful world. There was no time or very little for heart desires. You have come to destroy that old pattern and bring back true feeling. Living from the heart, living out of a box and going for your inner longings. This often does not match with what parents think is the best. This can create disharmony in the family, to a point where the pain often gets to the soul level and we just want to leave. So what can we do?

#2. Acceptance. Knowing the truth and the reason why they cannot understand us. It depends on us to make the difference because that is our mission, making and living the difference. It begins with accepting the situation as not a personal one, but as a global evolutionary process. We are all going through it, no matter what nation, culture or education we have. In this phase we begin to understand that we are part of a bigger plan, every single one of us. You too.

#3. How to overcome soul pain. Once we can feel that truth in our hearts we begin to relax, as we know, that our parents, just don't know what to do with us. We do not fit into their old educational concept of obedience. We are free spirits and need to express that. Our deeper understanding leads us to the power of forgiveness. They just do not know what they are to do. They are lost with our unconventional reactions and wishes. Forgiveness is the biggest power of healing as we set ourselves free from that pain of asking "why", because now we know and can understand them. We can let go the feeling of being a victim.

#4. Finding your own inner values. Don't judge yourself or others. We learn to stop judging our parents and ourselves, because we have learned to focus on the best way to maintain peace and stop fighting against them. Fighting creates an even bigger mess. The most intelligent way is to focus on our own inner values. Even if we hear all the time that we are not able or worthy or whatever they think they have to tell us. Don't react on these words, forgive and let go and focus on the values. YOU know in your heart. Focus on the talents you have.

#5. Think about your life dreams. Take a journal and write all your feelings down and then work on them. One by one. Do the same with your talents. In this way, you will find out what you wish to do in your life. Let your heart decide, as the mind will miss guide you.

#6. The power of vision. Once you find your life dream, shift it into a vision that becomes alive within your heart, soul and your entire being. In that state you do not bother any more about what others think. Let them be. Stay focused on your vision.

#7. Making a decision. That is a crucial moment, because a decision is the first step of realizing your dream life. You decide to go for it no matter what comes your way.

#8. How to overcome the feeling to give up. There will be moments that appear like invincible obstacles. These are moments in which you are trained to trust in yourself, in your vision and in your talent. These moments are very important as they make us strong. So take them as tools of learning and the obstacles will disappear.

#9. How and why to open up from your heart. You are born as a heart based person and the functional world tries to shut our heart down. We only can realize ourselves in full potential when we learn how to live from our heart, connected to the soul and the higher realms. It is our way to live, that makes us authentic beings, ready to express ourselves as we are.

#10. Go for your goal and keep your dream alive. Each time something happens, focus on your dream, your goal and let opinions of others just be a tool of self control. Accept them and when it does not feel right, let go and keep your dream alive, without hard defence. This is a process of re-evolution inside of you.

What you need, you have within yourself – do not seek it outside, that only creates more pain and suffering. In order to receive we have to learn how to give and to forgive and remember: You are different because you came to make a difference and live from your heart. Be and let others be what they have chosen to live. As long as you need your parents, be gentle and respectful as they give you a bed, food and a shelter. They are more lost than you are. You will find a peaceful way to live your dream. Be grateful for every experience, as they make you grow.

I did – and you can too – it turns out to be a blessing to be different. You will find that out on your own, step by step. Go for it and live your difference. You are wonderful. Allow yourself to be the love you are. Blessing on your way.

By **Regina E.H.Ariel** www.globallightparadise.com
www.2thepowerofspirit6.com
www.arielangelartandphotography.com
http://www.awakenedradio.net/ariels-golden-key.php

♥ ♥ ♥ ♥ ♥

10 TIPS TO FEEL GREAT ABOUT YOUR LIFE

Being a teenager can be rough, it's a transitional time from childhood into adulthood. Quite often teenagers feel misunderstood for this reason and the peer pressure can be overwhelming. Here are 10 tips to help them feel great about their lives.

#1. Have a great support network. Support in life is important. It allows you to explore, knowing that you have people backing you up. I was fortunate to have my parents. If you don't have this, then seek out others that are willing to support your dreams.

#2. Find a mentor. People who are successful are generally ready and willing to give back. Find someone in the field that you think you want to explore and connect with them. They will have much to teach you and they will also shorten the learning curve.

#3. Explore things that you enjoy. We often hear the phrase, "Do what you are passionate about" I say reduce this to the most simplistic, because let's face it, sometimes you don't know. Explore what interests you. This will lead you to know and understand what brings you joy. It is also a known fact that when we are doing what we enjoy and love, our confidence increases.

#4. Find your own cool. It takes courage to be you. I remember dressing a certain way at school and not really caring much what others thought...this was ballsy and fun. Finding your own cool is really about exploring who you are. Give yourself permission.

#5. Set out markers. Climbing Mount Everest is daunting. Taking one step at a time is how it's done. Setting out markers (mini-goals) allows you to see that you are making progress and will inevitably get you to where you are going. Baby steps.

#6. Give back. It's a very strong theory that when we feel low in our lives, we are instructed to give back. The feeling of contribution is one of the six human emotions that we all crave. Become a Big Sister, volunteer in your community. Not only will they thank you for it, but it will leave you with an everlasting sense of contribution - trust me.

#7. Self-care. My friend Leanne Young is adamant about self-nurture - self-care. Do your nails, spend time alone, write in your journal. It all goes in your emotional bank account for you to draw on when things get pissy (and they will get pissy).

#8. You get to start over - at any point. It is unfortunate that we are taught that making mistakes (I call it learning) is frowned upon. Life is all about learning and the only way we learn is by doing. Error -> correct -> error -> correct. That's how it's done.

#9. Guiding principles. This goes without saying that all of the above should be done with these in mind. Guiding principles in life are your pillars with which you stand. What is important to you? What are your non-negotiables? Speaking your truth was never more important.

#10...and lastly, have fun! Taking life too seriously makes everyone a bore. Your life, your book. What do you want written in it? Everyone is a story, I can't wait to read yours - be blessed. Life's a daring adventure or nothing at all - Helen Keller.

PS: I will read this and continue to take my own advice

Kimberly Berges is an associate who specializes in International Property sales, specifically Trujillo Honduras. She has sold 9 million dollars' worth of real estate in Trujillo and has a working knowledge of all facets of the purchasing process. She is a wife, mother and grandmother (5 grandchildren and counting) Her passion lies in helping people realize their goals and dreams. She has competed in natural body building competition placing second in the women's heavy weight division for Western Canada. With a determined attitude and focus, she believes anything is possible. http://HondurasLiving.com/

10 TIPS ON BUILDING SELF-CONFIDENCE

Self-confidence relates to self-assuredness in one's personal judgment, ability and power. Being confident in yourself is infectious if you present well, others will want to follow in your footsteps towards success. (Wikipedia)

#1. Have one hobby and become competent on this topic! Competence needs curiosity. Positive is that your curiosity will automatically lead you to this hobby. Learn about it! Study its history, view the broadness and practice it.

#2. Know WHAT you are because right now you are too young to realize WHO you are! Know your talents and your favorite school subjects. Know the source of your hobby: WHY do you love it? What is your special talent on this? Language? Technology? Creativity? Art? Be aware: whenever someone verbally attacks you on it or say, challenges you to keep it positive, have at least 3 answers! If your challenger makes it asking you three questions, which you can all answer with a smile, make sure to end up in a conversation. Competence on one stage in life is a great basic.

#3. Find three things you very much like or love of your body! This is the core of your growing self-love! Is it the colour of your eyes? Your height? Got those cute small ears? Love the tip of your nose? Your voice? The freckles on your cheek? Can you hold your breath real long under water? Love your broad shoulders?

#4. Have at least four friends with whom you share your time & challenges! Meet personally. Exchange with them, discuss things and support yourself. This is important to learn and keep your self-honesty. Be honest, it will ease your soul.

#5. Find a role model if you're up to something in life! Not everyone knows about it at this time in life, but some already do. If you are one of these few teenagers, keep your eyes open for someone to follow. A passive mentor is a good support for your mental stability. If you can rely on someone´s success, you will build your self-confidence faster than others.

#6. Have a job, even if it is only for six weeks! Make some money! Test yourself, choose your job and seek inside WHY you want to THIS right now. Secondary have a plan for what you will do with money wisely.

#7. Set your first "high" goal in life and go for it! This high goal should at least challenge you for 1-2 years before you can reach it, and to get there you should undergo at least some decisions in life. This will teach you to deal with consequences. Decisions and its consequences will strongly build your self-confidence.

#8. Create a positive, healthy self-communication! Be a good director in the beginning while programming yourself. Watch out how you speak to yourself, always. If you don´t like how your parents talk to you, change it. Write a new text, which gives you a better feeling and be honest. Study this text. Read your first book on psychology. Be aware of being a programmer yourself and how you will influence yourself. If you like the way your parents communicate with you, stay with it in your mind and grow it into more.

#9. Have dreams and a first plan for your future! Take all challenges in life to get there! No excuses. Start looking forward! It is hard to see something for many of us as teenagers, but the craziest thought, which is escorting you since quite a while or even since some years, is your "inception". It stays with you and becomes your dream. It won´t let go! Did you find it already? Write it down.

#10. Generate success! Success is the best leader to self-confidence, but it´s only 1 leadership item of 9 others to get to the full potential of self-confidence. Use the stage of sports, your hobby, a contest and any other interesting competition to get there. Learn from others to reach your first 100%! If you once made it to 100% on 1 stage in your young life, you reach the tip of the first mountain. And you know what? You'll love that VIEW!! Make sure to be ready for the valley which comes next, and use it to relax and communicate with others for a while - before you think of the next mental mountain to climb.

Professor Raj Persaud posits that true self-confidence comes from an attitude where you promise yourself, no matter how difficult the problem life throws at you, that you will try as hard as you can to help yourself. You acknowledge that sometimes your efforts to help yourself may not result in success, as often being properly rewarded is not in your control.

Rita Jaskolla was born in 1962 in Germany. She already was a strong minded child and now turned into a skilled woman who walked through chaos in life -on one stage. A tough disease Career as a teenager set her direction. As a young adult she started working full time in the Automotive Supply Chain with worldwide tasks and added up 25 years by now. Fate struck her more often and when checking the lessons learned in life she realized it was her extraordinary "chaos intelligence" which she developed under all those challenging circumstances. By now she is offering her abilities to others and works on an international career with the topics: Leadership in Chaos, Ideas and Decision making (in chaos). http://arrivinginchicagoritajaskollabook.com/

10 TIPS TO BEING COOL AND CREATIVE

#1. Be yourself. You are unique in the fact that you are the only you. What are your likes and dislikes? Stand by what you enjoy doing and you will attract friends who do the same.

#2. Wear clothes that suit your personality. To show your creativity, be unique in how you dress. If you are artsy, look for clothing that has an interesting detail or vintage inspired. Don't limit yourself to what everyone else is wearing. Wear a cool tie, with a jacket and cool runners. Experiment with your look. Go to vintage or second hand stores and look for cool combinations.

#3. Socialize. Spend quality time with your friends and family. Go out to movies, listen to music, and don't let other's opinions of you become more important than your opinion of yourself.

#4. Take care of your body. I know you have heard this before but exercising and eating properly will make you more confident, happier and healthier. Don't get caught up with the scale. My son was a chubby guy when he was young and now is over 6 feet and 175lbs. Lean and mean...and he was a creative kid too.

#5. Have a unique, expressive hairstyle. I know your parents may kill me for saying this, but this is an easy thing to change and it is fun. If your parents don't agree to let you do fun colors, add bows, headbands, ribbons and hats are awesome.

#6. Just be happy. I know cliché, but you have a choice to be miserable or not. Don't hang on to anger, let it go, go talk to whoever about whatever is bothering you and clear the air. Write in a journal or take a run and blow off some energy. And don't gossip about your friends, this just makes it worse. You will attract friends if you are friendly and happy.

#7. Explore your creativity. Try different medians, paint, draw, do pottery, write poetry, take a weaving class. Take a class or just go to YouTube, there is a video for everything.

#8. Attend a theatre camp. Most cities run programs throughout the year and in the summer. A great way to meet friends with similar interests and it is a riot.

#9. Take a dance class or start music lessons. Hip hop classes are everyone, try a beginners class. Great for your body and dancers are the best! Take a music class or attend a music program. A music program may give you a better chance of meeting creative and musical friends.

#10. Take a computer class in Adobe Photoshop or in Illustrator. This may also be a good way to build on a future career in design.

BONUS TIP: Just one more: If you really feel like you don't fit in your school or social circle, there is always the opportunity to attend an Arts School. This is becoming really popular and the acceptance of unique individuals is much better in the arts environment.

Dianna Bowes is the Founder and President of Fabulous@50 and Creative On The Move. She has had a creative spirit since a child, but has recently started to paint again. Her artistic talent led her into a career of graphic design and floral design. She sees the world in colors and shapes and connects with her creativity every day when she rides her bike through the river valley. Find out more about Dianna and her interests at www.fabulousat50.com or www.creativeonthemove.com

10 TIPS TO FEELING GREAT ABOUT YOUR LIFE

#1. Never seek to find your value in the opinions of others. That is a matter of your own heart and it is within you to know it.

#2. Don't put yourself above others. It can be a long way down with a hard landing.

#3. Don't put yourself below others. The soles of other's shoes hurt too much when they step on you. Stand up and take your place.

#4. Give back. Helping others is a great way to find out about who you are, what your talents, gifts and abilities are and how you can help change the world for the better.

#5. Remember that the more others try to bring you down, the more they are hurting inside. Have compassion for them because if they knew what love was and could love themselves, they would love you too.

#6. We all have a purpose for being here. Don't waste yours because you don't know who else it could affect if you do.

#7. There are people that we need in our life. There are people that we don't need in our life. Never be afraid to open the door for the right people and close the door to the wrong people.

#8. Think about this, how boring would the world be if we all looked and acted the same? Embrace your uniqueness and your individuality. Those are the qualities that will set you apart.

#9. Just because your grandparents, aunts, uncles, or parents did something a certain way doesn't mean you have to. The generations before us influence who we are, they don't define who we are.

#10. Don't label yourself and don't let others put labels on you. Labels are limiting. You are a living, breathing miracle with hope and a future. You can't put that in a box!

Shannon Berry is a wife and mother of three children, one who is 17 and in her graduating year of high school. She is also the owner and Director of Services of Capital Concierge. Every day she uses her talents and skills to help people have more time and less stress. She plans an event or two from time to time to help them have some fun too. Believe it or not, she was also a teenager once! Having witnessed these formative years from both perspectives she has seen and experienced how others can sometimes take us for granted or discount our potential simply because of our age. Her hope is that through this book, many will be inspired to realize their potential and live up to it, no matter what. www.CapConcierge.ca

10 TIPS TO LIVING SIMPLY

#1. Phone someone.

#2. Go for a walk.

#3. Go to the park or other nature spot.

#4. Read something motivating.

#5. Talk to parents/family.

#6. Write down what you are grateful for and say it out loud.

#7. Help someone else who is less fortunate.

#8. Visit with animals – show them love.

#9. Take a shower and wash away all the things that are bothering you.

#10. Distract yourself from your issues.

BONUS TIPS:
* Smile at people, they smile back.
* Hug someone you love.

Lisa McCarthy founded MeyeVU Interactive, Inc. to bring the Affirmations Mirror to the world. Working with technology, large organizations, membership groups and partners has prepared Lisa to launch her ideas into the consumer products marketplace. With over 20 years of experience in management, marketing, projects, teams and bringing ideas to life, it makes her the ideal person to launch MeyeVU Interactive.

Sent into foster care at a young age, Lisa suffered abuse and neglect, including burns over 40% of her body. She became a single mom at 21, but was determined to break the cycle of abuse, self-hate, and stifling dreams, to give her daughter a different life. Lisa put her two life-changing tools together into one powerful product: the Affirmations Mirror. MeyeVU Interactive is located in Burbank, CA. More information and products can be found at www.meyevu.com.

10 TIPS FOR PREVENTING CYBER BULLYING

#1. Education is power. Know exactly what cyber bullying is! Cyber bullying is the use of electronic communications to intimidate, control, manipulate, put down, falsely discredit, or humiliate another. These actions are deliberate, repeated, hostile, and intended to harm another. Electronic devices include cell phones, gaming systems, tablets, laptops and computers all which utilize the internet.

#2. Be a detective. "Google" yourself! Make sure to search your name in search engines on a regular basis. See if any of your personal information or photos are online that might be used as ammunition for a cyber bully to target you. If you find something make sure to remove it before there is a problem – after all, you don't want to help out the cyber bully.

#3. Take a breath. Think before you post! A split second decision can be instantly forwarded to millions in cyberspace and cause irreparable, permanent damage. If you wouldn't say it in person, don't post it online. You are constantly judged online and can ultimately be denied future scholarships, job opportunities, etc. based on what you posted online.

#4. Be conservative. Keep your photos PG! Always consider if you would want your family to see your images. Many lives have been ruined by "ex" boyfriends and girlfriends forwarding sexually explicit photos that were intended for their eyes only. Always remember – if it's digital – it can be sent to millions in a split second and your reputation can end up in the trash.

#5. Protect your password. Treat it like your toothbrush! You would never share your toothbrush right? Treat your password the same way. Don't leave it out for others to see and don't store it in a place that is easily accessed by others. Never give your information out to anyone – even your best friend. It is also a good practice to change your passwords at the minimum of once per month.

#6. Use your privacy controls. Better safe than sorry! Online social media sites offer you various options to protect yourself from online predators. Many predators pose as teenagers to get your information and your trust. You can never be too sure when it comes to cyberspace. On facebook, etc., go to your privacy settings to change your default setting to friends only.

#7. Always log out. Just like taking the key out of the ignition! Cyber bullies love to pose as others to threaten another undetected. Don't "save" your passwords in the log in fields – yes, it is convenient, but it also makes it that much easier for someone to log on to your account. Most importantly, make sure to never walk away from your electronic device while you are still logged in.

#8. Beware of false gifts. Cyber bullies are very tricky! Never open emails, text messages, etc. from people you don't know. Have the self- discipline to go ahead and delete them before reading. These links could have horrible repercussions such as tracking software, viruses, malware, etc. that could detect all your personal information, and/or destroy your computer.

#9. Save but don't respond. The Golden Rule! If you find that you are a victim of cyber bullying – DON'T RESPOND! They are looking for, and betting on, a reaction from you – so don't give them the satisfaction. Be sure to save the evidence and show it to your parents. If you are cyber stalked or threatened you made need to contact your school, an attorney and/or the police.

#10. Don't fight fire with fire. You just might get burned! Again, if you find that you are a victim of cyber bullying – DON'T RESPOND! Many victims have retaliated only to be accused of the original crime! Cyber bullies are very cunning and can even use the victim's parents as unwitting accomplices. They provoke the victim and when the victim lashes back they forward it to the parents of the victim who now think that their own kid started everything!

Gaill Blackburn is a wife and mother as well as author, healer, speaker, and non-profit co-founder. She considers herself a rather eclectic entrepreneur, with a BS in Business Management, an AA in Construction Drafting, and a diverse background consisting of art, graphics, construction, business, project management, computers, web design, writing, and various forms of energy healing. Her lofty career ambitions took a drastic turn when she gave birth to a beautiful, differently-abled daughter in 1997 and realized what was truly important in life. She left corporate America to care for her daughter and subsequently immersed herself in the world of Volunteerism.

Gaill is happily married to Bret, a two-time traumatic brain injury survivor, and mom to Britney, who has already endured over 20 surgeries. Her family is her life, and she revels in her husband and daughter's determination to not let anything get them down. She is the Co-Founder of Motivational Small Talk Inc., a non-profit corporation that specializes in bully prevention, diversity and dwarfism awareness, disability education, and motivational speaking. Gaill started asking God to use her as a vessel to share his love and a vehicle to spread his word over a decade ago and has been led on a spiritual quest ever since. She has studied a variety of healing methods, and as most healers, developed her own style encompassing parts of each of them.

Gaill absolutely loves helping others, and feels incredibly blessed to achieve this through her God given gifts for which she is eternally grateful. You can find out more about Gaill online at www.GaillBlackburn.com, www.MotivationalSmallTalk.org, and www.AngelicHealingsLLC.com. More tips can be found online at www.Bullying.MotivationalSmallTalk.org

10 TIPS FROM YOUR ANGELS

#1. We are always around You.

#2. We love You dearly.

#3. We know You are special.

#4. We see your heart and know how kind You really are.

#5. We see Your path and know that while it may look like a roller coaster to You, we are here to tell You that at Your deepest down remember, there is only UP to go.

#6. We know You are strong enough to handle everything, You'll see.

#7. We love that You have created your life to send You many opportunities to grow ~ which You will do amazingly well.

#8. Sometimes You will feel us brush your cheek or create a breeze when there is none, just a little reminder that yes, we are still with You.

#9. You are the most important person in our lives.

#10. Love yourself as much as we love You.

Cynthia Segal is a renowned International Intuitive Consultant. Her innate ability, to accurately see into her Clients lives and effectively guide them, covers everything from matters of the heart through medical conditions, and business dealings to guidance for their beloved pets.

Cynthia's accuracy has earned her a prestigious spot on the list of the World's Best Intuitives, Psychics and Mediums where she is ranked in the top 20. Her gifts have been featured in an award winning documentary movie, in several books written by her Clients and are shared in her books and on radio shows throughout the world. Cynthia's sense of purpose and passion for her work is evident in the ease and joy she brings to each Client Session.

Her eternal optimism and glowing smile leave you feeling comforted and secure. Cynthia's clients lovingly call their Sessions with her "The Red Phone To God". Find out more about her at www.CynthiaSegal.com or www.TheRedPhoneToGod.com

♥ ♥ ♥ ♥ ♥

10 TIPS TO BEING TRUE TO YOUR IDENTITY

#1. Be true to who you are. Gay, str8, bi, not interested, it doesn't define you.

#2. Party responsibly. Be aware of family history, addiction is deadly.

#3. Learn to forgive, take the blame off everyone else and look at your part.

#4. Always ask "Do I want to be right, or do I want to be happy?"

#5. No matter the mistakes they make, family is a gift, and should be cherished.

#6. Never think any job is beneath you.

#7. When speaking ask, "Is it kind, is it necessary, does it make the situation better?"

#8. Take action, no matter how small, for action is the key to making any dream come true.

#9. Service to others with no expectation of a return, will bring dividends far greater than you could imagine.

#10. No matter how hard you try to avoid it, you will at some point sound exactly like the parents you are rebelling against...embrace it.

By **Michael McDonnell**

The following is written by Kelly Falardeau: **Michael McDonnell** is one of my oldest friends from high school. We both had our challenges because we were both considered "different" from the rest of the teenagers in school. Michael was gay and I was burnt. We used to hang out in the school lounge and talk about life. The school rumour was that Michael was gay, but back in those days, it wasn't acceptable to be gay in any way and so he kept his true identity hidden, even amongst all the rumours. I didn't care whether he was gay or not, he was still my friend and deserved to have a life no matter what he was.

At 18 Michael had his first drink. He told me he was determined he would be on the same road as the rest of his family... lots of fights, drinking and craziness growing up. Not only did he have to deal with his family, but his younger brother had committed suicide, right after graduating from high school. When he took the first drink life became bearable and the pain he felt melted away. He was funny, popular and ready to conquer the world, until the drinking took over his life. Then his life became unbearable again and he lost his family and even moved away to another country to escape, losing touch with his family. He thought they were lost forever until the day that I found Michael only three weeks before our 25 year high school reunion.

One of my proudest moments in my life is helping Michael find his family. When I finally found him on facebook, I asked if he wanted me to see if his parents' and grandparents' phone numbers were still in the phone book (I still lived in the same town as we grew up in) and he said sure. I gave him two phone numbers and he called them. Sure enough, he got to talk to his mom, grandma and uncle for the first time in 25 years and since has been reunited with his long lost family. His mom, dad and grandma all came and thanked me for helping to reconnect their long lost son/grandson with them. They didn't know how to find him and thought he was gone forever.

Michael has since quit drinking and has six years of sobriety, moved back to Canada to be with his family and now has his own house. To connect with Michael, email him at sober07@me.com.

10 TIPS IN SEARCH OF YOUR OWN UNIQUE IDENTITY!

Every living person, regardless of age, has their own unique self and unique way of doing things. Each person has their own likes and dislikes, preferences, perception, dress code...the list goes on. Some things can easily be changed like hair color, for example. Some things can't easily be changed like height, for example.

Has anyone ever tried to 'change' you or have you ever tried to change yourself to be like someone else? If you like something like the color green, you will tend to be drawn more to things with that color. If you don't like something like animals you will tend to stay away from anything that involves animals. Are those preferences good or bad, right or wrong? No! Is it okay to like or not like something. You don't 'have to' change for anyone.

There will not be another person on this planet like you! No other person will feel like you or have the same family circumstances and dynamics as you. That makes you unique and different, which is absolutely okay. In a world where people tend to want to 'be the same as...' you still have aspects and qualities that make up you. It's fun to have friends who like the things you like or want to wear the same clothes as you do and yet you still have a unique difference.

As much as you are growing into being a teenager or changing into being a young adult, one thing is certain...there will always be change. There will be a stage in your life where you don't want to be like other people around you and you will try to find your own identity. This is an important stage to walk through. We share 10 tips to assist you in searching for your own unique identity.

#1. Grow to trust your self! No one knows you like you are coming to know yourself. You take you wherever you go 24/7/365. You know in any moment if you are not feeling good or something doesn't feel right. You also know in any moment if you are telling the truth or if you are telling a little white lie. You also know when you sense something doesn't feel so good or if fear is taking over because you are afraid of something. You will be the only one you can truly count on through your whole life. For those reasons alone, you are so worth getting to know, trust and love.

#2. Treat everyone uniquely! How would you feel if 'all the kids' were treated the same? If one teenager likes pizza, all the teenagers have to have pizza. If one kid lies or cheats, all kids are liars and cheaters. Does that make sense? Not all teenagers are the same, just like not all adults are the same. People may enforce the same rules or guidelines but as you are coming to see in life people are different in their temperaments, their upbringing, their reactions and behaviors. Start to notice what is unique in the people around you as well as what is unique within you.

#3. Relationships are required to live! One thing that will be consistent in your life is relationships with people. If you want or need to buy something, other people will be involved! That is a reality. Relationships show you so much about yourself. Through other people, you can learn what you like and don't like about many things...things like how to treat people, to how you like to dress. Relationships can help you find clarity with your own identity.

#4. Communication. Communication is necessary and takes place on so many levels. You communicate through so many things including your body language, your words or silence, song or dance, art, clothing and even your energy. What is being spoken? Someone can look like they are having a good time at a party and yet you feel how they are bothered about being there. Someone can say they feel happy and yet you can see they aren't. Communicating doesn't only take place through words. How you feel can speak volumes even if you don't say anything.

#5. Love your physical body. Your body is a powerful communicator and a miracle machine! What is causing your body to do what it is doing? How does it get your attention? You take your body with you everywhere you go 24/7/365. Your body will communicate to you when something isn't right. Through your aches or pains there will be a message for you about what is going on around you or in you. Over time you will hear what your body has to tell you. In that moment your body will 'right' itself and heal whatever was ailing you.

#6. Inner guidance. Your inner guidance is available to you every minute of every day. What does it feel like, look like, sound like? Start to become aware of how your inner guidance works for and with you. As you experience life, play with little messages you may be getting and notice what comes of it. With that awareness, you will grow to trust yourself. Over time working with those 'nudges that you have all the answers within regardless of what others may or may not say.

#7. Working with your six senses. Your senses are the most powerful tools you have. Your senses include your intuition and feelings. Not everyone is sensitive. Information that comes to you through your intuition may be totally different from everyone else. That doesn't make it 'wrong information'. What you do with that information makes all the difference for you. Along your journey you may learn different techniques and methods in doing things. They can be like tools to work with and considered part of your tool belt but they will not 'be you.'

#8. Your whole self. Your whole self includes a body, mind and spirit. There is your physical body and your non-physical mind and spirit. You are a package which works together perfectly for your own learning and growing.

#9. Searching and finding. Once you start to notice that you are unique in your own way, you will find you won't be searching so much to change your unique identity.

#10. It's okay to be alone. You will have many times in life where you will be alone to think things through or to do something on your own. Those times will be when there is no one around to tell you what to do. It's in those moments when you are making your own decisions where you truly find your self.

Life is not a 'once and done.' You don't go to school and then you are done. You don't get a job and then you are done. You don't clean up your bedroom and then you are done. Just like you continue to wash your clothes and continue to straighten up your room, life goes on. You are continually living the process of life. You move through life no matter what comes up to deal with. As identical twins we have spent our whole lives trying to be and do things the same. It has been through our experiences that we encourage you to find your own unique identity and live that uniqueness.

By The Twins, Sheila Unique and Sharon Thom

Being together all their lives, Sheila and Sharon have come to find their own inner strength. Although they appeared to have walked the same path, their experiences were anything but the same and through these experiences they have come to realize that everyone is unique. They did everything together and then had to learn how do things separately. In the process they found their own individuality. The Twins, Sheila and Sharon have a vision of assisting individuals/groups to be in a place where they can move through their blocks with ease and grace. Each Twin approaches their work in a unique wonderful way complimenting each other, offering a unique powerful healing experience for anyone who chooses to be part of the clearing process. For more information on The Twins, Sheila Unique and Sharon Thom, go to: www.UniqueEnergy.ca

♥ ♥ ♥ ♥ ♥

10 TIPS TO BEING BOLD, BRILLIANT AND YOU!

#1. Life is full of twists and turns, ups and downs. It's all on how you choose to live your life.

#2. Life isn't about crying when you fall down (and you will). Life is about learning and choosing how to get back up and dance in the rain.

#3. Life is the dance, and you are the dancer in that dance. How will you choose to choreograph your dance of life?

#4. Just keep putting one foot in front of the other. Believe in yourself, and let others help you.

#5. Dance is a metaphor for life. Will you watch the dance from the audience of the beautiful dancer on stage, or will you choose to be that dancer in the spot light of your life?

#6. Strut your stuff, dance your dance. YOU were born to shine!

#7. Be brave! Be bold! Be YOU!

#8. YOU are not alone! Someone is always waiting, willing, and able to listen to ANYTHING you need to share or talk about.

#9. What you have to share with the world, is important. YOU matter!

#10. Miracles are everywhere, just be willing to look and believe in them!

Aime Hutton is known to many around the world as an inspirational dancer, speaker and author. She has been published in two international e-zines, one for women in business and one on the subject of inspiring women. As well, she has published her first co-authored book "Take Flight ~ True Stories of how Dreams Shape Our Lives" with her chapter called "Looking Like a Dancer". She has also been a featured speaker for eWomen Network at Provincial events, inspiring women to get in touch with their inner dancer for a play date. She owns her own business of Awakening Goddess, inspiring radiant play and confidence through dance. Aime has also recently started a 'little sister' company called Wonder Girls Camp for girls in grades 6 - 9 to develop self-confidence, self-esteem, and celebrating being bold, brilliant and unique! www.AwakeningGoddess.com

10 TIPS TO FORGIVENESS AND LETTING GO

Letting go of the past is not easy I know, but let me guide you through some steps to do so. The steps involved are forgiveness, truth, & self-love.

When I was a child I was bullied. They thought it was funny, but for me, it was extremely hurtful. I remember coming home from school crying and trying to explain to my mom what had transpired that day but I never felt heard. Not her fault in the least as she had never experienced this and had no clue what to do. It was a lonely time but I thought I would get over it, eventually. I didn't! Years later I came to realize that every time I had been beat down, my soul and my self-esteem had been wounded. For every wound I had built a wall around my heart to protect me, so I thought. One day those walls came crashing down and all the hurt came back. As a very mature adult I had to work through those past events in order to regain my self-worth and my self-esteem. I was not stupid, ugly, and worthless!

Sure I was a skinny, short kid with coke bottle glasses but I was caring, loving, and giving. So why did it matter what the exterior package looked like? As a child and later a teen I didn't have the tools to help me get past the hurt, embarrassment, and the self-doubt. Only later did I realize what this all meant and how it had affected my adult life. The following tips are what I know to be true for me!

#1. Before you can let go of the past you must speak the truth about it. This doesn't mean that you have to stand in the downtown plaza and shout out the wrongs that were done to you. It means that you must first acknowledge the wounds to yourself. It is true, it did happen, and it's ok. The past is over and will only repeat itself if you let it. You have the control.

#2. Now that you've spoken your truth, the next thing is to look within. Talk about how it hurt you then and how it hurts you now.

#3. Get a journal and start writing about how you feel etc. This is for your eyes only. Tip: anything negative that I write I rip the pages out and then burn them.

#4. Truth told, now what? This is what you must understand....the event happened and there's nothing you can do about it! Why? Cause it's a past event and guess what you can't go back unless you have the time machine from the movie Back to the Future! Let it go!

#5. Accept the fact that the event or events have hurt you and probably have hurt badly. This is also part of telling the truth. People do what they do because of their own issues and sorry to say but the same goes for you! Yes, a whole lot of stuff to work on!

#6. Now I hear some of you saying "I'm not forgiving so and so". What happened is unforgivable" and yep you're right, it is. Here's the secret, "you do not have to forgive the act nor the person. This is not about them, it's about you." I'm not kidding! Forgiveness is for you and your healing not theirs.

#7. You're probably mad at me now and hey sorry to break it to you but this is what I know to be true for me and from the work I've done. Accept it to be so!

#8. Forgiveness is about forgiving yourself for hanging on to it. Let the person that hurt you go. Trust and believe that this wasn't about you, it was about them and their own issues. Once you embrace this part, the healing begins.

#9. Last thing I'd like to add is this: Once you identify hurts or wounds, and the nasty people in your life, write them a apology letter. No, you are not going to give it to them, so have no fear. The letter is about releasing all that pent up anger and shame that you are holding in your soul and heart. You no longer want to hang on to it, right? So, let it go!!! Write it, then burn it!

#10. This is the self-love part. Repeat after me "I love myself enough to let go of the past and others that have hurt me. I am worthy of love, acceptance, and forgiveness. I am a child of GOD and I have a purpose and a mission in this world and I plan on making it so!!!" Go forth and change your world cause I know you can. Your wounds are your greatest gifts.

Denise Ouellette is a Reiki Master/Practitioner, Certified DREAM COACH®, speaker, workshop facilitator, and author. Through her coaching practice, Soulful Discoveries Wholistic Therapy & Mentoring Inc., she inspires and empowers women of all ages. Working through the things that hold you back, she works with you to create the life that you want and deserve! For more information visit: www.SoulfulDiscoveries.ca

10 TIPS FOR TEENAGERS TO GIVE WHERE THEY LIVE

Being beautiful for teenagers isn't always easy but one of the best ways I've found to love myself is to show everything around me a little love. My home, my community, and the earth. Sounds like a huge task? Not as hard as one would think.

#1. Fill your space with things you love. It's not about the latest trends, what television or your peers think you should have, price isn't the point. Simply ask yourself, "Do I love it?" I happen to have the geeky obsession of loving buttons. Yes the ones sewn on your clothes. Why? Why not. They're small, unique, simple, and functional. Around my rooms you'll find jars of them, and jars of rocks, antique marbles, and pretty much anything I love to look at, touch, and be surrounded by. Granted my friends don't share my love of vintage owls and old books but when they're in my space they always feel comfortable. My "stuff" isn't what they would have chosen to buy but it is a reflection of me; if they're comfortable with me they're comfortable with my treasures.

#2. Love your yard. Nature was here first. If you mow it, sow it, and grow it it'll thank you back by being the first beautiful thing that feeds your heart when you come home.

#3. Give yourself to family. Be open and loving with family and they'll return the favor. Life is too short to battle the little stuff with people that share your space and have your best interest. They may not always be right but neither are you.

#4. Be kind to your school. It may not always be the easiest place to spend your days; homework, peer pressure, and a whole lot of your time. It is the place to give a huge amount of the tools you need for adulthood, go and learn all you can!

#5. Volunteer!!!! You may think the teen years are rough, and a lot of times they are, but there is always someone out there who has it worse than you. A person or organization is looking for a little hand up and you can give it.

#6. Consume less. Less is more is true. Quit worrying about what everybody else has, freak out about where it's going when they're done with it. Our landfills are bursting at the seams and nobody gets a do over if we wreck the planet. Is that name brand pair of jeans, to go with the other 10 pairs you already have, worth trying to figure out how to fix the earth in your adult years?

#7. If you have to shop, buy locally. All those small businesses you see around town are the ones supporting your sports teams, high school grads, silent auctions etc. Those small business owners give it all, often at the expense of their own paycheques because they have chosen to open a business in a community they love. Show a little love back and buy your stuff from them before the big stores.

#8. Don't litter! Stop laughing and look around. You might think that's a no brainer but looking at the garbage floating around my neighbourhood, "somebody's littering", and that brings down the beauty factor huge.

#9. Give yourself permission to be authentic. If you give your true spirit to everyone you meet you'd be surprised by the return. You have contact with tons of people every day. If you give your true self at every interaction you'll start creating a world that is simply amazing. Everyone wants to be surrounded by a clean and beautiful place full of happy people that have help when they need it and give help where they can.

#10. Give to yourself. Give yourself the gift of time with yourself. A little time every week to reflect on what kind of world you want to grow up in and how you can start making that a reality is a wonderful gift. Journal it, vision board it, sing it if you need to. You get to grow up in the most amazing generation but it's going to take a lot of work from amazing teens like you.

My tips to be a beautiful teen are to make a beautiful world; dream it, work for it, and create it. It seems like a lot of work, I know but someone has to start it, be a leader. When you start showing the love and respect for your home, community , and earth others will want to be a part of that and work with you. You'll be beautiful and so will everything around you.

By **Barb Scully**

10 TIPS TO COPE WITH GRIEF AND LOSS

Adversity is never ending. Just when you've overcome one of life's challenges, another is soon to follow. You can bet on it. It's important to remember this so that you can learn how to cope and conquer, especially with grief and loss. I can't say that I've always been strong or that I've always known how to put this into action, but what's important is that I CAN today. You can, too! I use the terms "cope" and "conquer" because they define how I've handled some of my greatest challenges. I have had to cope with loss, change, sadness, and stress, among other things, and while going through the process, I then conquered. I conquered my fears, conquered depression and conquered any self-defeating thoughts that would keep me from creating happiness in my life.

My tips come from my pain and experience. In 2005, I lost my mother to suicide. I was only 22-years-old. In an instant I became a motherless child lost in what I thought was a very cruel and unfair world. At age 23, I narrowly escaped a kidnapping by jumping out of the trunk of a moving car. Only months later, I was brutally assaulted with acid, resulting in 3rd degree full-thickness burns to 30% of my body. Recovering from the loss of my mother and the loss of my identity was not an easy process. I went through all of the stages of grief. I was angry, sad, shocked, in denial and scared until the day I accepted what had happened. I had to allow myself to feel, sometimes forcing myself to really go through it, internalize it, and then learn from the experience and move forward. That's not to say that I moved forward unaffected or that it wasn't incredibly difficult, but I did it.

I am not a psychiatrist, doctor, or in any way special. I am a perfectly imperfect person who's overcome some pretty unbelievable challenges. In many ways, I am just like you. I hope that you find my tips to be useful and helpful, and I hope that you know that you are not alone.

#1. Bad things happen to good people every day, and you could be one of them. Remember, it's not always what happens to you, but how you react that matters most. Just like the Japanese Proverb says, "Fall down seven times, stand up eight." It is possible to move forward.

#2. It's important to have a good support system while going through your trying time. Surround yourself with people who care about you—close family and friends, a mentor or confidante. It's important to have someone to talk to and support you when you feel discouraged and alone.

#3. Seek out resources for coping with grief and loss, whether it is a therapist or a support group. Surrounding yourself with people who can empathize with you will give you a sense of community, and may give you hope that better days will come. Meeting with others who've been through something similar and seeing that they've managed to overcome sadness and shock may help you see that it's possible to get through it.

#4. Wholeheartedly believe in yourself and the possibility of moving forward. Some people call this faith. Know that you have a purpose and that your experiences make you stronger.

#5. It's important to have a plan. Map out some short-term and long-term goals for yourself and ways that you will deal with your grief. Occupy your time with things that make you happy or bring you comfort. Finding constructive ways to channel your sadness will not only help you feel better, it will help you move past the pain and accomplish goals in the process. (I found that having a plan was very important for me around family holidays. My mom made our holidays very special, so thinking about celebrating them without her was very hard. Having a plan for how I'd celebrate and incorporate her memory into the holidays made them more manageable.)

#6. Hold tightly to your memories. As Maya Angelou so eloquently stated, "People will forget what you said, people will forget what you did, but people will never forget how you made them feel." This can be said for your loved one. You will always remember how they made you feel and no one can take that away from you.

#7. Find ways to celebrate your loved one's life. Whether it's a celebratory dinner where stories are shared or a candle light vigil, you are remembering that person and the impact they had on you. It's a great way to keep their memory alive and share your love for them with others.

#8. Own your feelings, be honest about them, and share them when you need to. There is nothing worse than holding something in or saying "I'm fine" when you're really not. Especially when you're sad or in pain. You're not always going to want to be strong and that's okay. So cry when you need to. It's all a part of the process.

#9. Remember that you and *only* you are in control of your own happiness. That's why you must be proactive about consistently creating happiness in your life.

#10. You may never "get over" the loss of a loved one, but in time you will find ways to cope with it. "Do the best that you can, with what you have, where you are." Theodore Roosevelt.

Karli Butler is a survivor. A DePaul University graduate with a BA in Communication, Karli received her MA in Organizational and Multicultural Communication in June 2010. She is a certified Peer Supporter of the University of Chicago Hospital's Survivors Offering Assistance in Recovery (SOAR) program, as well as an Illinois Fire Safety Alliance member, Camp Counselor and Mentor for *Camp I Am Me.* In 2008, she began her public and inspirational speaking career targeting young women. Her primary focus is discussion-based lectures pertaining to self-esteem, self-respect, forgiveness, and being a survivor of violence. She provides tips on overcoming trauma and any obstacle that life may hand you. Most importantly, she demonstrates how self-esteem comes from within and can empower and heal the body and mind.

In March and May of 2006 Karli Butler was the target of two vicious attacks made in retaliation against her boyfriend at the time. The first attack began with a violent beating that escalated to kidnapping by the three male attackers. Karli was able to escape from the trunk of her car while it was in motion. The second attack, by two females, resulted in acid being poured over her body leaving her severely scarred physically and emotionally. This experience has given Karli the exclusive gift of being a voice to others. Her presence and willingness to share her story is a manifestation of her strength and determination to not let her attackers limit her life by fear of violence.

Karli's story was featured on an episode of the Biography Channel's "I Survived" on December 1, 2008. She has also appeared on a number of radio shows. One of her most noted speeches was delivered to 200 assistant state's attorneys about her experience as a survivor of violence. She is most proud of the key role she played in the passing of Illinois House Bill 2193, a bill that requires those buying commercial-grade hydrochloric or sulfuric acid to show photo identification and have their data entered into a state database. KarliSpeaks@gmail.com

10 TIPS TO MAKING YOUR LIFE SNAP, CRACKLE & POP!!

Wow! To be a teenager again! So you're probably wondering what in the heck it really means to make your life "snap, crackle & pop?" You're probably wondering who in the world came up with that title? Well, let's start at the beginning.

A life, yes --even at your age, that "snap, crackles & pops!!" is a life that is exciting, it's full of adventure, it's filled with dips, curves and surprising bends in the road.

Here are some tips that will help you along the way.

#1. Say what you mean and mean what you say. There is nothing more powerful than being a young man or young woman of your word. As you continue to grow and learn about your life and the world around you, you'll begin to notice and determine the true character and quality of others who share your space. One of the biggest benchmarks of the depth of one's character is the integrity of their word.

#2. Do at least one thing per day that scares you or takes you out of your comfort zone. Now stepping out of your comfort zone doesn't mean you have to go and bungee jump tomorrow. However, it does mean to take stock of what really intimidates you. If you're not sure if something intimidates you just check your heart beat when you're in that situation or better yet check your sweaty palms! There you go -- you've hit the jackpot and identified what scares/intimidates you. Now...all you simply have to do ...is well JUST DO IT! (Let's keep it safe and smart!)

#3. Surround yourself with people that bring out the best in you. Think about how you would like to feel when you are in the company of your peers. Think about those friends/people who help you to feel strong, secure, confident, thoughtful ...etc. etc. etc. (you get the drift!). Now ask yourself how often are you in their company? Is there anyone on that list that you've simply admired from afar but you've secretly wished you could spend more time with them? Those "peeps" you listed -- yea, those -- those are the people you really should be spending your time with.

#4. Take time every day to do one thing that brings you joy, makes you laugh, smile or feel happy. Do you know what actually makes you happy? What do you enjoy doing when you are alone and no one is watching? Yup, thought so -- not so easy, huh? Why is it important to learn to enjoy your own company? Simple -- learning to first become your own "best friend" is one of the most powerful things you can do in your life. You not only learn more about yourself, but you also learn what REALLY works for you and what doesn't. Then you can spend more time doing what you love and lose the other stuff.

#5. Let your yes be yes, and your no mean no. Imagine if your best friend continually said yes to hanging out after school or going with you to see the latest blockbuster hit only to change his/her mind at the last minute? Wouldn't you be disappointed maybe even really pissed off? Imagine if this was a habit that you put up with over a long period of time? Now imagine months down the road. Would you trust that person? What if you really needed help with a school project that made up 50% of your grade and your "best friend" offered to spend after school helping you with that project? Would you rely on him/her? Would you trust this time would be different? NO! Exactly the point.

#6. Wake up every day and tell yourself at least one thing you really like/love about yourself. Okay we're almost there --hang in there! Let's have fun with this one. Again, this may seem simple, but ask yourself "How often do I actually and deliberately acknowledge (without sarcasm, hype or bravado) my strengths?" When was the last time you wrote down (on a consistent basis) the things you really and truly ROCK at? Yes, you read me right. What are you a bonafide, flat out, no questions asked ROCK STAR at? What can you do that no one else can do, quite like you? Yea, that thing! Nope, don't you dare sweep it away to the back of your mind. Pull it forward and look at it --honestly.

So, take a few moments, either at the beginning, end or middle of the day, and make a note of something amazing you remembered about yourself.

#7. Treat everyone around you the way you want and expect to be treated. Here is a quick and easy application tip. Think of the things that bring happiness, laughter, joy and feelings of safety to your world. Now, when you're done thinking about this and maybe even writing it down, practice performing random or deliberate acts of kindness to family and friends in your corner of the Universe. You see, a funny thing happens on the way to living your life this way. You will find these same kindnesses being returned.

#8. Practice performing random acts of kindness to those who can do nothing in return for you. Practicing random acts of kindness does the heart good! It helps you to develop and maintain a heart of compassion. Believe it or not, what you say to people all your life (and yes, I do mean for your entire life) will hardly make as much a difference or leave as much impact as how you make people feel. Remember this tip as it will serve you well as you walk your own individual path in life.

#9. Every once in a while give yourself a break -- you're not perfect, just human. Aaaaah! A tip I'm certain you'll love upon instant read. Yes, believe it or not, part of living your life and allowing it to "snap, crackle and pop" is not verbally bashing yourself. Give up putting yourself on the guilt trip treadmaster and definitely stop using words like "stupid," "fat," "slow," Don't say things like: "What's my deal?", "That was dumb!" or even "Duh!" to yourself. Of course I KNOW I don't have to go into great detail as to why words and phrases like this are SO NOT COOL to say to oneself...Ever!

It's about being the best YOU that you can be every day and as often as you can. As long as you strive for your best, then that's what counts.

#10. Repeat Tips #1 - Tips #9 on a regular basis! :) Practice makes perfect. What can I say? Will you remember to do all these tips every day, all day long? Probably not. However, it's a great guideline for you to take with you wherever you go.

Remember, life is meant to be lived...and in my opinion with a whole lot of SNAP, CRACLE and POP!!

Michele 'Ubercoach' Ashley is Founder and CEO of COEUR Compass Coaching where she works as chief facilitator of women's empowerment workshops and seminars globally.

Michele created COEUR Compass Coaching to serve as a platform to provide a 'safe haven' for women to learn key life skills and tools to define their lives to live their true passion. COEUR is about providing life-coaching services that allow women to connect to their truth so as to make the best choices for their lives the first time around.

Ms. Ashley served as Chairman of the Board of Directors for WEST Inc. (Women of Excellence, Strength & Tenacity, Inc.), a non-profit organization based in New York City in 2011. She is a member of the Women's Information Network (WIN) and has recently been appointed the Event Director for the Global Women's Summits 2012 for the North Eastern Region of the US. www.COEURCompassCoaching.com

10 LIFE TIPS FOR THE EVERYDAY TEENAGER

#1. Don't let others write your story. Not everyone is going to support or understand your life choices, BUT they are yours to make. Great things come from perseverance and dedication. Stay confident and don't be afraid to fail every once in a while.

#2. You choose YOUR reaction. Many times in life you will experience situations that you cannot control. For example, an uncontrollable car accident could change your life. But you have two choices, sit in a room depressed, or FIGHT to live. Choose your reaction.

#3. Don't forget to take the long path every now and then. You will be told all your life to make a life plan or path. But don't forget to wander off every now and then and smell the roses. Sometimes the longer path will end at the best destination.

#4. Don't worry if you don't know what you want to be just yet, just focus on being the best YOU. Most people end up falling into their careers as they grow older. Through experience, life choices and sometimes being at the right place at the right time. Make sure to use EVERY experience to the fullest and do the best job YOU can do...no matter what it is. Be the best at cleaning a barn on your path to being the best horse back rider.

#5. Heroes aren't people who wear a cape, they are everyday people who stand up for what they believe in. Every single person has the ability to do GREAT things. Even if it's as small as volunteering for your local community soup kitchen; be someone else's hero EVERY day if you can.

#6. No one has all the answers. No matter if you are 12, 17, 24, 38, 49 or 87, no one has the answers to everything, so don't stress. But be intelligent and listen to advice from your elders. They have seen a few things in their time.

#7. YOU decide what is beautiful/handsome. Every culture has its own definition of beauty. Who says you have to agree?

#8. Almost anything is possible in life if you are willing to work hard enough for it. Hard work DOES pay off. It may not always be an immediate thing, but even bad experiences give you an opportunity to tweak your approach and perfect your landing for next time.

#9. Always put yourself in the other person's shoes. It is hard to always understand why people act the way they do. But if you are willing to put emotions aside for a moment and look at things from someone else's perspective, you will find it's far easier to relate. Not only will this help you gain perspective on things, but also compassion and intelligence.

#10. You get far more in life with sugar than vinegar. Throughout life you will find yourself face to face with situations that make you want to lose control. But a good rule of thumb is to always try the 'sweet' route first. Yelling for something you want, in most cases, clouds your objective.

BONUS TIP: Never put others down to raise yourself up.

Catherine Oshanek is a professional workaholic. She is currently working under the name White Cedar as a fashion and commercial photographer and as a motivational campaign founder with I'VE BEEN BULLIED. Growing up with a severe learning disability, Catherine struggled in school after failing grade one, but never let that hold her back. Graduating from Journalism in 2005 as her college's valedictorian, she spent a few years working as a reporter and photojournalist. She then found herself working with a small team on the technical process to convert movies from 2D into 3D, testing movies such as Titanic, Lion King and Star Wars for the major Hollywood studios. Today she spends much of her time inspiring and motivating others to work hard and accomplish great things. facebook.com/wcedar www.ivebeenbullied.ca www.facebook.com/beenbullied

10 TIPS BY PAUL

#1. Have a dream and chase it.

#2. Do unto others as you have done to you.

#3. Think about 3 things you are thankful for every day. Positivity rules!

#4. Don't go to bed mad.

#5. Wait before you worry.

#6. Never stop asking why and how questions. The world is full of cool things to learn.

#7. Don't laugh at others before laughing at yourself!

#8. Never stop reading!

#9. Pay it forward! Simply buy donuts for the person behind you the next time you're at your favorite donut shop.

#10. One of my all-time favorites, courtesy of my dad: Think before you do it!

By **Paul Edwards**

TIP: Never be afraid to show the world the real you in you, for that's what makes you you. By **Deokie Birbal**

---

10 TIPS BY LIZ

#1. Don't rush through your life, enjoy the journey.

#2. If you are about to do something and your gut doesn't feel good, don't do it!

#3. Be a leader, not a follower.

#4. Know that it takes all sorts of people to make the world go round.

#5. Don't judge, but be accepting.

#6. Don't let anyone ever tell you that you can't make your dreams come true. Trust in yourself and your skills.

#7. Dreams are gifts you give yourself, goals are dreams with a deadline.

#8. If you are not comfortable talking to your partner about birth control or the consequences of being in a sexual relationship, you are not ready to be in a sexual relationship.

#9. Don't disregard seniors, for they are a wealth of information and can share true history events.

#10. Read, read, read for there is much to learn.

BONUS TIP:

Find your passion in the work you do, it will give you a reason to get out of bed in the morning.

Liz Raymond, born and raised in Ottawa, Liz has enjoyed an accounting career for close to 30 years. During her career she has gone from working at accounting firms such as Thorne, Ernst & Whinney, to opening her own accounting business in 1993. Since 1993 Liz has been providing a variety of accounting services (including training, set up, year-end preparation and computer and network maintenance) to her customers. Currently she is using her accounting business as a spring board to help other women become empowered and build their own businesses.

Liz has served as a board member for associations including the Vars Community Association, Carleton Heights Daycare and Carillon Co-op.

Liz has also been involved in the Network formerly known as ReSolutions Ottawa community since 2009. Having struggled through events in her life that had taken her to a place where she felt stuck, isolated and hopeless, it was with the support of the positive community, resources and workshops that she has been able to make success a habit in her life. A single mother of two boys, it was important to Liz to find a positive, pay it forward community. It is as a result of her continued "education" with these workshops that Liz has learned how to dream again and became a facilitator. You can visit her website at www.YourDreamsEmpowered.ca

---

When you change the way you look at things, the things you look at change – an oldie but a goodie! By **Brenda Netter**

---

10 TIPS TO SURVIVING HIGH SCHOOL

#1. The fact that you are afraid makes you like everyone else at this time. Remember this when you don't receive fair treatment. Mistreatment from others comes from a place of fear. It might show up as anger, bullying or gossip, but it's all based in fear.

#2. It's normal to feel strange about being neither a child nor an adult. One minute you want to be treated like a grown up and when it get scary you want to be a child again. Feeling caught between these two phases is normal.

#3. The really "cool" people in grade nine are seldom the cool crowd in grade 12. My own daughter thanks me for this information. The grade 9 geek that she was, became the high school president in grade 12.

#4. Popularity and friendship are totally different. Popularity is like playing "king of the castle". One minute you're up, and then you get pushed down. It has absolutely nothing to do with others actually liking you for who you are. A true friend stands by you whether you're at the top or the bottom.

#5. As much as you think people are looking at you, they're not. They are just like you are. They're busy thinking that people are looking at them and trying to look cool! Crazy huh?

#6. We can't control others. We can control ourselves. No matter what happens, we get to choose what we think about it. Attitude is everything. Henry Ford said: "If you think you can, or you think you can't... you're right!"

#7. Instead of trying to show your friends that you're a cool person, try listening to them. Make it about them and learn everything there is to know. Ask questions and be genuinely interested in them, not yourself. You will have more friends than you could ever imagine. Being listened to is so close to being loved that most people can't tell the difference.

#8. If you treat everybody you know and meet as if they were hurting inside, you would almost always be right. Your smile and kindness can truly touch a life.

#9. Always take the high road. Don't stoop to the level of those who treat you unfairly. Gossip and revenge will come back to bite you! Stand up for yourself without lashing out at them. My Grandfather always used to say: "Remember that the guy who is getting a kick in the rear is always ahead of the guy who is dishing it out". Others will see you as a better person when you stand your ground without trying to get back at them.

#10. Always be yourself. Nobody can do "you" better than "you". Follow your heart and dream big dreams. Then take the actions needed to make them happen. Work at making them fit you, rather than trying to "fit in". Remember that no failure is ever final, neither is any success. Often we just need to step aside and look at the big picture when things get tough. Remember that the darker it gets, the brighter the stars shine. You are a star, made to rise above, made to sparkle!

I would like to share with you words that have kept going through the storms of life.

"And now here is my secret, a very simple secret; it is only with the heart that one can see rightly, what is essential is invisible to the eye." – Antoine de Saint-Exupery

"You will get all you want in life if you help enough other people get what they want... If you go looking for a friend, you're going to find they're very scarce. If you go out to be a friend, you'll find them everywhere." – Zig Ziglar

Helene Shaw. As far as my "history" goes, I live in Victoria BC and I am the Director of a wonderful group of ladies with Jockey Person to Person. In my former life, I was a teacher and most of my career I taught in a high school in Ontario. www.Myjockeyp2p.ca/helenshaw.victoria

10 TIPS FOR BEATING A BULLY
(10 Tips for Staying Positive)

#1. Look inside, outside, above, under and around the box. Look for the possibilities. There is always a solution to a problem.

#2. Talk to and consult with as many people as possible. Tell someone what is happening. If the person you thought can't help you, there is someone out there who can. Don't stop until you find them. Just one friend or ally is often enough to get you through.

#3. "Omoikomi" (the Japanese word for thinking or believing things without checking whether they are valid or not) is often the root to many unnecessary, sad memories. Bullies feed on your weakest point. Finding out that you really are loved when you thought you weren't, finding out that fight you had with someone was just from a misunderstanding, or finding out that other people have the same feelings and problems that you do, can lighten your load and brighten your disposition. Unfortunately, "omoikomi" is often the root cause from the bullying side, too. Try and dispel your bully's invalid beliefs about you. Prove them wrong.

#4. Do something that makes you happy. Sing, dance, paint, build, create, run, read, try and improve yourself. A positive cancels out a negative. Do it to preserve your own balance and sanity.

#5. Confront your problems. Avoiding them only makes them worse. Think why this is happening and what your options are.

#6. Never forget that you are as important and relevant as anyone. You have a right to be happy, too. Go and find your happiness.

#7. Tomorrow is another day. Tomorrow is not written in stone. Knowing that things can and will be different, if not now but in the near future, can be empowering.

#8. Find your place in the world. Find the people you love, the place you feel safe, the things you like to do, and a place or cause you can contribute to.

#9. Envision your ideal life. Imagining and seeing what you want is half of the battle, and your most important step to take you there.

#10. Run, escape, flee! When things get so bad you think there is no way out or you are in danger, run! Get away from the situation. Never give the bully or the problem the satisfaction of taking your happiness or your life.

Shelley Suzuki completed her Bachelor of Education in with a minor in Intercultural Education in 1990. She then taught grade four and English as a second language for 2 years before becoming an assistant language teacher for the JET program in

Japan. In 1992 she became a full-time English teacher at Sakuragaoka Junior High School in Toyohashi, Japan. Currently she is the owner of a self-run, private, English language school in Toyokawa, Japan and teaches all ages from two to adult. Check out her website at www.PurpleCrayon.jp

10 TIPS TEENS STRUGGLING WITH DEPRESSION OR OVERCOMING LOSS

#1. Journal your thoughts and feelings as often as you can. Getting your feelings out on paper, whether you keep the paper or throw it away, will help release them.

#2. Seek help, whether it is from an understanding friend or family member, school counsellor, or a psychologist. Do not feel ashamed seeing a professional, you should not be expected to understand the grieving process.

#3. Give yourself healing time; it will not happen overnight, in months, or even in years. The grieving process and depression are like a roller coaster, and you will have ups and downs for a long time.

#4. When you're having a good day, embrace it and let your body feel good, if only for a few minutes. Do not allow yourself to feel guilty for this.

#5. Do not dismiss or hide your feelings. They are valid and need to be recognized. Grief is not a weakness, in fact it will become a very valuable life lesson, if you let it.

#6. Do not take on more than you can handle. Adding to the pressure you are already under can make the grieving process longer and harder.

#7. Be selective in who you chose to be emotional with. Some people just do not understand, and it can be hard to get negative feedback when you are already overwhelmed with sadness.

#8. Every morning when you wake up, look in the mirror and remind yourself of how many wonderful things you have in your life. Say positive affirmations out loud as often as necessary, many times a day. It will lift your mood and focus your energy, even if it is for a few seconds. Have faith, trust that you will be happy again. The black hole of sadness will not last forever, have faith that you will heal and that your future is wide open and positive.

#9. Eat healthy and keep active. Sometimes even a quiet walk can ease the pressure of grief. Negativity and sadness opens the door for sickness and exhaustion, and your body will have a harder time coping.

#10. DREAM BIG. You have every right to live a beautiful life.

Sheena Johnson empowers women with the ultimate bra shopping experience! Award winning customer service and the world's best in fine lingerie. www.TheBraLounge.ca

10 TIPS FOR A HEALTHIER LIFESTYLE

#1. Set a routine. Setting specific times throughout the day for meals, school, exercise, homework, quiet time and bedtime can improve concentration and reduce the overall tension and stress of everyday life.

#2. Eat healthy. You've heard the saying "you are what you eat", well this is true. Food is the fuel for your brain and body, which is why healthy eating leads to better performance. Eating healthy is all about balance and eating three balanced, nutritious meals and two or three healthy snacks per day. The most important meal of the day is breakfast, which many of us have the tendency to skip because of the early morning rush to get to school. Eating in the morning improves your memory, as well as boosts your physical and academic performance and lowers your risk of becoming overweight. Healthy eating doesn't have to be difficult, you can still eat the foods you love, in moderation. Make sure you are getting the nutrients that your body and brain need to work at prime levels.

#3. Get a good night's sleep. If you aren't waking up refreshed and alert in the morning, then you may not be getting enough sleep. The average teenager needs at least nine hours of sleep per night.

#4. Become active. As well as eating healthy and getting the rest you need, the best way to keep yourself healthy and feeling good is to keep your body moving. Daily physical activity can have many benefits including more energy, improved mood and lessened anxiety and tension. Exercise gives you strong bones and muscles, improves concentration and focus, helps with maintaining a healthy weight and helps to minimize your risk of developing chronic diseases like diabetes and heart disease.

#5. Manage your time. Making sure to manage your time can help to reduce stress, try not to take on too much. Keep a day timer, schedule your activities, but do make time for relaxation and fun activities every day.

#6. Learn to relax. There are many relaxation strategies that help you to lower stress levels. Maybe try taking a yoga or meditation class if you find that you are having a hard time relaxing. Spend a lot of time outdoors biking, hiking, tossing a ball around with friends or any other outdoor sports that interest you.

#7. Social supports. It is very important to surround yourself with people that you can count on, whether it is your parents, a good friend or even school counsellors. Having a great social network can be linked to greater well-being. Having at least one good friend can make all the difference.

#8. Reduce stimulants. Avoid caffeinated drinks, they can cause many side effects like irritability and difficulty sleeping.

#9. Avoid alcohol & drugs. Alcohol, drugs and cigarettes can be strong stimulants, which can lead to problems with stress and anxiety. There are also many other health risks involved with using drugs and alcohol, such as addiction, overdose and death.

#10. Reduce stress. Sometimes the demands of school and friends can become too much. Stress and anxiety can have negative impacts on your health and well-being. Try to deal with your problems, lean on your friends and family and take time for yourself. Daily exercise and diet can help to reduce the stress of everyday life as well as improve your overall health.

Making small changes can have a huge impact on your life, don't try to do it all at once. Pick one or two things and try them consistently, then when you think you're ready, add a new strategy. Set realistic goals for yourself and be patient, these changes can take time but they will have a positive effect on your life.

Dana Gamble. I am a wife and a mother; 25 years ago I married my high school sweetheart and we had two beautiful children. At the age of 39, I realized I had to make some changes to my life, so embarked on a complete lifestyle change and lost 40 lbs. Now I exercise daily and try to follow a healthy eating plan, I feel better and know that I will be around for my family for many years. I try to surround myself with positive, upbeat people who I know will be there for me when I need them. As well, I can be there when they need me.

10 TIPS FROM KELLY'S FORMER JUNIOR HIGH SCHOOL TEACHER

#1. Look at yourself in the mirror each day and say "I am simply the best I can be."

#2. Don't judge yourself through what others think. It is how we think about ourselves. No one else pays our rent!

#3. Allow others to solve their own problems. We can lend an ear, but only they can solve their own issues. Validate other people by being a good listener.

#4. Read about all those leaders who made a difference in the world. Take all of the good qualities and apply them to your life.

#5. Focus on your strengths not your weaknesses. Make your weaknesses your strengths.

#6. When the going gets tough dig deeper. Flip things around and turn things into a positive.

#7. Live in the moment not the past or the future. Make each moment count because this is what we have.

#8. Remember that you are a gift to the world. Bless what your gifts are and don't focus on what you don't have.

#9. Live your life through love not anger and self-pity. It is about the law of attraction. No one is attracted to someone who is always wallowing in self-pity.

#10. The way to love anything in this world is to realize it may be lost. Don't let anything be unsaid. Trust your heart.

By **Gail Bamford**, a former school teacher and principal

10 TIPS TO FOLLOW YOUR DREAMS

#1. Discover your passion & values. Do what you love to do and do it well. Make time for your passion. Strive to educate yourself and gain knowledge through studying, expressing, exploring and experimenting. Whether it be playing sports, painting, designing, researching or wanting to fly a plane; it is for you to decide what makes you the happy. Remember to Dream Big!

#2. Attitude & gratitude Attitude is everything. With a positive attitude, anything is possible. Be gentle with yourself and always feed your brain with positive thoughts. This will increase your productivity toward reaching your dreams. Step by step, with pure dedication you can easily accomplish your dream. If you fall, get back up again. Have the end in sight and truly visualize with your imagination what it is you want. Be grateful in every situation for everything. Be present in the moment. Be grateful how opportunity helps you to grow stronger and successful.

#3. Resist peer pressure. Always remember there will be outside influences and never let anyone tell you can't do something, because you can. When you care about what you do and who you are, you will remind yourself to do your best.

#4. Respect your parents/guardians. When you can appreciate and respect your elders this will go a long ways for the rest of your lives. Parents have a deep love for their children and want to create a better life for them. Understand that your parents do the best they can with what they have and know. Build a solid foundation and create synergy. Think of it as a Win-Win. When you have respect for them, they respect you.

#5. Set goals to achieve results. Set realistic goals that are attainable, you are more likely to reach them. Have persistence and determination. Use a daily weekly planner for one month and stick to your plan. If you have an exam, study early and do not procrastinate. Studying improves your memory. Have the courage to say no to friends; do what it takes to get closer to your goals. Be accountable for your actions, your words and follow through.

#6. Healthy body & healthy mind. When you take care of your body and eat healthy nutritious foods, your body and mind will function better. It is important to get your mind to work for you, not against you. Read positive books, look in the mirror and love what you see. Say affirmations, tell yourself everything is ok. Exercising regularly with a routine will help build a stronger body and a stronger mind.

#7. Self-Confidence. The key is to believe in yourself by loving every part of you. When walking, keep your head up and look forward in the distance. This will help increase a positive vibration. Looking forward into the future will keep you on target with your goals. Having high self-confidence allows you to concentrate on your goals, desires and dreams faster and more effectively. A positive attitude gives you permission to make the right decisions that enable you to do what is best. Create efficiency for productive powerful results.

#8. Develop motivating relationships. Surround yourself with people of positive influence. Be around people that build you up with sincere compliments. Have a role model with integrity and who is easy to talk to and confide in. Ask for advice when needed. Also, motivational books and videos will keep you focused while feeling great about you and your life!

#9. Education/job-position/have a business. Stay educated and knowledgeable on what it is you want and desire. Strive for high grades and a balance in your schedule. While in the workforce, be excited to generate income for yourself. Know you are worthy and deserve to have your dreams come true. Ask for what you want. If you need help, ask. Learn to save more money and spend less money. Develop successful habits to create wealth. Always marketing yourself on a daily basis. Learn and evolve as you grow. Be genuine and smile often!

#10. Travel/volunteer. In life, you are surrounded by people with different cultures, traditions, ethics, and languages. Respect them, learn from them and volunteer to make this world a better place. Be proactive. There is a time for focus and fun.

"*The World is a book and those who do not travel, only read a page.*" *–St. Augustine.*

Always do your best.

Nadine Shenher is an International Fine Artist. Her art is in Calgary Galleries and around the world. Nadine also has a background as a Certified Advanced & Master Hypnotherapist. Her passion is to create art and make a difference in people's lives with a positive impact. www.shen-om.com www.NadineShenher.com

10 TIPS FOR DEALING WITH LOSS

I read your post about wanting submissions for teenagers dealing with loss and wrote up 10 things I learned. I'm not sure if they are what you are looking for. They aren't pretty, but I can tell you that they are absolutely sincere to my experience. I lost my Mum at 11-years-old, so I was dealing with a lot of grief through my early teen years.

#1. Give yourself permission to cry when you need to. (and always carry a handy pack of Kleenex).

#2. Give yourself permission to be angry. Life isn't fair and that sucks. You should be angry. Just try to channel your anger appropriately (i.e. rail against the universe and all its' injustice, viciously shred newspapers, bash bananas and apples with a baseball bat, but try not to yell at your friends/family).

#3. Be brutally honest with yourself. Talk to yourself. Make sure you know how you feel. Ask yourself what you need. If you feel too weird talking to yourself, draw, paint, sculpt, write. Whatever, however, just get it out.

#4. People aren't mind readers. If you need something, ask. If you want to be alone and your little Brother is glued to your side, ask a family member to take him to the zoo. If you need help working through things, ask your school counsellor if they can recommend a grief counselling group, etc.

#5. Many people think they are mind readers and say, "I know how you feel". Try not to maim them. Nobody really knows what you are going through because you are unique and so is your loss. What they mean to say is that they care about you; it's just coming out weird because people say strange things when they don't know what to say.

#6. Let the pieces fall where they may. Some people will feel awkward around you because they don't know how to act. The good ones will stick with you and figure it out, the ones you are better off without will drift away.

#7. Friends are neutral ground, talk to them. After losing my Mum, I was surrounded by my family's grief and the only way I could talk without feeling like I was adding to everyone's sadness was to talk to my friends. They were my lifeline.

#8. Take a break from your grief. Do something fun, go to a movie with friends, be silly, laugh, forget about everything for a while. Also, if you are talking to your friends, they might appreciate the break too.

#9. WARNING -blunt truth: "Time heals all" is a crock. The hole in your heart after losing someone you love doesn't miraculously heal after a month or a year. You have to learn to live your life without that person. It's hard and it's slow and it hurts like hell, but you will get there. Take the love and lessons they gave you and carry them forward.

#10. Appreciate and love the good people you have in your life for as long as you've got them. Make sure they know how much they mean to you.

By **Rebecca Brae** www.braevitae.com

10 GUIDING PRINCIPLES FROM TROY

#1. Be here now. "Life is what happens to you while you're busy making other plans." - John Lennon. Many of us create beliefs that life will begin after we reach a certain goal, level of success or obtain something that we are trying to attract. Life won't wait for you, it's happening right now. Creating goals, aspirations and intentions of what we wish to manifest is a beautiful space to be in. The danger is projecting ourselves so far into the future that this moment slips away. Find comfort in knowing that this moment is setting the stage for those future moments. Always embrace the present moment and tune into what the universe is trying to show you.

#2. Create an attitude of gratitude. We all have experiences, people, or moments in our lives to be grateful for. Sometimes they can be hard to see but they are there, even if it is just the sun shining on your face. The truly amazing thing about gratitude is that when you really play in the energy of being grateful, you attract more positive things into your life to be grateful for. Life is all about energy and attraction. If we radiate positive, high vibrating energy, we will attract exactly that right back at us. Find gratitude for everything and everyone that is important to you, then take it one step further and let them know you are grateful for them and what they bring to your life. I don't even allow myself to get out of the bed in the morning until I find at least one thing to be grateful for. It makes for some pretty amazing days.

#3. Seek out teachers. We all need love, support, guidance, encouragement, and wisdom from others in order to continue moving forward. There is no shame in admitting we don't know it all. We will never know everything, but with the help of others we can learn so much. Connect with teachers, mentors, coaches, and gurus and never stop seeking them out throughout every stage of your life. When the opportunity is right be a teacher to someone else and share your wisdom and life learning's.

#4. Dare to dream. Open your heart and your mind to the limitless opportunities available to you. Creating the life you truly desire begins with setting intentions of what that life looks like. Our only limits are our own self-defeating beliefs of what we are worth, what we deserve, or what we can do. Throw those beliefs right out the window and dream BIG. Regardless of where you've come from, where you live, or where you are in this life, you can truly create anything you aspire if you believe in your dream.

#5. Discover the power of forgiveness. Think about the people who have hurt you the most. Are you holding onto any pain, sadness, or anger? Holding onto those emotions actually does the opposite. They fester in our bodies and impact our emotional, spiritual, and physical health. We cannot change our past but we can find peace in the moments we have right now. Being a real man is being able to let go of our past. Creating space and opportunities of true forgiveness releases the blocks that are preventing you from experiencing the peace, love, and joy you are seeking.

#6. Practice random acts of kindness. Find opportunities to do something nice for someone and have no expectation of receiving anything in return. When you do something out of kindness for someone, you will encounter experiences that will fill your heart and possibly change your life forever. Opportunities to practice kindness surround us every day. What can you do to make a difference in someone's life today? It doesn't have to be a grand gestures and it doesn't have to cost you money. Kindness can be found in lending a hand or offering a smile.

#7. Love. Love life, love people, love the earth and everything in it. We are all connected; we are all brothers and sisters. The more love we offer the more love we receive. Everything we do to our environment and to other people has an impact. Do you want to create positive impacts or negative impacts in this world? Don't be afraid to offer love to anyone. I hug, embrace, and tell all my male friends that I love them. I receive the same from them and we have the most powerful friendships.

#8. Be the best YOU. There is only one of you in this universe and we need you to be the best you possible. It's great to aspire to be more like someone you respect, admire, or look up to but honor yourself by loving and admiring who you are. We all have our unique gifts and talents. Share yours with the world.

#9. Keep your mind open. Open your heart and mind to new concepts, ideas, beliefs and ways of doing things. Most of our values have been influenced by our society, culture and the religious teachings of our elders. Ask yourself, are these my truths? You may find that your current values do not resonate with you. Just because a value or belief has been passed down from generation to generation does not mean it is a truth. We must move away from traditional beliefs of what is right and what is wrong and instead be willing to entertain multiple possibilities and ideals.

#10. Embrace your feminine energies. Every single person in the world is made up of a combination of feminine and masculine energies. Regardless of gender, some people are more driven by their feminine energies, others by their masculine energies, and some are fairly balanced between both. Throughout history, men have typically only embraced their masculine energies of strength, power, force and competition while completely ignoring their feminine energies such as nurturing, gentleness, healing, and love. The global impact is evident in our quests of power and dominance through wars and violence. The individual impact is equally as devastating with so many men never experiencing this lifetime with the fullness of beauty and love that is available to all of us. We need to create new belief systems where real men are gentle, kind, and nurturing while still radiating strength.

Troy Payne, Inspirational Speaker, International Bestselling Author, and Musician. Troy is an inspirational speaker, international bestselling author, music producer, singer and guitarist. Troy started his career as a youth and family counselor with the intention of helping people overcome adversity.

In 2004 he launched his company Wellness Realization and began speaking professionally. Troy has dedicated himself to Encouraging, Engaging and Empowering youth and adults to overcome adversity and find resilience. He released his book 'The

Road to Resiliency' in 2011 which quickly became an international best seller.

As a musician he has always believed in the healing power of music and became the creator of the band 'Aside from Sorrow'. They recently released their first album 'Out of the Darkness, Into the Light' which is the soundtrack to Troy's book. Their music depicts the struggles we are all faced with but also inspires hope, change, and healing. Their music is being featured in film and television. http://www.WellnessRealization.net

10 TIPS TO CONNECT WITH YOUR SPIRIT

#1. Hang in nature ~ that which connects us to the Creator ~ Spirit speaks through the birds and the trees ~ step outside each day and put your mind at ease.

#2. Listen in love to those around ~ resist the urge to make a sound ~ and if you do, you may just find ~ the special messages that lay behind ~ for everyone else is simply a mirror ~ if you listen carefully ~ you will truly hear ~ and as a result, get very clear ~ when you honor others in such a way ~ they will indeed return the favor someday.

#3. Be silent, be still ~ surrender all your conscious will ~ take some time every day ~to meditate, appreciate or simply pray ~ for in the stillness, all alone ~ you will discover a warm safe place inside your soul ~ that is always there for you to go. When you're stuck flailing to and fro, ~ just stop, go inside and soon you'll know ~ this state of being will guide you home.

#4. Release all unwanted emotions ~ I swear it's like a secret potion ~ instead of pushing down how you really feel ~ cry, be angry, be you, be real ~for when you invite the storm to come ~ the more you get to appreciate the rainbow and the glistening sun.

#5. Stretch out the blocks, physically ~ the more you move ~ the more you are free ~ the body connects us to the Divine ~ treat it with love and you'll always be fine ~and when you are feeling rather tired ~ just know, this is also a message from higher ~ your physical feelings are spiritual guidance ~ feel your way towards the bliss, this will take you the highest.

#6. Ask to be shown the way ~ feelings can be confusing and you may wander astray ~ in the moments of stress, frustration or despair ~ remember there is a Universal energy that truly does care ~ when you say "Please help me along" ~ the answer will come, perhaps through a friend, animal, computer or song ~ allow it to flow in whichever way ~ it may be next week, it may be today ~ and when it comes, you'll be out of the blue ~ back to your joyous, loving self ~ the only one that is true.

#7. Epsom salt water baths, or a swim in a lake ~ both are guaranteed to ensure you feel great ~ the water cleanses the negativity from your soul ~ and reconnects you with the knowing that each precious moment is gold.

#8. Music and dancing ~ are key for the spiritual self ~ crank up your favorite tunes and just let it out ~ sing, shake or just meditate ~ give much thanks for the beats that float you away ~ and help to release all the cares from your day ~ these magical tools will surely assist ~ the attainment of a wondrous new level of bliss.

#9. Let the plants be thy food ~ recommended with reason by many a guru ~ these tasty superstars are what really nourish you ~ the more fruits, veg & healthy dose of grains ~ the more vibrance and fun your body can sustain ~ the animals, environment & economy will thank you much too ~ veg choices are the most loving and compassionate to do ~ for the entire planet and certainly you.

#10. Create, play, create ~ whether you prefer to write, ski, act or illustrate ~ your passions are the gifts of Spirit ~ which make you so great ~ You've come to shine your light in the most fun way for you ~ simply follow your heart and it is easy to choose ~ whenever you let out your uniqueness, your beautiful truth ~ Spirit bows down to thank you, in infinite gratitude ~ and as it is so, the world does too.

After years of stress, pain and illness **Erika Chell** took a trip to India to meet various spiritual Masters alongside Janet Attwood of The Passion Test. She then left her career in finance to pursue full time spiritual practice. Erika was initiated to practice meditation under a fully realized living Master and also studies a form of life coaching called Power Coaching with Mind Kinetics. Her passion now lies in the area of intuitive healing. She has extensively studied plant based nutrition, metaphysics, channeling and many forms of holistic well-being practices. Spirituality (aka Love!) forms the foundation of her daily life and healing practices. To connect with Erika Chell please message or subscribe to her on facebook. You may also contact her through e-mail at erika.chell@ultimateclarity.com.

10 TIPS TO UNLEASH YOUR INNER POWER

As a professional who has mentored teens and having moved out of the house when I was 12, I know how difficult teen years can be. Between hormones and peer pressure, trying to figure out where your life is going and just trying to keep your head together, it can really be a struggle. Here are things I've found that help.

#1. Find a mentor. Is there something you are interested in that you would like to learn more about? A mentor can show you how to take your skill into a business environment. Offer to work for free to start and develop their trust in you. Diving into something can help you really find your center.

#2. Find a hobby or something that really engrosses your attention, that you could do for hours. Nothing helps you be with yourself in a strong way more than something that's fun, relaxing and takes up all your attention.

#3. Uncover your passion. A passion can be like a hobby, but it lights your imagination on fire. It can be your life's work, or something in the moment, but giving yourself a venue to express who you are through some kind of activity is life-altering. For many people, passion lies in some kind of service to others. Experiment and see what really jazzes you up.

#4. Become a member. Find a group of like-minded people and join their community. This can be anything from a group based on shared hobbies to a group putting together a real business. Having a place to contribute will help you find ways to shine.

#5. Establish a community and lead it. There is little in life as empowering as leading a group of people. Start with a Meetup group or school club, and share your leadership, commitment and compassion with others. Don't give up if it gets hard - just find new and creative ways to keep people engaged and participating.

#6. Create stable friendships. Whether with other teens or a few select adults, you need a safe place to talk about what's going on with you without being judged. If there's no one in your environment, try talking with your school guidance counsellor and see if they might fit the bill for you.

#7. Work with animals or nature. When it comes to really letting your inner power out into the world, there is nothing quite so life-changing as working in nature, or working with animals. There are many ways to do this, from volunteering at an animal shelter, to pet-sitting (which you can get paid for if you're trustworthy), to just taking long walks in a park or forest. Volunteer at a local zoo or animal rescue facility. Try it and see what works for you. Animals require you to be honest and in touch with yourself, and they reward you well when you are.

#8. Tune into your spirituality. Regardless of your spiritual direction, there are groups and meeting places where you can share your spiritual beliefs with others, and become more deeply aware of what you do believe and what it means to you. These days, many spiritual people are ridiculed in school, but you can keep it to yourself there, and share it where it's safe, or develop your own practice at home.

#9. Tune into your physicality. This is a great one. How do you like to move your body? Whether you're into the martial arts, sports, dance, yoga... whatever your physical outlet, the deeper you go into it, the stronger you become inside. Don't be afraid to try different things until you find what works for you. Immerse yourself, and see what happens.

#10. Read, learn, grow & evolve. There is always someone who has been down the path before you, and by reading and learning, you can move forward easier and faster, developing a deeper understanding of the process. Then in time, you may become the leader for someone else. No matter what you're interested in, spending time learning more about it is always time well spent, and will help you make better decisions for yourself and your life.

BONUS TIP: Don't be afraid to let go of old friends who don't really fit in your life anymore. We all grow, all the time, and sometimes we outgrow our friends. Remember that people may come into your life for an hour, a day, a month, a year, a decade... how long they stay is not the point. The point is to find the gifts they bring into your life, and make that worthwhile. You will be that person in other peoples' worlds as well.

Each of us has within us a well of inner power, and finding the key to unlock it, so that we can use it in our life, can be a fun and challenging puzzle. Try a few things, and see how you feel. You'll know you're in the right place when time passes really quickly, when you feel strong and balanced inside, where there is no 'pushing', just 'being' in the moment. We all have something that unlocks that door.

Jana E. Beeman, CHHP, CHP, AADP is a Board Certified Holistic Health, Nutrition & Fitness Practitioner, certified in Hypnosis and Restorative Yoga. She is an EFT and Meditation Trainer, life coach and spiritual counsellor, as well as a stress relief and migraine expert. She is also an avid animal rights activist. She is an active teen mentor. www.BalancedLifeToday.com

10 TIPS TO ACE THE TEST OF LIFE

#1. Dream. Be prepared to do whatever it takes to live those dreams. The human experience is only as interesting as you make it. If you choose to plant yourself in front of the TV, expending fewer calories than if you were sleeping, while eating genetically modified grains fried in genetically modified hydrogenated oils, don't expect to be "living the dream". You only get out what you put in. Caution: not everyone will agree with your dreams. Dream anyway.

#2. Love. The highest purpose for us on this earth is love, unconditional love: the hardest and sweetest kind. It takes great practice to remember unconditional love. (We have it as children but it is often chided, scolded, or beaten out of us by adulthood.) Unconditional love and its ensuing kindnesses can transform the hardest heart and heal the rockiest relationships.

#3. Laugh. Whatever you choose to be, do and have in your life, be sure it makes you smile. A few "my-cheeks-hurt" belly laughs every day will help you get through the darkest storms. The people in your life should bring you peace and joy; if they don't, you need new people. We don't have to live in misery; we generally choose it for ourselves and then we blame others (see Point #6).

#4. Learn. In business they say if your company is not growing, it's dying. The same principle applies to your brain. If you're not learning, you're dying. Not having a post-secondary education is not a legitimate obstacle. Everything taught in every class is written in a book so if you can read, you can have any education you want. Most of the important books are available at libraries for nothing but the cost of a library card. Or you can watch a video on how to do almost anything.

#5. Read. If you don't read well, get help. There are numerous courses you can take to improve your reading skills. If you don't like reading find topics you enjoy. Begin by reading about the things you love, your homeland, your hobby, your heritage. Then read broadly and deeply, across genres and generations, classics and cult classics, fiction and non, from left and right and up and down. Read books, newspapers, magazines, online and offline. If you follow this advice you will have an invaluable education and you can talk to anyone about anything by simply asking the right questions. The only cost is your time. There are many more frivolous ways to spend time.

#6. Take responsibility. One of the easiest habits to adopt is blame. I say habit because it is a choice. You can choose to look for ways in which you played a part in a particular failure, learn from those mistakes, and move onto bigger and better projects and experiences. Or you can choose a scapegoat to carry your share of the blame. No good comes from blaming others and wallowing in the subsequent inertia (resistance to change). When you fail to take responsibility, you miss the lesson and you are doomed to repeat the same lessons until you get it.

#7. Be respectful. If you respect yourself (and you must come first) and you respect others, you don't need any other "rules". Respect includes caring for yourself, nurturing your mind, body and soul. Forgive yourself. Give yourself credit when you accomplish something good and when someone praises you. If you can do these things for yourself, it will become natural to treat others with the same concern and dignity. Every human dilemma is, if not solved, improved, when garnished with respect.

#8. Art. Create and/or consume copious amounts of music, dance, paintings, sculptures, writings or any other art form that you enjoy. Avoiding psychotherapy is doable if you have a release for your soul's creative energy. Music sets me to dancing or helps me relax at the end of a trying day. Creating art is highly therapeutic; absorbing art is almost equally medicinal. Painter and patron: partners and mutual beneficiaries.

#9. Eat good food; drink lots of pure water. Let food be your medicine, as recommended by Hippocrates. Eat foods that are ingredients, not that HAVE ingredients. If it comes in a box or a brightly coloured bag, or if you can get fries with it, you probably shouldn't eat it. The best food is always as close to its natural state as possible. Eat mostly plants. Grow your own food or know your grower whenever possible.

#10. Think for yourself. History is fraught with extinct peoples that followed some wacko leader, who sometimes didn't seem so crazy, until we had the benefit of hindsight. Don't be a sheeple, heading in a certain direction simply because everybody else is doing it. You might be lonely sometimes but you will be alive!

Shelley Goldbeck is a Thinker, Writer, Speaker, and Marketer on a mission to wring every last experience from her life this time around through self-awareness, learning and discovery. Shelley is the author of three books so far, and because of her interest in a variety of subjects from health and wellness to real estate to marketing, she writes for a number of web sites. She is currently working towards her Toastmasters Advanced Communicator Gold designation. Shelley has two daughters and two grand-daughters and she is happily unmarried to Doug. Read Shelley's blog at www.OneWomansOpinion.com

10 FINANCIAL TIPS

#1. Start a Money Club to learn about the value of money with friends in your community or school. I don't mean building a big pot of money together and investing it as a group like adults do. This group is to educate each other on money matters such as how credit cards work, what does it mean to take a student loan out to go to school or by a car. Create three roles: Researcher, Educator and Coordinator. So pick a concept for example like bank accounts: the Researcher would Google find any information about the bank accounts, the Educator will collect all the information and summarize it so it is understood by the others in the group. The Coordinators role is to make sure everyone is on time, in the correct location and invites adults to the meeting if required. The group can be any size. Every few months switch roles. With the bank account example, someone from your local bank could explain how the process works.

#2. Every amount of money given, earned or allowance save 10% of it.

#3. Learn the concept time value of money.

#4. Know how compound interest works. This is a must! Mortgages and credit cards are the same lending product. Mortgages are just compounded at a lower rate. Once you learn this concept, depending on mortgage length you could be paying your mortgage amount three times the original amount.

#5. Learn how to cook (saving money). Cooking is necessary life skill, it can save your health, help you maintain normal weight and is cornerstone for social gatherings. If you want to save money the last thing you want to do is spend money eating out. You can go out and get a sub for $5. Yes its $5 today and then $5 another day and then another $5. The lesson learned you have just paid the owners a profit three times. Don't you think you should be keeping this profit for yourself?

#6. Shop wisely (save money and look for discount items). Don't impulse shop!!

#7. For the older teenagers with part-time jobs. Establish Credit but use it wisely. Apply for a credit card for the lowest limit. Buy one item a month on the credit card and pay it off before the payment due date. What you are doing is establishing a credit history? This credit history and score will follow you around for the rest of your life.

#8. A lot of teenagers want to travel once they have finished school. So if you make $40,000 and you take a year off that will impact you financially, the last year you don't work before retirement. Let's say in your retirement years you make $160,000. That means your earnings are now less $160,000 not $40,000.

#9. Before you leave school learn how to budget, life style and household expenses. When I first moved out I had my first cheque and went shopping bought unnecessary items for my bathroom. Once I was home, I realized I did not have money for groceries. So off to the store I went to return my purchased goods. I felt really embarrassed speaking to the clerk with my excuse why I had to make a return.

#10. Start saving for your retirement as soon as you can. People are living longer than the amount of retirement income saved. Let's say you start working at age 25 and work until 65, that is 40 years of saving and potentially you could live to 90 (25 years in retirement). Retirement is the most expensive time in your life.

Diane Shortridge is a dynamic, team oriented Certified Management Accountant with over twenty years business experience within diverse industries. She is a Life Licensed Insurance Broker who deals with advanced tax strategies using insurance products. Contact via Linkedin at ca.linked/pub/diane-shortridge-cma/15/989/267 or silverlininginsuranceservices.com

♥ ♥ ♥ ♥ ♥

10 TIPS TO HANDLE DIVORCE

Unfortunately, in today's world many families face divorce and with the divorce of our parents often comes re-marriage. For the few of us who can experience a positive outcome having a well-balanced and healthy step parent are those of us who will experience the opposite; the abusive step parent.

Abuse comes in many forms; physical, financial, sexual and emotional.

My parents separated when I was 12 and my mother partnered with a man who my family knew. His first language was not English, but he was well educated. He faced ridicule because he could not properly speak English. I did not agree with their arrangement and for many years he put me down for my love of the English language and writing and expressing myself through artwork. He had majored in Science in University and later went on to become a microbiology major; I decided to major in English when I graduated from high school. His constant puts down on my passion for writing took a toll on me and while I wrote and was published, his negative words took effect on me. He not only verbally abused me; he physically abused me and ridiculed all of my artistic endeavours as well. And I ended up marrying a man who physically threatened me and told me that I'd never come to anything.

As teens we cannot decide who our parents re-marry when they divorce. However, we can take charge on how we deal with what is going on. If you are facing the same kinds of circumstances you can choose to do the following:

#1. Talk to an understanding relative who champions who you are and your strengths. Having someone in your corner can strengthen you and give you courage during times when an abusive Step parent is telling you falsehoods about yourself.

#2. Remember you are a child of God who remembers who you were while in the womb and every hair on your head. He loves you and gave you a purpose in this life!

#3. Abusive people, no matter if they are a stepparent, bully at school or a co-worker are cowards at heart. They cannot face the pain and insecurities they feel within themselves so they turn on others.

#4. Tell your parent how you feel and if they don't respond.

#5. Talk to a school counsellor.

#6. Talk to a loving and responsive relative.

#7. Get involved with a support group for those with Step parents. An alternative could be Al-Anon who follow the twelve steps program.

#8. Keep a journal.

#9. Talk to a neighbour who you trust.

#10. Call the Police if things get out of hand. Physical abuse is NOT to be condoned.

Kimberley Langford overcame the effects of living with an abusive step father who abused her emotionally and physically. Subsequently she was able to leave an abusive marriage. She is the published author of the book, "The Evolving Woman Series….Daily Reflections, "which is a 31 day journey for women to examine the good, and not so good aspects of themselves that they can celebrate and make positive life affirming changes in their lives.

To read more of Kimberley's work, please follow her blog at; http://kimberleylangfordauthor.wordpress.com/

10 TIPS FOR AN AMAZING LIFE

#1. Choices. You are old enough to know which ones are wrong and which are right. Every choice you make has consequences, choose the good ones.

#2. Confidence. If I could go back in time, the one thing I would wish is that I was more confident as a teenager. I wouldn't allow myself to be bullied, and I would have stood up for myself way more. I wouldn't have cared what people thought of me as long as I was being true to myself.

#3. Respect. Have respect for your peers, for your elders, but most importantly for yourself.

#4. Friendships. You are only as good as the company you keep. This is so true, be choosy you are worth it!

#5. Gossip. There will always be people who talk behind your back and throw negativity your way. Learn to ignore it, don't take it to heart, it doesn't matter anyway.

#6. Be positive. This will change your life, think happy thoughts, be grateful and your life will be amazing.

#7. Enjoy yourself. Sleep in, be silly with friends, laugh at yourself. Don't be in such a hurry to grow up. Play hard.

#8. Find your passion. What floats your boat, what is it you can't stop thinking about? Art? Music? Embrace your talents and show the world what you are made of.

#9. Random acts of kindness. Try and do one nice thing every day for someone else, whether it's giving a compliment, opening a door, or smiling at a stranger. You can help make this world a better place, and I promise you will feel amazing.

#10. Never give up. Don't ever let anyone tell you it can't be done, don't tell yourself, don't make excuses, just keep going. I know from experience. I grew up on welfare (social assistance/income support) with a mom who dealt drugs and a father in jail for second degree murder. Because of those obstacles I tried harder, I formed my own opinions of myself, I forgave, and I overcame. I am now own my own magazine, have two healthy, happy little kids, and an amazing husband. Never give up!

By **Candace Lauman-Robichaud**

10 TIPS FROM TANNER THE 23-YEAR-OLD

#1. It is nice to take the time to ask yourself who you are, and who you would like to be.

#2. Don't hesitate to meditate! This is done simply by paying attention to one's breathing or listening to one's heartbeat.

#3. Be confident in your abilities and be open to recognizing your own capabilities, allowing them to grow naturally and unforced. It can be painful to try to force yourself to grow.

#4. Remember that you are part of nature, and you were born in freedom.

#5. Celebrate community and be honest in your communications, it saves you from much unnecessary fear.

#6. Let yourself be beautiful, creative and artistic. Allow others to do the same, for these are innate freedoms that are ours by nature.

#7. Keep in mind the balance between control and spontaneity, order and chaos, thinking and doing. An extreme in one produces extremes of the other.

#8. Moderation, even moderation.

#9. Focus.

#10. You are dearly loved by all of nature, and there are many in this world who, though may be limited by physical barriers, extend their love to you and you are free to have this love whenever you need a light in your life.

By **Tanner Michael Hartmann**
www.facebook.com/azraelsdream

10 TIPS FROM JASON

#1. Stay Loyal. First to yourself. Second to your goals. Thirdly to those who help you towards those goals.

#2. The only place where "success" comes before "work" is in the dictionary. Hard work ALWAYS pays off.

#3. Listen to your mom. Listen to your dad. They've been through what you are going through now. Learn from their experiences.

#4. Surround yourself with people that will challenge you. Followers don't help you get to the next level.

#5. Never stop learning.

#6. Posting on Social Media is not socializing. Get out and see people.

#7. Strive for excellence – not for perfection. Learn the difference.

#8. An open mind opens up new worlds.

#9. There are 24 hours in a day. 8 for working/school. 8 for relaxing. 8 for sleeping.

#10. Always treat others the way you want to be treated.

Jason Olandesca has over 14-years' experience working in the health care field. Starting his career as a registered nurse, helped define Jason's passion for helping people and health. He has worked with centres of excellence for innovative health solutions including Medicis and Sanofi-Aventis and has received numerous accolades and awards.

Today, Jason works with Strata Health Solutions' Business Development Team allowing him to "Make Positive Changes to Healthcare at The System Level".

His personal mantra is "Change Tomorrow, Today." He encourages everyone around him to be an agent of positive change doing things today to create a positive tomorrow for themselves, their families, friends and the community that surrounds them. www.linkedin.com/in/jasonolandesca

10 TIPS TO SELF-LOVE
Help! I've fallen in a feeling & I can't get out

What I have learned in this life is that we all can find value if we choose to look for it. When you find yourself stuck in one of those horrible, rotten, no good, very bad days here are a few things I try, that I find help me get unstuck.

#1. Breathe. Whether it's a pop quiz, sprung on you in math, or the day where you stub your toe, only to go on and bonk your funny bone, then walk right into the cute boy at school.... Breathe. Ever notice that when you dwell on the negative and focus on what's not going right, things seem to go worse? Breathe. Take a moment to clear your head. Refocus & carry on.

#2. Sweat. Sometimes we all get there, that feeling of stuckness –worry, heartache, and fear. One of my favorite ways to move through an emotion is to sweat. Hit up a hot yoga class (my personal fav), go for a run without a destination in mind, go play some basketball with friends – just get moving. I mean really moving. Sweat. It's really easy to get stuck when we don't move. Let the sweat take the worries, fears, and pain away. Cleanse your soul.

#3. Get creative. Switch sides of your brain. Get artsy crafty. Make a photo collage of the people you love. Work on a scrapbook for your mom. Build a dream board. Paint, sketch, journal. Find a way to get your feelings out on paper. When you put time & energy into a project, you redirect the stuck energy into purpose.

#4. Laugh. Notice that giggles are contagious? If we all take a moment to think, we can all find a memory that brings a smile to our face. Push it farther. Giggle, chuckle. That simple little exercise changes the whole make up of our body. Try it. It's hard to go back to the same state of being upset with a smile on your face. Surround yourself with people who make you laugh. It's good for your health.

#5. Crank it!! "If it's too loud you're too old" may be the adage of your parents' generation, notice though they don't seem to hold the oath anymore when it comes to your music? Regardless

142

the same connection & value is still there, music has the ability to bring us through so much. Heal & transform. It can give the words we struggle to find. My love of music & lyrics I can relate to, was a gift from my dad; it was he who taught me there's no such thing as too loud. Maybe consider investing in a good pair of headphones if your music tastes differ in the family, otherwise use it as a platform to communicate and connect. Take a listen. Ask questions.

#6. Phone a friend. Different people come into our lives at different times. Be conscious of those you surround yourself with & how you feel around them. Ever notice that after a really great squawk with Negative Nellie, you don't actually feel any better, you're just kinda placid? Find awareness in your own feelings. Figure out what you want & need from others. It's okay to have a vent session about how unfair your parents are, but a true friend listens & validates your feelings –that's friendship. A great friend makes you forget how frustrated you are with them in her presence. Surround yourself with people who make you feel better about you.

#7. "Me" time. We are so busy in our society; school, part time jobs, dating, friends, family time. It doesn't ever seem like there's enough hours in the week to get it all done, where everyone is happy. How are you doing? Not you the student, not you the employee, not you the son/daughter. How are YOU doing? Take some "me" time for you. Give yourself a break. Take 5 minutes longer in the shower, read a book, paint your toes. Rest. Relax. Recharge.

#8. Grab a snack. Hunger = Grumpy. Eat something, grab a glass of water. Get back to the basics. 8 glasses of water a day, 8 hours of sleep at night & a balanced diet. Try it. Often when we become more conscious of what we put into our body to fuel it & how we feel with different foods, we take better care of ourselves.

#9. Be a kid again. Oh the good ole' days. Ha! We used to laugh or squirm at our parents reminiscing over the good ole' days, since they don't seem to be the most understanding creatures sometimes (parents), how come they can't remember what it's like to be a teen but recall so fondly the good ole' days. Don't they realize that one day this will be my good ole' days?

Wait a minute. Don't I realize one day that these will be MY good ole' days? Make the most out of them. I guarantee your parents or grandparents who so fondly remember the good ole' days had responsibilities too at your age, maybe different ones, but notice they recall the good times. The having fun, laughing. Live your life making memories so that one day, you too can bore your children with tales of the good ole' days.

#10. Remember, it's only a day. One day I was having a crap day & reached out to my facebook peeps. I had a girlfriend I hadn't spoken to share on my wall a beautiful adage:

"Don't let a bad day make you feel like you have a bad life" What a great reminder to stay present. This is only a day. Sometimes it's a few back to back or even longer, but even for the things we cannot control, we always have the ability to choose how we respond. Strive to create value in all things.

Always remember, you are so very loved my friend, by **Jaclyn Olsen** Teen & Family Coach info@diffusionsolutions.ca

10 TIPS FOR LIVING YOUR TRUE BEAUTY!

#1. You are one of a kind. PERIOD- Fact: Population 7 billion – YOU are the only one in the entire universe with your finger prints; can't give you any other fact that proves your uniqueness.

#2. Be YOU. It's your job. Don't believe me? See #1.

#3. Smile – True beauty automatically RADIATES.

#4. Treat yourself like youa re worth millions. Here's why: One of a kind pieces of art (e.g. The Mona Lisa) are worth MILLIONS of dollars. Why? Because it is one of a kind – and so are you!

#5. Listen to what is in your heart and soul. This is who you truly are. It is guiding you. True beauty will shine if you listen to what it is trying to show you. Listen and live it!

#6. See beauty in everything and everyone. Beauty is what you choose to see. Choose compassionately and from a place of love!

#7. You were created perfectly perfect!! Not honoring your WORTH and YOUR true beauty is disrespectful. Imagine telling an artist (creator) that their creating was ugly?

#8. Put zero worth in what you see in the media. Take those magazines and videos and celebrity photos very lightly. Educate yourself on the truth behind those images. (most of them are Photoshopped)

#9. Power up your looks but don't let it consume you! Your true beauty should shine from your soul – not from what makeup or clothes you choose to put on.

#10. True beauty is living who you are on the inside. Find what you love about you, what comes naturally to you, what makes you feel empowered and LIVE IT! Remember...... it's your job!

Leanne Power is the author of the award winning children's book, "You Are Sooooo Beautiful", founder and CEO of Soulstice Book Company. Her passion is Empowering Esteem for women ages 4 to 104.

Her book has sold over 2500 copies internationally and is now in 3rd edition print. You Are Sooooo Beautiful was also nominated for the 2011 Canadian Library Associations Children's Book of the Year.

Leanne is a successful and driven entrepreneur of two Canadian companies, the mother of one daughter and has had the honor of guest blogging for www.parentingpink.com, the world's #1 resource for parenting girls.

She is an author, and speaker and national facilitator for the Dove Real Beauty Campaign Workshops. Her passion is now in speaking and hosting her workshop called "EmPOWERED Esteem". Taken as a daughter/mom/mentor team, communication, trust and bonds and open discussion happens with fun and insightful activities that perhaps may go otherwise unaddressed. She has also had numerous interviews for television, as well as print across North America, most recently,

CTV News, Breakfast Television and the Edmonton Journal. Leanne's gentle yet powerful approach in relaying her message is captivating and thought provoking. This woman is going to change the face and definition of beauty one girl at a time! (which explains why her Leanne's "EmPOWERed Esteem" Workshops are sold out months in advance).

Recently, she has been approved for the internationally recognized PTPA Media (Parent Tested Parent Approved) Seal of Approval. She has declared it her lifelong mission to share with children her experiences of having very successful and high achievements, yet very low self-esteem and what can be done to change it. To learn more about Leanne Power, her book "You Are Sooooo Beautiful" and her workshops, go to www.LeannePower.com

10 TIPS FROM DEB

#1. Giggle. It's that simple.

#2. When you have a choice to be kind or mean, be kind. It will make your heart sing.

#3. Never get too old to play. Dance in puddles; make a snowman; colour; skip rope......

#4. Tell the people who have made a difference in your life that they did.

#5. Do random acts of kindness. You will feel better than the person you do it for.

#6. Remember there is a perfect plan for your life. You just need faith.

#7. Be amazed by the beauty in the world. Never forget to look at the stars.

#8. Don't be a bully! It makes you a small person.

#9. Hug your family every day.

#10. Be the first to say "I'm sorry!"

By **Deb Cautley** Youth Empowerment & Support Services www.yess.org

♥ ♥ ♥ ♥ ♥

10 TIPS FOR TEENS BY KIM

#1. Remember every person on this planet will start and end life the same way. We all come into this world a blank slate; helpless and needy, ready to be formed, and we will all exit the same way. Who we become is a product of our experiences, parenting, education, and eventually our choices. Feelings of superiority *("I'm better/smarter/prettier.")* – or inferiority *("I'll never be that good/smart/good looking.")* – are lies we tell ourselves. You are no less, and no better than anyone else.

#2. Be kind to your body. Your body is part genetics, part choices. Your body is a miracle that works perfectly without a lot of supervision. It is durable, and tough, but it is not immune to brutality. Like a beautiful car, treat it like crap, and you'll soon see wear and tear. Learn to thank your body for its loyalty to you; legs that move, lips that kiss, arms that hug. You only get one body. Do yourself a favour and learn to appreciate all it does for you without asking.

#3. There are no do-overs. Some things – like actions and words – are permanent. Sometimes 'sorry' and 'oops' don't cut it. Rebel against it if you want to, but as the quote goes: "There are three things you cannot recover in life: the moment after it's gone, the word after it's said, and the time after it's wasted." I wish I knew who said that. Likely, it was my mother. She was almost always right.

#4. Your parents are only human. Parents are essentially big children, and they are flawed like the rest of us. Deal with it. If you were blessed with perfect parents, lucky you. If you have them on a pedestal, they might disappoint. If you feel like you are the adult at your house, be kind to yourself, learn to set healthy boundaries and plan your escape. You can choose to move on with love when the time is right. *Many* of us have.

#5. Never stop laughing at dumb stuff. I mean it. Fart jokes, weird faces and vulgar comedians. Don't take yourself too seriously. Have at least one friend who will let you act like a complete nutbar. Don't ever lose the light hearted, yuk it up,

147

young side of you. Deep, low, belly laughter is powerful medicine.

#6. Develop a strong moral code. Know your own value system; what you will and won't tolerate in treatment. Know how you will 'show up' for others. Be incorruptible. Pride yourself on trustworthiness. Practice kindness and neatness. Do what you say you'll do. Do it because it's the right thing to do. Be unwavering in consistency. Accountable people inspire others and are solid leaders.

#7. Learn to be still. Those of us born with a smart phone in our hands never will know a silent moment – even on vibrate. We are bombarded with messages day and night. Flashing screens and dinging alarms, YouTube videos and instant gratification will mean you are distracted and over stimulated, constantly seeking meaningful connection and internet answers to your questions. Stillness is where peace lives. Learn to sit unplugged. Breathe deeply and listen. The only answers that matter come from inside, but you have to be quiet to hear them.

#8. Fall in love with yourself. What if the first person you fell in love with was you? What if you loved your weird curly toes? Accepted the fact that you suck at math? Or treasured your ability to listen to others? What if you put your dreams first? Forgave your mistakes? Welcomed your fears? Expected good treatment from others? Learned to self-soothe? People who learn to love and accept themselves are happy, confident people.

#9. Believe. Call it what you want - God, Buddha, the Universe or Creator – just believe in a good and loving, creative power bigger than yourself. The spark that makes your heart beat is the same spark that makes flowers bloom, raspberries sweet and lemons sour and is the magic behind why baby sea-turtles know how to find the safety of the ocean without their momma. It's a miracle and so are you.

#10. Let your light shine. You weren't born into this world to follow, conform or fade into the background. You were born with a unique gift to share in your lifetime. Your job is to figure out what your gift is (you could have more than one) and then rock it like a superstar. Your gift might be physics, or gymnastics or it might be making others feel beautiful. You might build beautiful buildings, whisper to animals or grow potatoes. You will know your gift when it makes your heart full and happy to do it. The greatest gift you can give to others is to be you.

By 23, **Kim Berube** was a single mother of two under two, living on welfare. She has overcome her own life challenges including addiction, two auto-immune diseases, dysfunctional and abusive relationships and a lack of self-worth that literally left her homeless. Over the last dozen years, she has figured out how to successfully manage anxiety disorder, OCD and depression, in addition to the personal demons of guilt and shame and has discovered the power of choice.

She now lives in central Alberta with her handsome husband of 13 years, and her four kids, ages 10 - 20. She published a quarter of a million copies of real woman magazine; a monthly, full colour print magazine that was devoted to recognizing and celebrating the accomplishments of 'real' women. Now she works as executive director of the Lacombe and District Chamber of Commerce, but fills life with creativity and loving endeavours. Kim credits her determination and personal success to a long line of 'pro-female' family members and mentors who've paved the way with strength and love - those both male and female. She is consistently busy with family, business, music and words. www.BigLoveForGirlsAtRisk.wordpress.com

10 AMAZING AND PROVEN SUCCESSFUL TIPS FOR TEENAGERS!

#1. Have fun as long as it doesn't hurt anyone else.

#2. Read books and articles that others think are stupid as long as it will take you toward your dreams.

#3. Question EVERYTHING until you discover your truth, not theirs.

#4. Keep everyone's email and phone numbers forever.

#5. Use ConstantContact to stay in touch with every person you ever meet.

#6. Get involved in events/organizations happenings that will help you meet the right people.

#7. Always ask for more than you want.

#8. ASK ASK ASK for everything and all things.

#9. Ask again. If you don't ask the answer is already no.

#10. Believe you CAN because I believe in you.

Steve Sapato is a Speaker, Author, Trainer, Entrepreneur and World Traveller out of the Tampa, Florida area who teaches people how to become the best they can be. He is a successful and proven speaker whose motto is, "*I can change your life in 60 minutes if you want it to change.*" Contact Steve at steve@stevesapato.com

10 TIPS FOR SELF-EMPOWERMENT

#1. Be fully responsible and take control. I know this tip sounds like it may have come from your parents or teachers but it is so important to becoming self-empowered. Think about it, if you don't take responsibility for you, then you are allowing someone else to be in charge! That takes the "self" out of self-empowerment! Let's say you want to get better grades in school. I would suggest beginning by finding out what your current grades are and taking responsibility for them. It's not your teacher's fault you chose not to do your homework, or not to study for a test, right? By taking responsibility for them you empower yourself to make different choices which will end up with you receiving different results...better grades! It's easy to do and it's all about YOU!

#2. Think powerfully. People who are self-empowered realize that what you think about and focus on is what tends to show up in your life, so they pay close attention to their thoughts. This is how life works....think positive, happy thoughts, things will go that way. But if you are a negative thinker, always expecting the worst, complaining about what you don't like, then you can expect more of that to show up. Using an example of getting better grades, begin thinking positively about earning higher grades, for example, "I can do this, I know I can!" Do this as often as you can, make a habit of thinking positively about you and grades and the success you seek will be yours!

#3. Speak powerfully. This goes together with tip #2. The words you say have power in them so use then carefully. If you are thinking positively and focusing on things that you want more of, then back it up with powerful words. There are many people, who start out thinking positive, but then they speak about what's wrong or about reasons why what they want cannot really happen. Back up your good, happy thoughts with praise and positive comments! Your thoughts about better grades feel good, so support them by telling yourself and others that you can do this and it's just a matter of time.

#4. Act powerfully. Now that you are thinking and speaking powerfully, it's time to act with empowering behavior. Talking and speaking well about earning better grades is awesome, but if you don't follow that with good choices then your dream dies there. You can think about changing and talk about changing but nothing actually changes until action takes place! Before you Do anything, ask yourself, "Is this going to help me get closer to my goal or not?" If you answer, "Yes," then do it, and if you answer, "No," then make a better choice. (If you always try your best, you should never be disappointed!)

#5. Trust how you FEEL. Your feelings are very important and paying attention to them will help you make empowering choices. Trust your feelings! If you are not sure about making a particular decision, sit for a moment quietly and think about it, noticing how you feel. Does it scare you in a bad feeling way? Does it scare you but with a sense of excitement? Do you feel you should just go for it? Or do your feelings tell you that now is just not the right time? Only you have the right answers for you. Trusting yourself is a must for those who want to be self-empowered.

#6. Stop comparing yourself to others. You are unique and amazing! Even if you are an identical twin, you have your own thoughts, feelings and perceptions. In other words, no one sees and experiences the world exactly the same as you, so trust yourself. It's fine to ask others for advice, but don't allow them to make up your mind for you. Empowered people make up their own minds.

#7. Failing doesn't make you a failure. <u>Everyone</u> fails sometimes. But it is how you think of failing that makes the difference. Failing is nothing more than an event that takes place; it is something that happens TO you. Thinking you are a failure, that somehow you change because you failed at something, is a negative way of choosing to see yourself. We know what happens with our thoughts...right. (See Tip #2)

#8. Get to know you and celebrate. You are uniquely awesome and filled with greatness. You are born this way and there isn't anything you have to prove to anyone. You are the most important person in your life, so get to know you and be your own best friend!

#9. Be Kind to others for no reason. Do you want to feel super empowered? Start being kind to people for no reason and without expecting them to repay you! Start small if you want, by smiling at someone and saying "HI", especially if they don't know you. Hold open the door, pick up something dropped, or complement someone on their clothes...it will make them feel good and you feel empowered!

#10. Keep things fun! Self-Empowered people choose to stay powered up by keeping things fun! No matter where you are or what you are doing or who you are doing it with, you can choose to keep it fun.

BONUS TIP: Love! This is the most important tip ever. You must start with love for yourself. If you don't have it, how can you give it away?! Once you have it, give it away to everyone you know, everyone you meet, and every time...and you will live an extraordinary life, guaranteed!

Hello, my name is **Joe Kovach** and I know that YOU have GREATNESS within you right now! Life is an amazing journey! I truly believe that there is nothing we cannot Be, Do or Have if we learn how to use the tools of our thoughts, feelings and actions. The greatest feeling for me is to empower those who wish to discover their own unique greatness and live their life to the fullest! As a school counsellor for over 15 years and a Life Coach, I have successfully helped children, teenagers, parents and even inmates work through their personal challenges and turn their obstacles into opportunities and live from their highest wishes! I know how challenging being a teen can be and I can still remember my own struggles of being bullied, picked on and feeling alone and lost. With help, I learned that all my challenges brought amazing gifts and to help you along your journey I offer my 10 tips for self-empowerment. May your highest wishes be fulfilled! www.TheClearDesire.com

10 TIPS FROM FAWNA

#1. Enjoy the present (time wanting to be older or younger makes you miss the awesomeness).

#2. Don't forget how confident you were at some point-Kindergarten? Before that- when you were going to be an astronaut, a clown and a fireman.

#3. Listen to your rants, you are right, don't forget, don't give up, the world is f*#%@^ up.

#4. You are perfect. Just the way you are.

#5. Everyone is too busy thinking about what you are thinking about them to think about you.

#6. Your parents will not always seem so annoying. You may like them again.

#7. Start living now, if there are things that you know you will do in your life. Do them now if you can, you don't have to wait to be an adult for all of your dreams.

#8. Kindness matters at every age.

#9. You are more supported and loved than you could even imagine.

#10. The energy of the teenage years is important to the world- you matter.

Fawna Bews: This world says: Bachelor of Science, Physical Therapy, Master of Arts in Counseling, Craniosacral Therapy,

Somatoemotional Release, Certified Reflexologist, Reiki Practitioner, Certified Angel Therapy Practitioner, Co-Manager Stampede Ranch for Kids, coach training with Inspired Future, Student of A Course in Miracles.

Like you, my life lessons have been just as valuable, I am a mom of 3, a wife and an 11 year cancer survivor. What I have learned from all of this?

- I don't know anything!
- I believe that you are whole and complete.
- I believe that you can live a peaceful and super fun life.
- I believe that you have the answers on how to do this inside of you.
- I believe that you and I will find our way home.

www.FawnaBews.com

10 TIPS TO GET IN TOUCH

#1. Feel the emotion. Emotions are connected to experiences. Like plant roots in our senses; hearing, sight, taste, smell and touch. Close your eyes and recall an event. Remember:

- The sounds that were around you.
- The scent that comes to mind.
- The images - what did you see?
- The way your body felt – inside and out.
- The taste in your mouth.

#2. Talk about it. Find a friend or family member you know it is safe to share the experience with. Think of others, someone else has troubles too. Find a solution or let it go. Get away from your thoughts by talking to someone about their situation. Everyone needs understanding, inspiration, motivation and support. You are not alone!

#3. Walk it out. Go for a walk with a friend or on your own. Silence, space and nature have many gifts. Disconnect from electronics; computer, phone, text, tv, and games. Turn off the noise. Sit for a moment and let nature play with your senses. A flower's sight and smell, the flight of a butterfly, the wind in your hair, and the sun on your skin can instantly help you feel better. Slow down and savor moments.

#4. Appreciate – Take time to thank someone. Find things and people you are grateful for. Watch a child play (join in). Find a cause to support. Giving to others feels good. There is much in life that brings happiness – what is it for you?

#5. MOVE -Listen to music and dance – your favorite feel good tunes are great to dance to. If you have to dance alone in private, so be it. Feel the music and let the negative energy out. The gentle exercise provides feel good endorphins. Time moves, it is not permanent, nor is the moment that caused how you might be feeling. Let it flow, bounce, roll or simply fade away. Try it with your eyes closed.

#6. Own it - the way you feel is a result of the meaning you have given the moment. It's your responsibility to feel good. Consider every moment as an opportunity or possibility in disguise. Every miss understanding is an interpretation, as an individual you have attached your own meaning to the situation. Adversity, negativity and challenge provide you with a choice. Will you chose to be happy?

#7. Create - use your imagination to express yourself. We are all different somehow. Thank goodness. Find what appeals to you - take a magazine and rip out some photos, visit the library and check out something new. Inspiration is everywhere. Paint, draw, doodle, collage, design, perform and build your own original work of art. No rules. The sky is okay purple if that is what you imagine. It's yours! Now create a simple plan, set a small goal. Lay out the steps that it will take to reach that goal. Then take the steps, slowly one by one. Change the plan along the way if you need to.

#8. Write – journal a story in 3rd person. Observe who, what, where, when and how. Reread it. You may find a new perspective that takes the thoughts off constant replay.

#9. Celebrate – your successes and those of others. Celebrating others can be very inspirational. We all enjoy words of encouragement. Your successes deserve acknowledgement and a pat on the back, as much as anyone else's. You are an inspiration to others. When things don't work out, try again, modify if necessary. Every effort is worth celebration and recognition. A reward does not have to be monetary or large to be meaningful. Satisfaction and/or gratification can be enough.

#10. Love yourself, life and others. Look into your own eyes, in the mirror and say "I Love You!" Mean it. Believe it. Do something just for you. Find your feel good. Watch a funny movie. Laugh at yourself – can you find the funny-side? It's okay to be silly. Loving others can start with wishing them well regardless of the situation. We all want love, acceptance, attention, freedom of expression, some sense of control, individuality, connection, play, celebration, to be seen and heard, and to contribute; but we all make mistakes. Forgive yourself for mistakes – we are all here to learn, besides perfection can be boring.

Jennifer Cockton started working at age 14 in hospitality. She was an entrepreneur right out of high school. Before becoming the founder of SystemsGirl, she spent 18 years in financial planning. She was once asked to summarize her life in six words. The words that she feels comfortable with are - woman, mother, entrepreneur, that Loves Play! Jennifer truly Loves Play and believes that every small business owner became one to add that sense of play back into their lives. She shares simple system solutions with clients and helps implement, beginning with contact management. Jenn believes in Quality vs Quantity in your social media and database strategies, as a tool to minimize marketing efforts, boost sales and save time. Getting to know people better develops connections that go deeper and it's Fun! Her greatest joy in life is time spent with her family and friends, especially her beautiful daughter. www.SystemsGirl.com

10 TIPS TO BELIEVING IN YOURSELF

What is magic?

"Magic is believing in yourself. If you can do that, you can make anything happen." ~Johann Wolfgang von Goethe

Here are some life-changing tips to increase your belief in yourself:

#1. Know that no matter what you look like, how you dress or what your marks are in school, you are perfect the way you are. You are beautiful – or handsome! You are a smart and unique teen. Always remember that you bring something special to this world that no one else can.

#2. Listen to your heart and intuition. Be open to new friends who are different than you because everyone has something special to offer. Here's a secret: friends you make as a teen often become your lifelong friends!

#3. Make sure you love, cherish and nourish your friends. Encourage them with love and compassion because they are wonderful and important.

Even more important, make sure you love, cherish and nourish *yourself.* Encourage yourself with love and compassion because *you* are wonderful and important.

#4. Pray or meditate daily. Accept with gratitude, the Joy and Peace of Mind that comes from connecting with your higher power.

#5. Celebrate *all* your successes today, even the small ones. Celebrate getting a B instead of a C in chemistry. Celebrate having the courage to say hi to your attractive new neighbour. Celebrate learning Pythagoras' theorem because it's *so* exciting! Each success builds upon the others and before you know it, you are incredibly confident.

#6. Cultivate a sense of humour. We are all meant to enjoy life and a sense of humour makes all our lives easier. No one is perfect and we all make mistakes.

#7. Discover your courage. Many people think of courage as being brave enough to fight. Courage can also mean walking away from that same fight. It takes courage to take a different path than your peers when you feel their path is not right for you, to speak up when there is a wrong happening or to visit a dying relative in the hospital. You *are* courageous - you have more courage than you think.

#8. It is important to feel good about yourself. If someone puts you down or bullies you, it says a whole lot more about them than about you. When someone puts you down, most likely that person has low self-confidence and low self-esteem. In other words, they feel terrible about themselves and putting someone else down makes them feel better. They need psychological help.

#9. Keep a daily or weekly journal and review it often. In it, write what you are grateful for; what makes you happy and your a-ha moments or the sudden insights you have about yourself, others, or life.

#10. Believe in yourself and know you can be, do or have *anything* you put your mind to. Set huge goals and take a stand for greatness today. Have a vision for what you want in your life and get a mentor to help you get there much faster. As your belief in yourself increases, have fun creating a life of deliberate abundance.

"Your belief determines your action and your action determines your results, but first you have to believe." ~Mark Victor Hansen

Elizabeth Clark is a life coach, business coach, and trainer who has coached over 600 people to achieve their goals. If you are deciding what you want in life, or looking for creative and fun ways to reach your goals, sign up for her online newsletter at www.DeliberateAbundance.com.

10 TIPS TO FEEL GREAT ABOUT YOUR LIFE

#1. Eat healthy and stay active. Take care of YOU!

#2. Go for a walk, get involved in a sport and get outside where you have the ground beneath your feet and fresh air in your lungs.

#3. Surround yourself with people who take you up. Spend time with people who make you smile and who support you.

#4. **Create a personal Board of Directors.** Who do you go to for advice on relationships, on school work, on family matters, on money matters?

#5. If you can't tell people what you are doing? Don't do it!

#6. **Study hard, do your best, be proud of your achievements.** The end result will be great, so long as you put your best effort into whatever you are doing. Whether you are trying out for the basketball team, doing an assignment, working on a project or taking an exam; when you do your best effort you will always be proud of the end results.

#7. Get involved! Help out in your school and community. Pay it forward. The greatest gifts in life come when you are helping others.

#8. Set goals. Set goals for all areas of your life, 30 day goals, 60 day goals, 90 day goals (to keep you on track) and then 1, 3 and 5 year goals! Remember nothing stays the same, you can subconsciously move through your life or you can create your journey!

#9. Write it down. Go old school; dig out a pen and paper and Journal. Journal about the good, the bad and the ugly. When you put a pen to paper and start writing about what is going on in your life you can have amazing clarity!

#10. **Don't take life so seriously.** Remember to have FUN, enjoy every moment; this is not a dress rehearsal.

Donna Reid Helping YOU Lose Weight Get Fit and Stay Healthy! www.ellequin.com

10 TIPS ON BEING YOU!

#1. Be true to you. As important as it may seem right now to fit in, what is really important is being able to look in the mirror each morning and to recognize the person that you see. This is a great time to discover who you really are. Trust yourself. Listen to how you really feel about things and never forget that the uniqueness in you is what really makes you cool.

#2. Be ingenious. Think differently. Ask tough questions. Dig down deep so that you can explore, discover, create and share. *Your* ideas are the currency of *your* future. The more you have, the richer you will be.

#3. Be grateful. Look around you. What do you have that others do not? There is always something to be grateful for. Maybe it's a friend, an experience or simply a feeling. Or maybe you found $10 in the subway. Why not make a Grateful Journal and write down at least one thing each day that you are thankful for?

#4. Be sure. In spite of how urgent everything may feel right now, just remember that there is time. Many of the decisions that you are going to be faced with will follow you forever. Don't let anyone pressure you into something because it's supposedly "cool". It's ok to take a few more days, weeks or months to think them through – to know if this is really what you want to do. Be careful. Be safe. Be sure. Be cool on your own terms.

#5. Be amazed. While you're busy growing up, don't forget to hold on to the child inside. Be crazy. Be creative. Be curious. Be amazed. After all, if you don't nurture that side of you now, you just might lose it forever.

#6. Be wrong. No one is right all of the time and thank goodness. Being wrong is one of the ways that we learn what's right. So when you're right, be right. But when you're wrong, have the courage to admit it, apologize if necessary and move on. Don't forget to write down what you've learned in your Grateful Journal!

#7. Be generous of spirit. True generosity is when we give without any expectation of being given in return. Ideas. Love. Respect. Friendship. Understanding. Knowledge. Share as much of these as you can and the universe will make sure that you receive more than your share when you need it most.

#8. Be the one. The one to speak out for what is right; the one to defend those who cannot defend themselves; the one who is there when others are not; the one who speaks the truth when others cannot find the courage.

#9. Be strong but remember that it is absolutely ok to need help. To reach out for advice and sometimes, even for comfort. It's not easy to be in the middle of the discovery of you but you do not need to do this alone. No matter who you are and no matter what challenges you will face, there will always be someone somewhere who is ready to listen and to help. Please have the strength to find them.

#10. Believe in yourself. Believe in the incredible person that you are and will continue to become. Believe in the power of the possibilities that lie waiting to be discovered. Believe in those who see the best in you and never let those who don't stand in the way of what you know in your heart to be true. You are beautiful and you are capable of amazing things.

BONUS TIP: Be nice. Really - just be nice. Be nice to others and remember to be nice to yourself. It's so simple and yet so powerful. Nice is cool. Nice is beautiful. Our world would be such a better place if everyone would just remember to be nice.

A five-time award winning business owner **Toni Newman** is passionate about the power of ideas. A highly sought after speaker and Innovation Catalyst, Toni has an uncanny ability to help her clients turn inspiration into innovation and ideas into results.

Toni travels extensively working with audiences who are committed to change and ready for results. Her approach is quite simply a breath a fresh air. Entertaining and highly knowledgeable, authentic and exceptionally relevant, Toni brings a uniquely powerful mix of proven strategies, extraordinary creativity and real world insight to the platform. www.ToniNewman.com

"Because what if the only thing standing between where you are today and where you have always believed you could be, is the courage to let go of where you have already been!"
~ Toni Newman

10 TIPS ON LIVING YOUR DREAMS

#1. Decide to do the things that ignite you. What are you passionate about? What do you enjoy doing? What lights you up? What talents and gifts are within you that you would like to share with the world? Decide to spend more time on the things that ignite you. The key word is "decide." It will always be your decisions that will decide your destiny. Choose wisely. It's time.

#2. Believe in yourself. Believe in yourself 100%! Truly believe in you. Believe that you are capable of achieving great things in this world. I say this because you can, but only if you believe it. Your 100% faith in yourself can eliminate all your fears. With faith the possibilities are endless. It's time.

#3. Write down your goals. Don't just think about your goals. Write them down. Write down all the goals you would like to achieve. Life will go as far as your thoughts so don't be afraid to think big or dream big. The key element for goal-setting is to be specific. The more specific you are the more it is real for you. Don't forget to create deadlines for your goals because without deadlines they usually don't get completed. It's time.

#4. Take action now. An idea will always stay an idea until you take action. It is always the actions you take that will help you move forward. This is what separates the winners and the losers. Whether it is small steps or big steps, just stay in motion. Don't delay. Do it today. Do it now. It's time.

#5. Persistence pays off. There will be times when things become difficult and you want to quit. Just stay with it. Stay in the game. Champions are created because they work hard and stick with it...no matter what. Remember, every "no" is a step closer to "yes." Keep it going. Keep moving forward. Don't let anyone or anything stop you from doing so. It's time.

#6. Keep it positive. Focus on the positive rather than the negative for the positive will lift you up and the negative will bring you down. Spend most of your time thinking what is possible, what you are capable of, what you have accomplished and how you can get better. There will be those negative voices in your head that will try to bring you down, but don't listen to them. Your thoughts are a powerful tool so be sure to shift them in ways to lift you up. It's time.

#7. Always be a student. Always stay in learning mode. The greatest leaders are also the greatest students. Read books. Attend workshops and trainings. Learn from other people. Never stop learning. Remember, the more you know the more you grow. Do it for your life, liberty, and the pursuit of your greatness. It's time.

#8. Build your dream team. It takes teamwork to make the dream work. With a team you have access to more resources and more importantly, it makes the journey a lot more fun. The people you want on your "dream team" are those that believe in you, challenge you, encourage you, celebrate you and appreciate you. It's time.

#9. Find a mentor. Find someone that can help you. Seek out someone that has accomplished whatever it is you want to achieve. Great mentors guide you in the right direction and can save you years of learning. It is the mentors in your life that show you greater possibilities. The best way to get one is to just ask. It's time.

#10. Be kind and give thanks. Being kind to others goes a long way. Sounds simple but most don't do it. Kindness allows people to want to work with you and can also bring you more opportunities. Don't forget to be grateful. Be grateful for what you have and what you have accomplished. Give thanks to your family, friends, teachers, mentors, dream team and others that help you along the way. Your gratitude is always appreciated. It is this attitude that will help you live the life of your dreams. It's time.

Romeo Marquez Jr. is an international speaker and leading authority on Success and Leadership who has presented to over 200,000+ Students, Parents & Educators across the United States and the world in 1000+ events. He is a former UCLA student, TED conference speaker, and recent workshop facilitator with the internationally known teen program, Challenge Day.

As an actor, acting coach and college professor, Romeo has worked with notable names such as Jim Carrey, Anthony Hopkins & the Black Eyed Peas as well as having clients appear in major productions on Disney, Nickelodeon, Cartoon Network, and various commercials.

He has written numerous projects and is currently on tour with his inspirational one-man show, entitled "It's Time," empowering all people to take action on their passions which is now in the developmental stages of being turned into an inspirational film/documentary to remind the world why it is important to take action on their greatness now. Romeo continues to expand his journey with love to be of service to help all humanity for the universal good.

www.RomeoMarquezJr.com www.YoRomeoTV.com

10 TIPS FOR OVERCOMING ANXIETY

Being a student in today's world can trigger all kinds of anxiety. Have you ever had sweaty palms, tightness in your chest, tension in your body or nausea in your stomach when facing a situation? If so, you know what it means to feel anxious.

Sometimes the anxiety is tied to something you have to do – like a sport or a speech or a concert. That's called "performance anxiety." Other times the anxiety just seems to linger or be triggered by people. That's okay!

The great news is – You're not alone! The most successful people in the world have felt the exact same way. The even better news is that yes, you can overcome anxiety to live, love and play with freedom.

#1. Stop seeing anxiety as an enemy. Instead, view it as your dear body's way of saying, "Hey, this might be dangerous!" That way you can thank your body for speaking up and trying to protect you.

#2. Acknowledge all those distressing emotions and symptoms. Again, your subconscious mind just wants to make itself heard. So for a few moments, indulge your flesh and focus on those feelings to they can feel free to leave.

#3. Breathe deeply, at least 3 times. By "deeply," I mean breathe in to the count of four, hold it for the count of four, exhale to the count of four, and hold that before breathing in again. This process will actually slow your heart rate back down.

#4. Love and accept yourself fully right now. Anxiety can be so uncomfortable, that when we feel it, we can't stand ourselves. That's so mixed up! Instead, imagine your body filling up with rivers of love that come straight from heaven through your heart. Love always drives out fear.

#5. Choose to forgive anything or anyone who has contributed to your pain. You can just whisper this, "I forgive you. I release it. I let it go." You may want to say this to yourself while doing the breathing mentioned above. If someone has genuinely hurt you, this does not mean what they did was okay. It means YOU are okay, and you're taking back the power you gave them over your emotions.

#6. Choose your own empowering state. If you want to feel calm and confident, say so! If you want to feel strong and powerful, say so. Imagine your body filling up with power as you say, "I release it and let it go, and I choose to be calm and confident!"

#7. Visualize your ideal outcome. Get crystal clear on what you really want and why. Visualize your success until it's so real that just thinking about it makes you happy. When thoughts of the "worst thing possible" pop into your mind, quickly replace them with your happy images of success.

#8. Pray and declare, "Let this or something better happen – no matter what!" This way, no matter what happens, you can know it's part of your greater good. Indeed, it all plays into your personal success story.

#9. Get totally in touch with the present moment and savor it. Refuse to worry about yesterday, tomorrow or five minutes from now. Instead, revel in the moment with a sense of wonder about all you see, feel, smell and experience. This may be a moment you looked forward to long ago. You'd hate to miss it.

#10. Practice gratitude in all things. Since we get more of what we focus on, focus on what is going well. Think of what is wonderful about your situation and say to yourself, "I LOVE IT HERE!"

When you do those things, the anxiety will slip away and be replaced with enthusiasm. Then you will be the one inspiring others just by the way you live. That may the biggest anxiety reliever of all; realizing that it's not all about you , but about the lives that are touched through you. Now, go play. You've got this!

Gina Parris is a speaker and performance coach who helps people overcome anxiety to reach their full potential -joyfully. Her clients include professional athletes and musicians as well as students and entrepreneurs. She has free gifts available on her website at www.BuiltToWin.com

♥ ♥ ♥ ♥ ♥

10 TOP THINGS I LEARNED WHILE ENROLLED IN THE SCHOOL O' LIFE

#1. Endings are beginnings in disguise. Once upon a time I had both a job and a relationship end within 24 hours. True story. It was pretty hard to get out of bed for a wee bit. Now looking back on that fun-filled day (sarcasm can soften the edges of what at the time was a bit of a rocky day), I see why. Neither the gig nor the guy were ideal for me. Thank God for unanswered prayers. Trust that things really do happen FOR you, and that those back door blessings are just around the bend!

#2. Life is lived forwards but understood backwards. I was 35 when I figured that one out. So you may need to put that one in your back pocket for a bit. There will be times that things make no sense whatsoever – but the upside of 'getting older' is that age really does provide some perspective as to once again, why things do happen FOR you. I had a job producing a reality show that I didn't like working on. Yet, I took it soooo personally when I didn't get asked back the next season. Do not confuse who you are with what you do. Our jobs and careers are expressions of our talents and skills, and it certainly bites when you are stuck in a job that doesn't work for you, BUT it's not our everything. Wish I'd learned that a little sooner and I hope you learn that one early on. There was something better and brighter around the corner. Trust BIG.

#3. That which is to the highest good of self, is to the highest good of others. One of my most favourite and wisest teachers, Gila, taught me that and I quote her all of the time. It REALLY helps when I use that as my litmus test when making decisions. It's pretty easy to get hung up on trying to make everyone else happy and forget about ourselves.

#4. Regardless if it's a job, a relationship or a pair of jeans, if you have to talk yourself into it, it's not a good fit. End of story.

#5. Put FUN first.

#6. Let go or be dragged. It's a ZEN proverb and if I were to ever get a tattoo, I'd put that on my forehead. Letting go of what we think we have to have, creates the space for what is best to find its way to us.

#7. Another one from Gila – the only meaning anything has is the meaning you give it. Perception is everything. For example, a guy and a gal are making out on a street corner and one person walks by and says 'how romantic', a second person walks by and says 'that's disgusting, get a room', a third person walks by and says 'wow, where did she get that sweater'.

#8. Every opportunity has a cost and there is always a downside to every opportunity. You can't have one side of a magnet. The glass isn't half full or half empty, in reality it is both. Check out John Demartini for more on that!

#9. This too shall pass.

#10. Trust how it feels in your body.

By **Kari Dunlop** www.GlindaGirls.com

10 TIPS FOR TEENS BY ALLISON

#1. If a relationship has to be kept a secret, you shouldn't be in it. This is especially true if the people you are hiding it from are the ones who truly care about you the most.

#2. Go ahead and gossip; as long as you don't mind it coming back to bite you big time!! Remember people who do it WITH you will also do it ABOUT you!!

#3. Comparing yourself to others is the fastest way to misery. You will always find someone smarter, more beautiful, thinner, richer, etc. Instead, see yourself how God sees you... He created you to be the best YOU that you can be. The world would not be the same if you did not exist... God created you special and put you here for a reason... You have unique ideas, unique strengths and unique and beautiful things to offer the world so keep dreaming, keep giving and keep sharing YOU with the world.

#4. It's okay to wallow, but limit the time you allow yourself to "go there." Everyone has heartaches, disappointments and bad days... expect them, accept them, cry your eyes out and give yourself some TLC to get through them. Just don't wait for the pain to be gone before you take the next step or you may find yourself stuck there for years.

#5. Be kind to all, but choose your best friends wisely!! Surround yourself with true friends who accept you as you are, celebrate your successes, comfort you in your pain, keep you safe from harmful situations and bring out the best in you. Far too many lives are ruined from poor friend choices.

#6. The fastest way out of a pity party is to focus on someone else in need. There is always someone worse off than you so focusing your heart and attention to help another person who is struggling always brings needed perspective to your own problems and quite often results in a great new friendship.

#7. Holding onto anger is like carrying around a 100 pound backpack. It will drag you down, cause you pain and never let you really fly. The funny thing is you can choose when to slip anger off your back and walk away... and when someone or something puts it back on your shoulders, remember, you are not obligated to carry it!

#8. Don't do something permanently stupid just because you are temporarily upset! Give yourself some time for perspective to set in before you retaliate, make decisions, hit the send button, react based on assumptions or hurt another person. Seriously consider all consequences first before taking any actions when upset.

#9. Failure is the back door to success. Don't let fear of failure stop you from accomplishing your dreams. But as you follow your heart, don't forget to take your brain with you!! It is always good to have a Plan B (and C and D just in case!)

#10. It will get better. It doesn't matter what "it" is, it will always get better. Give a difficult situation time, give it sleep, give it prayer, give it perspective from a true friend and give yourself some TLC and remember... you made it through yesterday didn't you? You can make it through today too and with God's help you really can make it through anything. God loves you whether you believe in Him or not... and sometimes in life He is the only one you can turn to. Trust Him to work things out in the best way for you.

Allison Orthner wears many hats including portrait photographer, high school teacher, event planner, wife to a gorgeous man and mother to two utterly wonderful teenagers!! She also appears regularly on TV in Canada, writes for Canadian Scrapbooker Magazine and has been widely published including 13 front covers. Her heart's passions, however, are her faith, her family, her friends, fun and travel (in that order). Allison's deepest desire is to live a life full of passion, love, generosity, forgiveness and hope... a life that inspires others to do the same. You can learn more at www.AllisonOrthner.com

10 TIPS FOR HEALTHY TEENS

I want to share some "secrets" about being "skinny" with you. They come from a video series I created called "The B.S. Of Skinny". Most of you are probably thinking, "What! The **B.S.** of Skinny?" Yes, but the "B.S." does not stand for what you probably think it does. :-) The B.S. I am referring to is actually two different things: the **B**ogus **S**ecrets and the **B**est **S**trategies.

First of all, let me tell you a bit about myself. I was the "skinny" kid at school. This may sound "perfect", but it wasn't fun at all. I was called "carpenter's dream" because I was "flat as a board" and "sticks" because my legs looked like two toothpicks. Yeah...it was so much fun being "skinny". :-) One of the reasons I was "skinny" was because I was very active, too active according to my teachers. Another reason: my genetics. Additionally, my mom fed us really healthy food! I LOVE being healthy! My whole career (for the last 25+ years) has been helping people become healthy, happy and whole! I especially love working with kids! (I raised 16 of them... but that's another story!)

So here is "The B.S. of Skinny" for Teens:

#1. Bogus Secret: "There is a Perfect Body." **Best Strategy:** No, there is not! You were made perfectly for *you*. All you have to do is take care of what you've been given and it will be perfect!

#2. Bogus Secret: "Skinny is sexy." **Best Strategy:** Skinny is NOT sexy; it is DANGEROUS! Your goal should not be to be "skinny" but to be *healthy*. Did you know that anorexia is the third most common chronic illness in female teens? Did you know that **everyone** who is anorexic and does not get help **WILL** die? Here's what happens with an eating disorder... you get:

- dry skin
- brittle nails
- thinning hair that breaks or falls out
- growth of fine body hair covering the *entire* body
- tired easily
- dizzy or faint
- dehydrated (early wrinkles)
- organ, heart and stomach damage
- loss of tooth enamel (yellow, weak teeth)
- bloating (so much for the "skinny" look!)
- frequent sore throat and/or swollen glands
- bloodshot eyes or dark circles under the eyes
- sores or calluses on knuckles

Does any of that sound sexy? NO! You have to eat to be healthy!

#3. Bogus Secret: "I have to work out like a maniac to be skinny." **Best Strategy:** Actually, *what* you eat is 80% of what you *look* like. Exercise accounts for only 20%. So, the trick is to eat properly, plan ahead and practice healthy choices. So, what *should* you eat every day? I'm sure you've heard this a million times, but it is the truth. Eat lots of veggies, 2 – 3 servings of fruit, 2 – 4 servings of carbs (brown rice, potatoes, yams and corn, but NO WHEAT products), 3 – 4 servings of organic dairy, 2 – 3 servings of protein (red meat, white meat, fish, beans, lentils, eggs) and drink LOTS of water.

#4. Bogus Secret: "There are pills that will make me skinny." **Best Strategy:** Nope. There are pills that will make you edgy, nervous, irritable, grouchy, and dehydrated; give you bad breath and gas; damage your organs and heart; but NONE that will make you skinny. Sorry.

#5. Bogus Secret: "Surely, no company would sell me something that is bad for me!" **Best Strategy:** Businesses are built to make profit. If it will sell, it will be sold. When you were a kid, you had to rely on your parents for your health. Now that you are older, you can start making some food choices of your own. Whatever you do, don't waste your hard-earned money on "junk" food because that's exactly what it is, no matter how healthy they tell you it is. Eat as closely to nature as you can (the list in #3).

#6. Bogus Secret: "Fat-free is better for you." **Best Strategy:** Everyone needs healthy fats to have healthy hair, skin and even hormones. The trick is to eat healthy fats like avocado, nuts and nut butters, and organic virgin olive oil instead of whipping cream, hydrogenated fats (in most chips, chocolate bars, cookies, etc.) and burgers. Never opt for the "fat-free" stuff.

#7. Bogus Secret: "Sugar-free is better for you." **Best Strategy:** You are far better off consuming real sugar (if you have to) than to eat sugar replacements. In truth, your body responds to sugar replacements in the same way it does to sugar, only the replacements are *chemicals* instead of the real thing. Always opt for the real thing.

#8. Bogus Secret: "I need to go to the doctor every time I have a cold or headache." **Best Strategy:** Take care of yourself properly and you won't have to go to a doctor very often at all. If possible, stay away from antibiotics. The more you take them, the less effective they will be when you really need them. Some medications actually make you *gain* weight.

#9. Bogus Secret: "If I take vitamins, I don't need to eat properly." **Best Strategy:** Vitamins are just a form of health insurance. Nothing beats eating properly. It is important to take vitamins so make sure to take quality vitamins.

#10. Bogus Secret: "If I just drink liquids all day, I'll stay skinny." **Best Strategy:** I know a lady that is about 250 pounds. She told me she does not know why she weighs so much when all she does is drink all day. I asked her what she drinks and she brought me a "cold coffee mix" that she puts in milk. She drinks about 6 of them a day. Each drink has about 400 calories. She was drinking 2400 calories a day! The same thing can happen with special coffees, mixed cold drinks, etc. *Stick to water!*

Just remember...You are perfect the way you are! You are destined for great things, things only *you* can do. To do those great things, you need to be as healthy as possible!

Just B U!

Angela Sladen-deRox lives on an acreage outside of Sherwood Park, Alberta with her husband David. She helped raise 16 children and is "mom" to 10. She has four beautiful grandchildren. Angela has a long personal and professional history of helping people become healthy and fit, and she is passionate about it! Angela is a certified nutritional consultant, registered sports nutrition advisor, certified personal trainer, and former gym owner. www.totalhealthmethod.com.

10 TIPS FOR TEENS FROM
A BURN SURVIVOR

#1. First and foremost love you for who you are. Love everything about yourself. Until you love yourself no one else can! Be yourself!!!

#2. Believe in yourself and the accomplishments you will make. Redefine what is possible in your life.

#3. Dreams are so important. Fulfill dreams that you have and exceed your own expectations and no one else's.

#4. You will have struggles in your life. Confront them head on and deal with them. Don't push them aside. They will make you stronger in the long run.

#5. Love your body. Understand that your self-esteem and body image can affect and influence your relationships with yourself and with others.

#6. Take the time to understand the concept of body image and its importance in your daily life. It is the first step to feeling better about you.

#7. What you perceive, others will believe. What I mean by this is, what you perceive about yourself and put out to the world is what others will believe about you.

#8. Life is about lessons. Lessons will always be in your life. Take what you can from them and use them as you journey on. Remember you can learn from both good and bad lessons.

#9. Never give up!!! As my friend Kyle Maynard says "No Excuses"... Have the life you want. You are the only one that can re-write your story.

#10. Have hope, courage, determination, perseverance, willpower and self-motivation in all you do.

By **Cindy Rutter,** RN, BSN

I (Kelly Falardeau) met Cindy at the World Burn Congress many years ago. She also got burnt when she was a child and what I loved about her was that she taught me that burn survivors could have children too. I thought because of my scars I wouldn't be able to get pregnant. I didn't think my scars would stretch enough, but Cindy had two daughters of her own and was able to show me that I was wrong and would be able to have kids too. That's the power of knowing someone who is like you and the power of the internet. It's easy to find others who can help us and share our stories.

♥ ♥ ♥ ♥ ♥

10 TIPS TO CREATE INNER PEACE
AND HAPPINESS

As a certified life coach, I have laid out what I call 9 Steps to Inner Peace and Happiness. It is a set of highly effective tools I use to assist my clients in resolving or coming to peace with their ongoing problems.

I was excited to share these tips with teenagers because I believe that you're never too young to work on your personal growth and development. All that is ever required is a willingness to do the work.

#1. Make a daily appointment with your Higher Power. The very first step to creating inner peace and happiness is to make a daily appointment with your Higher Power and keep it! Whether you pray, meditate, walk in nature or go to church, the choice is yours. Acknowledging your Divinity and believing in a Power far greater than yourself to support and guide you, will prove to be your most powerful life tool.

#2. Practice forgiveness. The second step to creating inner peace and happiness is to practice forgiveness. Many of us believe that we don't have anyone we need to forgive. The truth is, we could probably find someone to forgive on a daily basis. It's often the little things that hurt us and yet sometimes we feel silly feeling the way we do. But the truth is, if your feelings are hurt, they're hurt... simple as that. Validate how you feel and practice forgiveness to those who have hurt you. Forgiveness isn't about other people; forgiveness is for you... so that you can move on.

#3. Create quality connections. The third step to creating inner peace and happiness is to create quality connections with people who treat you in the most loving and unconditional ways. Who you spend your time with is who you become so it's important that you choose wisely. Fair weather friendships aren't real... you want to be around people who've got your back even when you make mistakes.

#4. Look after your personal health. The fourth step to creating inner peace and happiness is to look after your personal health. This includes both your physical and mental health. Never, ever be embarrassed about getting help for these things! In today's culture we are abundant with so many wonderful alternative practitioners, coaches, therapists and doctors. Take advantages of these services and get the guidance and support you need to help you deal with whatever physical or mental challenges you are struggling with! It's not easy being a teenager but you are never alone!

#5. Move your body on a daily basis. The fifth step to creating inner peace and happiness is to start moving your body on a daily basis. Your body is just like a machine and it needs to be moved regularly. Finding an enjoyable way to move your body for 20 minutes or more per day will have a huge impact on your self-confidence, your energy and your overall well being. Stay active and keep moving!

#6. Create powerful boundaries. The sixth step to creating inner peace and happiness is to create powerful boundaries. Many of us are allowing unacceptable situations into our personal space. We are allowing people to walk all over us or we spend our time doing things in the hope that others will like us. This gives us absolutely no personal satisfaction or appreciation. When we set up powerful boundaries, we take back our control and we only allow into our lives what is acceptable and what feels right to us. Listen to your gut feelings... if they feel good you know you're on the right track, if they don't then stop what you're doing or say no! You are your own boss!

#7. Become aware of what you want in your life. The seventh step to creating inner peace and happiness is to become aware of what you want in your life. As a teenager it can be difficult to know what you want to do or where you want to go. This is completely normal. Take some time to daydream. What excites you? How would you like to serve other people? What are you really good at? What could you see yourself doing for the rest of your life?

#8. Acts of service or kindness. The eighth step to creating inner peace and happiness is called acts of service or kindness. Most people would agree that it feels better to give than it does to receive. There are so many ways we can apply this step in our lives. Ask yourself these questions: "What can I do for someone else today? How can I make a difference for someone today? Who could really use a boost right now?" When you have your answers, GO FOR IT!

#9. 21 day personal challenge. The ninth and final step to creating peace and happiness is to create 21 day personal challenges. These challenges are so important because they will keep you moving forward in life. What I love about them is that they are totally doable. For example, I once had a 21 day challenge to clean out my junk drawer! Sure it only took me a day, but it was a task that I kept ignoring and so the 21 day challenge really gave me the motivation I needed to get it done! It was definitely worth it! Your 21 day challenges can be anything you want them to be. Make a list of all the things you would like to get done in your life. Then, one by one, use the 21 day challenge system to accomplish them little by little.

#10. Love yourself no matter what! You're not perfect. You never will be. Do your best. Acknowledge your hard work. Never give up. Mwah!

Carmen Jubinville is a certified life coach, committed to helping women resolve their resentments, jealousies, heartaches, negative patterns, belief systems and more. To connect with Carmen visit her online at www.carmenjubinville.com or on facebook at facebook.com/CarmenJubinvilleMentorToWomen.

10 TIPS OF MOTHERLY ADVICE
TO TAKE SERIOUSLY

My mom was killed by a reckless driver who refused a breathalyzer which pretty much means he knew he would fail the test. My mom always had great advice that I am so thankful for, I am also grateful that I get to pass along her advice not only to my daughter but to millions of daughters everywhere. I had an amazing, caring, smart, beautiful and I can't forget to add, fun mom who taught me to love myself for me!

#1. The first thing I learned from my mom was that it didn't matter who my friends were as long as I was a good influence on them, I really felt a sense of responsibility to make sure I was making the right choices.

#2. The second important lesson was to treat people how I wanted them to treat me. I always put myself in other peoples' shoes.

#3. The third, don't count anyone out as a part of your life, even if it's just a smile exchanged during the day it could be making a difference in someone's life.

#4. Be involved, my mom told me to always take advantage of all the extra circular activities, it's the easiest way to meet new people and experience new things.

#5. Include everyone; you might realize how much you have in common with someone you've never talked to before.

#6. Don't be afraid to stand up for yourself, if you like a band that someone else isn't a fan of then agree to disagree. It's ok to like something different than your friends.

#7. Never start tomorrow with yesterday's problems was something I heard a lot from my mom and I never let something that happened the day before stick with me the next because every day is a new day.

#8. The eighth piece of motherly advice was that boys have feelings too. Being a young female, I never put a lot of thought into how I might affect my male friends/boyfriends. Who knew the opposite sex had feelings? Not me!!!

#9. Number nine, from the words of Miley Cyrus (I know so yesterday) but "Nobody's Perfect" it's the truth, everyone has something that they're self-conscious about, even the people you might think are perfect.

#10. Last but not least, you are in control of you, you decide who and what affects you and how you're going to handle things. I know that's a lot of responsibility but it is easy if you are making the choices that make you proud of who you are!

Always remember your mother is going to steer you in the right direction and no one will love you like she does.

By **Kelly Romanchuk**

10 TIPS ABOUT SELF-WORTH AND TO BELONG

For me, self-worth is that one does not compromise one's beliefs, morals and goals to belong. Self-worth comes from within. How you believe in yourself. How you manage your self-esteem.

#1. Be proud of who you are and where you come from regardless of size, shape and physical differences. Learn to embrace them. Accept you self. Love yourself.

#2. Keep self-respect. If you have that in place it will carry through to how you show respect to others.

#3. Smile. I find so many people do not smile enough. It is so important to embrace your smile. Your genuine smile will let others see love in your heart.

#4. Do not compromise your morals and your beliefs to belong to a popular group. Sometimes what appears to be popular or the in-thing turns out to be the not so good in-thing. Popularity contests are over rated.

#5. Your body is your temple. Don't sacrifice yourself to risky circumstances because others have done it or because you are being persuaded to do so. If your gut instinct tells you that it is not okay and that it does not feel right. Don't compromise those feelings by any means. You are the only one that has the final say when it comes to your body.

#6. Peer pressure is the worst possible thing to happen to a teenager. The only pressure you should be concerned about is from within and from your parents. Does it feel right to you? What are the consequences involved? If they continue on name-calling, are they truly your friends? You can walk away. It may hurt, it may be painful but you will recover.

#7. Learn to forgive. We tend to hold in resentment, hatred and bitterness over the most mundane scenarios. We must be able to forgive in order to live life and move on. We may not forget the hurt that caused us not to forgive but those wounds will heal. Yet, they can re-open throughout our life. That is why it is very important to be able to forgive. The more we are able to forgive, the more likely those wounds will remain closed. Most importantly be able to forgive yourself.

#8. Embrace your world. Embrace every moment of your daily life, your family, friends, pets and people who you interact with on a regular basis. We have one life that we know of.

#9. Judgment. Be very careful with your judgments. It is crucial to not get trapped into the vicious cycle of "who said, she said, he said." This leads to gossip. Don't be chatty, spiteful or judgmental of others.

#10. Mindful. Be aware of your surroundings, other people's emotions and of your own. Less is more. Sometimes the best person to be is to be the listener. Keep calm, cool and collective in your thoughts. C3 as I like to call it.

Hi I am **Lily Chatterjee**, I have been asked to write a brief bio about myself. Where do I begin? I guess I will start with the basics. I was born in Lansing, Michigan. My father was from Kolkata, India and my mother is from Austria. I was raised in East Lansing, Michigan. I have traveled many miles with in the states and around the world to explore, connect and learn from how other people live. I grew up experiencing firsthand what it was like to be bullied. In turn, I reacted as a bully myself in my pre-teens. It was awful.

Most of my life I looked for acceptance and love, mostly in the wrong places. When I had my accident, I went through more discovering, healing and acceptance issues. Almost 25 years later, I have found myself again and have learned to accept and love myself. It will forever be a work in progress. I would not have been able to write and share these tips with you were it not for being comfortable and loving who I am today. It took me a very long time. I hope that these tips will benefit you so it does not take you as long as it did me. Traveling and searching for self–love and self-worth brought me full circle back to East Lansing, where I reside with my mom in the house I grew up in. Definitely, "Home is where the heart is."

10 TIPS FOR TEENS FROM SHERI

#1. Be your authentic self. Be true to yourself always. March to the beat of your own unique drum and do the things that make you happy. Don't worry what other people will think. Many people are still searching for who they are and may not yet be embracing their uniqueness. Magical things happen when you're following your passions, the things that you really love in life.

#2. Accept and love yourself just the way you are. Each night before going to bed, look at yourself in the mirror. Look deep into your own eyes and verbally acknowledge and celebrate the things you accomplished that day. For example, you brushed your teeth, went to school and did your best on a quiz, turned down an opportunity that didn't feel right, encouraged a friend at lunch, drove your little brother home, did your homework, and played with your dog.

#3. Surround yourself with people who inspire you. Always seek to be around people who amplify your energy. After interacting with them, you feel uplifted and excited about life. Look for this reaction when considering friends, coaches, bosses, mentors, clients, coworkers, etc.

#4. Practice blissful thinking. Dream the biggest dream you can and then make it even bigger. Visualize the most amazing life you can imagine ... then multiply it by 10! It should be so huge that it simultaneously scares and excites you, inspiring you to really go for it. Don't play small in life and settle for less than you desire, go for what you really want and deserve and keep trying.

#5. Be courageous and ask for what you want. High achievers get where they are by asking for what they want. You'll be amazed how often you will get a 'yes' when you ask the right person from the heart in a respectful, non-entitled way. You don't lose anything by asking ... you don't have it now. Go ahead, try it!

#6. De-clutter your life. Let go of anyone, anything, any opportunity/event/activity/obligation, etc. that no longer serve you or fit into your vision for your ultimate life. Anything that drains your energy must go. Amazing things will come when you create the space for them in your schedule and your life. When in doubt, throw it out.

#7. Trust your intuition/inner voice. We are all equipped with an inner guidance system. Practice getting in touch with your inner self and listen for the whispers of your soul. Sitting in silence and enjoying nature is a great way to deepen your connection with your inner voice. When you receive an intuitive nudge, take inspired action as soon as possible and watch the magic that unfolds before you.

#8. Choose to amplify love, joy, and kindness in the world and trust that it will be reflected back to you. Sometimes it can feel like we're bombarded by negativity. Break the chain and refuse to be a part of it. Associate with people, places, things and events that make you feel good and fill you with hope and joy. Discontinue blaming, complaining, gossiping, and rationalizing. It's a waste of your precious energy. Champion the people who are making a positive difference in your world. Amplifying the positive will enhance your life and the lives of everyone around you.

#9. Express gratitude daily. There are so many things to be grateful for in our lives. Sometimes when we're busy or distracted, it's easy to lose sight of all of the amazing gifts we have. For example, our families, our friends, our ability to think, the beauty of nature, food to eat, etc. At the end of each day, think about the person, thing, event, or opportunity for which you're most grateful and then appreciate the impact on your life.

#10. Keep taking action in the direction of your dreams. You may feel nervous or scared when trying something new. That's completely normal. If you're really going for your dreams, you'll make a few mistakes along the way. Don't let them take you out of the game. If you feel pulled to pursue something, honor that feeling and continue taking action toward your goal despite your fears and doubts. You'll never know until you try.

When you commit to living the life of your dreams, you'll feel good knowing that you're working toward a challenge that's worthy of your efforts. Above all, do what makes you happy and enjoy this exciting journey!

Sheri Fink is a #1 best-selling, award-winning children's author and an international speaker. She writes books that inspire and delight children while planting the seeds of self-esteem that can have lifelong benefit. Discover more about Sheri and her books at: www.WhimsicalWorldofSheriFink.com

10 TIPS FOR HEALTHY TEENS

#1. You are a mirror reflection of who your friends are. It is of the utmost importance that you surround yourself with people who have like interests and goals. More often than not, we may find ourselves wishing to be part of a group just to achieve a certain status. We may be put into compromising situations that challenge our value systems so as to not lose our standing within that circle of influence. These decisions can be the ones we may most regret later.

If you find yourself in a group that gossips behind people's backs, tease others and partake in unhealthy risks, you have to ask yourself is that what you truly want and need in order to grow into the incredible person you are. Can you imagine a situation where you are honoured to have the friends you have where they support and encourage you to reach the greatness that lies deep within you? It is possible and you deserve it!

#2. Life is not a spectator sport. The happiest teens are those who find a passion and get involved. Of course, the obvious choices would be to join a sports team, participate in drama or music program but there are endless opportunities.

Some of the most powerful and rewarding experiences are those that involve service. Volunteering may seem like a task but those who do, reap the huge benefits and walk away empowered from the experience. There is no greater way to enhance self-esteem than bringing joy and making a difference in the life of another.

#3. Focus on five positives at the end of each and every day. Life is filled with obstacles and they can wear us down. When we are stressed, the tendency is to devote the greater part of our thoughts on the problem. It is human nature despite the fact there are moments of warmth and kindness that happen all around us each and every day if we choose to recognize them.

At the end of each day, take the time to reflect on a minimum of five positives that occurred. They can be a kind smile, funny banter with someone, a delicious meal, a compliment you received, a minor accomplishment or simply anything that brightened your day in the slightest amount. Make this a regular habit and you will find that there is a lot more to smile about than we often think. It gets easier over time doing this and it can chop down the negatives you think consume your life. Not only that, you'll sleep better and wake up feeling good about the next day.

#4. Work hard, play hard. Do everything you do with passion. Most people have the misperception that work is a negative thing and it makes life more difficult when it is truly the opposite. The harder you strive in any given area, the more it allows you to achieve success, thus making things easier and much more fun in the end.

As a mountain climber, approach trails can be long and tedious. In order to experience the highs (what a terrible pun) and all the excitement the day could offer, you have to slog your way through the ugliness. It is the same in life. So tackle the drudgery with joy and get ready for the ride of your life!

#5. Believe in the golden rule, with a slight change. We have all been told time and time again about the golden rule, "Treat others like the way you want to be treated." Although this looks so nice on paper, how it should read is, "How you treat others is how you will be treated."

Practice being the first to smile, the first to greet someone, the first to give a compliment, the first to help, the first to volunteer. Try this for a month and see what the results are like. You will notice people treating you with more respect which is exactly what you deserve. Remember, every day we are modeling how we want to be treated.

#6. Your attitude is a choice. Scientists the world over are making new discoveries in the power of belief and how it translates into everyday life. How we interpret the world around us is how it will correspondingly respond to us. What you choose to believe in will become your reality.

Believe things happen for a reason and it will serve to help you grow. Believe you have the power to make your dreams come true. Believe you deserve a great life and take the steps to make it happen.

#7. Keep growing. As young children, we found the world to be a fascinating place filled with wonders. As we get older, we may take things for granted or narrow our focus to just a microcosm of all that is around us.

The world is amazing. Continue to keep reading, explore, try new things, visit new places, take more calculated risks and go on new adventures. Every opportunity we take advantage of helps us to grow and to become all of the greatness we were destined to be.

#8. Let fear be an inspiration and not a deterrent. So often in life, we avoid the things that put fear in our hearts and thus, cause us to miss out on opportunities. There are so many phobias out there and for good reason. But what if we were to learn how to come face to face with that fear and how to work with it?

The fear of rejection denies us the chance to meet that special someone. The fear of speaking in public denies us the opportunity to inspire others or to live out our dream as a performer. (Trust me on this one as I am very well versed in it, unfortunately.) Any fear that prevents you from living the life you were meant to live cannot be the determining factor dictating your destiny.

Yes, there may be hurt and having to learn how to deal with "No!" So what? When we develop the strength to deal with it, windows of opportunities are opened creating magnificent scenarios we never dreamt possible. One of the greatest rushes is having gigantic butterflies floating around in your stomach and you stepping up and conquering the world. Try it and tell me what you think!

#9. Accept responsibility for your life and take control. So often, we feel like life simply unfolds and we are mere actors on a grand stage playing the role that we were destined for. Not true. We have to realize we are the producers and we determine in what direction this will play out. We have to go out and look for the scenarios we want and if we can't find them, we make them. One day, your life will flash before your eyes so it better be something worth watching. Take control now and make it happen!

#10. Love being you. You are a unique wonderful piece in the grand puzzle of humanity. Without you, something would be missing. There is no one else like you. So often we try to be someone we are not to gain acceptance but why? You have to be you because everyone else is taken. It's not to say we can't emulate some of the traits and characteristics from people we admire. Combine those qualities with the uniqueness of you and bam, you have the recipe for awesomeness. You are you and you are amazing.

By **Mark Ivancic,** a grade four teacher

10 TIPS FOR TEENS BY TISH

#1. Quit worrying about what others "think."

#2. You become like the top five people you surround yourself with, choose wisely!

#3. Would you rather be "right" or be "happy?"

#4. If you never try, you'll never know.

#5. True personal growth is hard work (keep growing!)

#6. Deal with life's challenges and focus on life's gifts.

#7. If you're always trying to be normal, you will never know how extraordinary you can be!

#8. Self-worth is measured by how you treat yourself.

#9. God gives us all a purpose, it's up to us to find it.

#10. "Bad company corrupts good character "choose your friends wisely and be yourself in good character and attract the right friends.

Tish Lethbridge was born and raised in an alcoholic family, and was the fourth born out of five siblings, all of which were boys and she was the only girl. She was never shown any love and was never told she was loved by her parents, which was very hard on a little girl who's personality was all about loving and sharing with others.

Right after graduating from high school, she met a guy, and he showed interest which she thought was "love" and she got pregnant at 19-years-old. She ended up getting married and having two babies in 11 and half months. That marriage lasted three years, as she had married a man who was an alcoholic and abused drugs. At 21 years of age she found herself alone and scared raising 2 little ones, as patterns go she met another man who she thought would love her and take care of her and her boys.

She was married for 20 years and had five sons together, with a lot of mental, verbal, and in the end physical abuse, not only to her but their children also. She finally found the strength to leave the marriage and has been a single mom of seven sons for four years. It has taken a lot of personal self-development, and surrounding herself with upbeat positive people. She has grown into a "strong worthy" woman.

Looking back she sees the destructive patterns that she was following and how it all started with her own upbringing as a child. She now knows that she has to "love herself before she can expect anyone else to love her, she needs to take that little girl who was never told that she was loved, and look in the mirror and tell her that she loves her every day! If something doesn't feel right, don't do it! It's true when they say listen to your "gut" feeling! Through all of this she has become an independent business woman, found a company to work for who changes many people's lives (personally, physically, financially), and a WOMAN who has been able to give her sons a safe, secure, happy home! Every day I look for ways to improve myself, and be a better person so that I can 'serve' others. May you all be "Blessed" on this journey that we call "life." www.naticiaforeveryoung.nsproducts.com

10 TIPS TO CREATE AN AWESOME LIFE!

#1. Realize that life is awesome. Right now, write down three things that are awesome in your life (maybe you have the best friends, your parents are super cool, or you have your favorite teacher at school). Even though life can be tricky sometimes and not seem like it is going your way, there is always something that is awesome about it.

#2. Create an *Awesome Life* list. This list is one of the coolest things to do to create your awesome life. This list is where you write down your dreams, desires, goals and the things you want to do. Write down 99 things (or get as close to 99 as you can), experiences and feelings that you want to have in your life.

Where are some places that you want to visit? How do you want to feel each day? Do you want to meet some new friends? Do you want to go skydiving or sing in front of an audience? Who do you want to meet (a celebrity, a scholar, a mentor, a business owner)? What kind of grades do you want to have in school? What activities do you want to participate in? Creating your *Awesome Life* list is like phoning or texting the universe with your request for what you want to happen in your life.

#3. Create an *Awesome Life* poster board or scrapbook. You can do this on your computer with graphics and images, on Pinterest (which would be really cool) or by cutting out magazines and downloading pictures and gluing them onto poster board or in a scrapbook. Look at this board or book every morning before you head off to school and every night before you go to bed. Be sure to put a checkmark or gold star beside the things on the list that have happened. This is the visual picture of your awesome life.

#4. Your actions need to match your desires, dreams and goals. This is really important! You have to take action and move towards your dream. If you want to sing, you need to practice and maybe look into singing lessons and figure out how you will pay for them.

If you want a more healthy body, you need to start exercising (try running, Zumba, join a soccer team or do some yoga) and make sure you are making healthy food choices. Ask an adult for help in these areas. If you want better grades, you have to study more and ask for help. You can't make your *Awesome Life* list, text the universe with it and then sit on the couch. You have to starting doing things to make your dreams come true!

#5. Share your *Awesome Life* list. Tell your friends, family and those who care about you about your *Awesome Life* list. You never know who can help you make some of those experiences come true.

#6. Don't be afraid to ask. Ask for advice, ideas and information on how to achieve some of your goals and dreams. Email or tweet someone famous, ask your friends who have the same interests, ask your relatives or your teachers at school. Ask. Ask. Ask. There are people out there who want to support you in creating your awesome life.

#7. Be grateful for the awesomeness of each day. It is important to realize what is awesome in your life every day. Before you go to bed each night, think about or write down three (or more) things in your journal that were awesome about your day. Some nights this might be tricky but try really hard to focus on the good parts of your day. Other nights, you might fill a whole page in your journal. Look for little things and big things that made your day awesome.

#8. Encourage your friends and family to live their *Awesome Life*. It is more fun to have people surrounding you as you reach for your dreams, desires and goals. Have an *Awesome Life* party and share your dreams and goals with your closest friends and family. Make your awesome life poster boards and scrapbooks together. Find out what is on their list and then help each other make it happen.

#9. Make changes to your *Awesome Life* list. The dreams and goals you once had may not fit now or aren't as important to you as they had been. That's ok, as you change, your *Awesome Life* list will change.

#10. Be positive. A positive attitude attracts positive experiences, people and things into your life; keep smiling and have fun. Your life is guaranteed to be *Awesome*.

Jill Ethier, BComm - I am a Creator Warrior. I bridge the gap between your dreams and your reality. I help you make it happen. I create change. I draw out the greatness in individuals and companies with the programs that I have developed. My toolbox combines my BComm in Marketing and Finance with the ancient wisdom of all things energy including Feng Shui, Dowsing and some other cool stuff. I created the Greatness in Action Experience which is used by individuals, families and corporations for personal growth and relationship building. It was designed for clients and businesses so they could identify and utilize the power of their Greatness every day. This experience is focused solely on unleashing the energy of Greatness to prosper, succeed and experience what living fully truly means.

www.GreatnessinAction.com

10 TIPS TO BEING A FABULOUS TEEN

#1. Quit waiting for someone else to do it for you. Bottom line - if you want something, you've got to make it happen for yourself. It's your passion, not theirs. Put on your big girl panties and woman-up!

#2. Failing does not mean you are a failure. Here's the secret decoder ring: You are only a failure when you don't learn from your mistakes. If you keep doing the same thing wrong over and over again, you are not going to get a different result. Take what you learned from your previous mistakes and make better choices next time. Failing is a necessary part of the journey that leads to your eventual greatness.

#3. Don't postpone joy. If there's one thing I can tell you, it is this. Life is too short. Wasting time doing something that you despise is a disservice to yourself and to others around you. Find your passion and success will follow.

#4. When opportunity knocks, open the darn door! You will be presented with many opportunities in your life, and some will have great appeal. Some you will hard work for, and some will come to you easily completely out of the blue. Recognize opportunity and seize it with both hands when it comes. True story: Last week, I offered a University fine arts student a small role in a TV show. She declined the offer because she was in class studying to become an actress. Huh? So, she was studying to become an actress to land a role like the one I had literally just offered her. Idiotic.

#5. Quit wasting your talent. I issue you this challenge: Many people, and not just teens, spend hours lamenting about their looks or what is wrong with them or what they'd like to change. For Pete's sake, get over yourself and quit wasting your talent! Use your time better. In business, we call this opportunity cost. While, you were choosing to spend your time on trivial matters like "do I look fat in these jeans?" you could have been doing something else that would have benefitted you and/or the world. For example, you could have helped someone with a learning disability learn to read or walked a dog at the pet shelter or planted a tree. I guarantee they won't even care what your hair or jeans look like and would be just grateful for the help.

#6. If fate closes the door, then climb through the window. Most people give up too soon or bail at the first sign of struggle. Seriously?! Nothing worth having comes easy. I swear if that were the case, most of the world would cease to exist as we know it. At the very least, we'd have nothing to watch on TV. Every day, I run into barriers—great big mountain size barriers! When we're filming it's a total gong show! You've got to be able to re-direct to get where you want to be, and quickly.

#7. Be a problem solver, not a problem. This one is fairly fresh in my mind. On our last shoot, we had several crew members vying to work on our show. We had several competing issues in the execution of the production. Some of the candidates couldn't get past the less than ideal situations that we were dealing with and kept harping on the problems, making the situation even worse. Two others saw the problems but came up with creative ways to handle it beautifully. Who do you think I hired?

#8. Be nice to people on your way up, because you're sure to see them again on your way down. I read this once somewhere and it always stuck with me because it's so true. Some people get a little success under their belts and get big egos. They step over people as they claw their way to the top, and it eventually comes back to haunt them.

#9. Re-frame. I recently had this conversation with my 10-year-old son who was complaining about having to take his medication. I told him that he should be happy to even have medication to take that would make him better. I practice the same technique when doing tasks that I dislike such as cooking dinner after a long day at work or cleaning the house on weekends. I remind myself, that at least I have food to cook and a house to clean.

#10. Fact: you can't be good at everything. Know your strengths and seek out others to backfill your weaknesses. Only a great person is honest enough with themselves to acknowledge their weaknesses and to do something about it. It also takes a great person to see greatness in others. Don't kid yourself, the opposite is also true.

BONUS TIP: Never forget kindness. Along your journey, many people will help you, support you and forgive you for those times when you behaved like an absolute moron. Sometimes, it's just a little thing that makes all the difference in your world, and other times it's something gargantuan that made you who you are today. Make sure to thank them immediately and with heartfelt gratitude. Then, going forward along your path, keep them in mind for any chance to help them back.

By **Janeen Norman**, CEO, Fabulous Corporation
TV and Film Entertainment, www.fabulouscorp.com
facebook.com/fabulouscorp twitter.com/FabulousCorp

10 TIPS FROM EMILY

#1. Wash your face regularly, with soap and water. It's cheaper than buying medicated acne wash, and just about as effective. Also, toothpaste applied overnight to a pimple can dry it up pretty well--just remember to wash it off in the morning.

#2. It's fine to go vegetarian (I've been vegetarian for eleven years, and vegan for a year and a half), but make sure you're doing it for your own reasons, whether it's for your own health or for animal rights and not just because all your friends are doing it. Also, if you JUST cut out meat, without actively trying to replace the protein with a protein source plus a whole grain (for example, peanut butter on whole wheat bread), you'll become anemic and feel dizzy, headachy and cold a lot of the time. Been there, done that, got the shirt.

#3. Speaking of shirts, if you splurge on a high-fashion item, make sure it goes with most of your other clothes. It's far better to buy "pieces" than "outfits," because that way, you'll be able to do more with less. Furthermore, you don't need a ton of money to have fun. For example, if you can't afford a "dinner-and-a-movie" date, a picnic in the park is just as enjoyable, and practically free.

#4. There are no "girl" activities and "boy" activities--if it makes you happy to play sports, cook, sew, paint, play a musical instrument, wear a certain colour, cry during movies, be affectionate with your friends, or whatever, then you should do it. Maybe you'll get flak for it, but chances are, there are other people who secretly want to be more of themselves, and less of what society tells them to be, who'll silently thank you, or better yet, come out of the woodwork and join you.

#5. Further to #4, don't be afraid to start or continue an activity because someone says it's "geeky." I've played the clarinet for many years (among other things), and I got called a "band geek" on a regular basis in high school, but I ignored it, and later earned two degrees in music.

#6. In the words of Ani Difranco, "Feminism ain't about women." Well, it is, but it isn't entirely. Feminism is also a great way to give men some insight into how to treat women. The best way to start with that is with communication and open dialogue. So, guys listen to your girlfriends, sisters, mothers, and female friend and you may be surprised at what they have to say. For example, you may think it's flattering to whistle at a pretty girl but honestly, most of us find it annoying. Sometimes, the smallest gesture can be meaningful to a woman. For example, it meant the world to me when my best guy friend from undergraduate signed a pledge to help stop violence against wome, during a special awareness week at our university. It showed that he cared about something that was important to me.

#7. Further to #6, passive-aggressiveness does nobody any good. You may think you're being "polite" or "trying not to make waves" by not speaking up about what you want and how you feel, but it breeds resentment. Don't expect people to read your mind.

#8. Do-it-yourself piercings are a BAAAAD idea. Under no circumstances should you allow a non-professional to impale any part of your body with a sharp object. You'd think most people would know this, but you'd be surprised at how many people think that a sewing needle and a potato are legitimate ear-piercing tools. Potatoes are dirty and breed infection, home (and school) bathrooms are much dirtier than proper piercing studios, and sewing needles are for fabric, not for skin.

#9. If you try to squeeze into a size three when you're not really a size three, the result will be unflattering. You don't have to love the size you are, but if you wear the size you are you'll look and feel better.

#10. If you think everyone is staring at you and judging you about how you dress, act, talk, etc. chances are, they aren't, because they're worrying about the exact same thing. Wouldn't it be better for everyone to acknowledge that, laugh at themselves a bit and then just let it go, and focus on being happy?

By **Emily Adams**

10 TIPS FOR TEENS BY SUZANNE

#1. YOU can do anything!

#2. YOU are not alone.

#3. YOU are beautiful.

#4. YOU make a difference.

#5. YOU are brave.

#6. YOU are strong.

#7. YOU are special.

#8. YOU are loved.

#9. YOU are worthy.

#10. YOU are perfect just the way you are!

Suzanne Mazzarella received a B.A. in Communications and TV/Radio Production with a Minor in Theatre. She also has 13 years of Corporate Experience in the areas of Finance and Legal Compliance.

In addition to her Corporate and Academic accomplishments, Suzanne has immersed herself in Personal Growth and Spirituality through her own unique journey. This journey includes a Personal Near-Death Experience and Significant Insights as a result of her practice of Meditation and Natural Ability to Lucid Dream. Suzanne also has an extensive knowledge and love for Numerology and its applications in everyday life.

Her greatest desire is to share the truths she has learned and continues to learn, in a positive and uplifting manor, while walking her own path of self-discovery. Find her at www.TheYayTeam.org

10 TIPS FROM CARLY

#1. Always remember that you are more important than your friends. If they are being disrespectful to you, they are not worth your time, energy or love.

#2. Try to create a small routine for washing and moisturizing your face. Keep it simple but make time for it every day.

#3. Know that you deserve to be loved and practice telling other people you love them. It should be shared.

#4. When you look in the mirror, especially if you're grumpy or "not in the mood" force yourself to smile. Instead of focusing on areas you don't like, say OUT LOUD four things you *do* love about yourself. Repeat this if necessary.

#5. Always make time for breakfast. Pack food the night before if you tend to rush in the mornings.

#6. If you like to dance, dance. If you like to dance but feel you can't, take a class and go! Even if you go alone, it's for you!

#7. Make use of your guidance counsellors. If they don't know, seek out other people (friends, parents, university professors, business owners, the Internet) to give you a better idea of what you want to do after high school and ask lots of questions so you can be more realistic in your expectations.

#8. Be aware of social media's power in your life: like anything that has the ability to reach millions, make sure that you believe what you say before you send it because it's with you forever. But don't get scared by this; find your voice for a good cause and be heard.

#9. Baggy jeans and sloppy jeans are two different things - know the difference.

#10. Put effort into how you look, work at how you define your own style and rock it - this effort and creativity will make for a more confident you. This doesn't always mean spend a fortune (unless you can/want to), it means feeling good about the impressions you make because it literally "fits."

BONUS TIPS:

Get involved in lots of activities in university if you can manage it. It might be uncomfortable if you are particularly shy but activity is an important and vital part to enjoying life. Get excited and join/start a club!

Travel. If you can, go while in university. Take advantage and learn outside of your comfort zone. Learn a language and connect. Travel broadens your mind and opens you up to opportunities.

By day **Carly Turner** is the "Support" piece to her wonderful Strategic Planning team at Business Instincts Group, while by night she is an art-loving superhero in knee high boots and a polka dot dress. (Most of that is true). Besides surrounding herself with a supportive, generous and witty collection of friends and family, Carly enjoys writing up a storm on just about anything in her blog. Experimenting with food, taking long walks (in Calgary) with her dog, Ginger and feeding that tenacious travel bug whenever the opportunity arises. She would like to thank Kelly Falardeau for the chance to give some tips to teenagers because she used to be one and has sincere sympathy for all they go through! Check out her blog at: misscarlyloo.ca

♥ ♥ ♥ ♥ ♥

10 TIPS TO CREATE YOUR THUMBPRINT

If there was something I wish I had learned at your age, it would have been learning and having a better sense of who I was, what was most important to me, and trusting myself and my decisions.

There is NO other person just like YOU! You were born for a special reason and purpose. Part of your job in life is to figure what your special 'thumbprint' is: who you are, what your unique gifts and talents are, developing the skills so you can then make your 'mark', your contribution in life! It's not always easy, but it also doesn't have to be hard!

I want you to know that YOUR LIFE MATTERS! Who you are makes a difference! The world is wanting and needing what you have to offer! No exceptions!

#1. Who are you? Looks like a simple question, but the answer may not be as obvious. You are at a wonderful time in your life to explore more of who YOU are! You have lived in a family environment, where, more than likely, you have been told what to do and how to do it. Even though your parents, teachers, even friends, have your best interest at heart, all too often you are not trained to think on your own. What makes you happy? What frustrates you? What do you love to do? What bothers you about our world today? Is there something that you personally are struggling with? The key to your 'thumbprint' may lie within a personal challenge, a heartache or even something that simply makes your heart SING! Listen to your HEART! What is YOUR truth?

#2. What is most important to you? Knowing what is most important to you, your values, what you believe in the most, are very important to know. They serve as your navigational system for making decisions. They will influence your actions. They will determine, in part, how you feel. Google to find a 'list of values.' Go through the list, checking those values that are important to you. Then identify the TOP FIVE that matter to you the most. Live by these values and your life's decisions will be much easier!

#3. Trust yourself. If there were ONE thing that I would suggest that you learn, cultivate and strengthen, is learning to listen to the 'quiet whispers of your heart,' and learning to trust

YOURSELF! You will always have people that are more than happy to share their thoughts and opinions. But for you to have a happy and successful life, you must trust YOUR JUDGEMENT! It's wise to learn from others. But at the end of your exploration, it's important to take a step back and FEEL what is going to be right for you! Trust is not necessarily a THINKING process. Gather your facts, sort through them and then determine what FEELS right for you! Your intuition, your 'gut', your internal guidance system will turn out to be your best friend in life. Learn how to listen to your intuitive wisdom, and you will experience great wealth, health and happiness!

#4. Take good care of yourself! You have been given only ONE body. Learn to nourish it well now. Eat foods that best support your health! Still enjoy 'treat' foods, but have them as treats! ☺ Rest well, nourish your body, make sure you drink plenty of water, and take time to MOVE your body! If you learn to take care of your body NOW, your body will continue to take care of YOU for a long time!

#5. Be a giving person. Find ways to lend a helping hand. There is nothing better than knowing you've helped someone in need. It will keep you feeling good about yourself and your life!

#6. Learn the 'art' of being disciplined. School is important. Even though you may not like doing some of your assignments, or even understand 'what's the point?,' do it anyway! There are going to be things in your life that you are always going to have to do and may not like but they will still be necessary. Learn to embrace those assignments and activities that you DON'T like doing. Be proud of yourself for doing them. Being disciplined about the things you love comes easier. Knowing you have what it takes, no matter what, will make ALL the difference in the world!

#7. Go for the gold! The wishes and dreams you have in your heart are your true inner guidance! They are there to keep you learning, growing and going after what you want! They are your TRUTH! But you may have to work hard to get there. However, when you are following the wishes and dreams of your heart, your 'work' becomes a labor of love!

#8. Help is not a 'four letter world!' Learning to ask for help will serve you in life! There is NO WAY you will ever know everything you need to know or be able to do everything you need to do. We were meant to work together! Recognize your talents, but also recognize what you are NOT good at! Find people that can help you sort through problems. Allow people to help you find clarity. If you are down and out, make certain to you let people in your life lift you up and offer a helping hand!

#9. Keep your eye on your 'target' and celebrate your successes! Always remember where you want to be going, what you want to be experiencing. It's also very important to BE GRATEFUL for the steps you've taken, the life you have NOW. It's SO important to appreciate the MOMENTS in life! Each day, before going to bed, find at least 5 things in your life that you are grateful for. This will add such a special richness to your life!

#10. Enjoy your life! Take good care of yourself, do the things that are important (like school!) and then HAVE FUN! Spend time with people who you enjoy. Smile a lot. Laugh a lot (especially in those moments you don't feel like it)! When needed, ask for help! We are all in this life TOGETHER. Strength is not just taking care of yourself. Being strong is also when YOU need support, guidance or just a hug!! You know how good it is to offer a support to others. Be certain not to deprive those who care about you the same kind of experience! We love to help!

LIFE IS AN ADVENTURE! If you open yourself to the wonder, the magic, the mystery and the joy of life, you will find happiness and success beyond your wildest imagination!

Wendy Darling is the founder of Thumbprints International LLC, a personal growth organization. She has over 30 years of experience as a life transformation coach, management and organizational development consultant, keynote speaker, radio talk show host, and columnist. Wendy's Thumbprint Method™ blends innovative practices with practical life skills. Wendy has been dubbed a "Fairy Godmother" by her clients because of her ability to support them in turning their dreams into reality. Wendy holds a Bachelor's, Master's and Specialist's Degrees from the University of Missouri-Columbia. For more information: www.YourThumbprint.com

10 TIPS FROM KIMBERLY

#1. Make yourself a "TAG LINE" that makes a statement about what you believe in and what you stand for. It's okay if it changes as you grow because your values will change, but it should be positive and motivating so every time you write it down or say it, it moves the energy within you. Mine is "Everything Counts, Make TODAY Matter!!"

#2. You'll never know how incredibly important the kids on a school bus are until your daughter is on one and you drive by a school bus and look for her smiling face.

#3. Your heart knows where you want to go and what you want to be. Allow yourself to follow your heart, never forgetting to listen to your inner wisdom that is your guiding light.

#4. When you work for others; the way to be more valuable than the next person is to incorporate yourself as your own internal business. When you give yourself permission to be your own driver, you will always take the lead and end up in front.

#5. Always focus on the result you want to achieve. If you want better results, then you are getting, you must find and implement change in your life.

#6. There is as much potential in front of you as there is behind you. Celebrate your successes and always go north.

#7. Don't be a wallflower. The people who accomplish greatness live a life of boldness, audacity and never stop testing where their comfort zone is.

#8. What could you do, every day in 60 seconds that would take An INSANE AMOUNT OF COURAGE to move you forward? If you do this every day, it will change your life forever.

#9. When speaking with others, no matter if it's on the phone or face to face always give them the gift of your presence and spirit. That is the magic to connecting with real people.

#10. If you have a dream and you are passionate about achieving it...be relentless!

Kimberly Schick-Puddicombe is the founder of www.MomsDadsAndKids.com as well as the Publisher and Fun Finding expert for the The 'Little Black Book' for busy families™, Alberta's ultimate resource guide from pregnancy to tween. Kimberly has two active kids and knows how frustrating it can be to find a new place or plan and outing. She shares the best places, stores and attractions; affordable, easy to plan outings; tips and ideas to spice up your family fun and has developed a "Family Bucket List" to help plan your adventures. She has turned her passion and wealth of Kid-Friendly knowledge into a consulting arm to assist retailers and the hospitality industry on how they can become more family friendly. Visit her at www.MomsDadsAndKids.com.

10 TIPS FOR GREAT SELF-ESTEEM

#1. Be yourself – others will admire you for it.

#2. Choose and be very picky about who you call a 'friend'. It is always better just to have one true genuine friend than a bunch of so called 'wannabes'.

#3. Stick to things YOU like to do or want to be, not what others are doing.

#4. Enjoy your age, it only lasts one year.

#5. Don't try to be someone you are not – it only hurts your spirit and self-worth. Lies that you tell yourself only bring you down and no one else. It's easier to just accept and be your true self.

#6. There is no purpose in worrying about yesterday because tomorrow you will be upset about something today. Live in the moment – it's an amazing fulfilling way to live.

#7. Self-esteem is how much you believe in yourself and your self-worth. Speaking up is your greatest ability that will help, support, and even protect you. You are worth it.

#8. If you hear often from people and friends around, 'you must be nice' then it is time to revaluate. A true friend says 'I'm so happy for you'.

#9. Learn about your finances, how credit works and what a balanced budget is at an early age. You will thank yourself greatly later in life. Money is about worth, yet balanced responsible finances equals healthy self-worth.

#10. Only rely on yourself. You are the only guarantee you have in life.

BONUS TIP: Compliment yourself and allow yourself to be complimented. Always reply 'Thank you' with a smile.

'Whatever your past has been, you have a spotless future' –
Carushka

Your friend,
Amanda Welliver, President/Founder, Paradigm Esteem
Multiple Award Winning Self-esteem Entrepreneur
www.ParadigmEsteem.com

10 TIPS FOR LIVING AN EMPOWERED AND AUTHENTIC LIFE FOR TEENS

How, in a world that has managed to forget and get so lost in greed and senseless competition can we remember and express who we really are, uncovering the loving, joyous perfection that lays within each of us? My hope is that these 10 tips that have presented themselves to me will spark some remembrance and inspiration within you. It is my honor and privilege to share this pivotal time of remembrance with each of you. Thank you for courageously and lovingly choosing to be here, now. These are exciting times of great shift toward a more heart centered way of being.

Here are my 10 tips to assist you in releasing your true and awesome self!

#1. Love yourself. We truly do teach others how to treat us by the way we treat ourselves. If someone is treating you badly and disrespecting you, chances are they are picking up on your low level of self-worth. Treat yourself with love, respect and especially compassion. I suggest doing the "mirror exercise" daily: Look in the mirror --into your eyes and express love and appreciation for yourself. See yourself as the unique and amazing Divine Creation that you are!

#2. Show up - fully present, as yourself. Show up as yourself and for YOURSELF. 90% of success is showing up! Share your truth and your light with others and BE REAL with them. Everyone can tell a fake and although it's scary at times, remove your masks whenever possible and be emotionally authentic in each moment. True friends will love and support you and will always allow and encourage you to be yourself...but how will those true friends ever recognize you if you don't show up...as you. "To be beautiful means to be yourself. You don't need to be accepted by others. You need to accept yourself." - Thich Nhat Hanh

#3. Breathe. Breathing is one of the most under-used but valuable tools we have. Breathing resets our nervous system, reduced stress, oxygenates our cells, helps us gain emotional control, and much more. Take deep conscious breaths right into your belly and then exhale fully several times a day. Breathe in love and healing white light and breathe out any negativity or everything that no longer serves you.

#4. Follow your heart. Our hearts connect us to the truth of who we are. Our heart's emotions TELL US when we are in alignment or out of alignment with our highest selves and with truth. TRUST that. Learn to listen to and trust your own intuition and your emotions. Move toward what makes you feel good and alive....even if it's different than what a parent, teacher, or other source is telling you. Our hearts hold the power to affect real change and to lead us exactly where we need to go to meet our higher self and live out our purpose and passion.

#5. Take risks & don't be afraid to make mistakes. If you aren't making mistakes, you likely aren't stepping out much or taking enough chances. Neale Donald Walsch says that "life begins at the end of your comfort zone" - I agree! That is where real learning and growth begin but you have to be willing to be uncomfortable at first.

#6. Look for the GOOD in everything! What you focus on grows and expands. Although it's easy to get caught up in the negative, the violence and the dysfunction in the world...it is always a choice. Make the choice to focus on what's right and good in the world. Every day before bed, take the time to list mentally or in writing 5 things that you are grateful for.

#7. Find your Clan. Find those people who will love and support you through thick and thin and who understand you or at least try to understand you. Jim Rohn says that we are the average of the five people we spend most of our time with. Who are you surrounding yourself with? Are they helping you or hindering you? Life will always have its ups and downs and these people are really key to supporting you, helping you up, and seeing you through challenging times.

#8. Lighten UP - We are here to enjoy life! The universe really does have your best interests at heart and yes...everything does happen for a reason; although the gift in the hardships and heartaches doesn't often reveal itself until later. Let go of the stuff that doesn't matter and that weighs you down. Have FUN, love one another, dance, sing, and play. I've found that it helps to see life as one big adventure or a giant experiment. Life is wonder-full!

"Life is either a daring adventure or nothing at all." - Helen Keller

#9. Practice true listening and acknowledgement. As humans, two of our core needs are to be seen and heard. True, heart-centered listening is giving our full and undivided attention to a person; releasing the self-talk, criticisms and judgment and simply listening to understand. This is truly one of the greatest gifts you can give another - that of being truly heard! Acknowledging yourself and others is also key to feeling like we matter. Look for the positive characteristics about a person, those specific gifts and characteristics that a person possesses and tell them!

#10. Never stop caring! LOVE is the answer, always. We all have a divine purpose here on this physical plane and we need to care for ourselves and for one another. Caring people make the biggest impact. Every thought word and action is energy and begins a ripple effect of vibration. Choose the positive thoughts, words and actions and lead the change you wish to see.

Namaste, Jeri

Jeri Tourand is a mother of three girls, teacher, author, speaker, radio host and founder of "Living from Heart Center" and "Parenting from H.E.A.R.T." Please connect with her at www.livingfromheartcenter.com

10 TIPS FROM IRYNA

#1. Love God. Loving God and having faith in God is an essential part of human nature, and human life. God is your Creator, you are bonded together by this invisible "cord"... just like a baby and a mother are one, and so are you and God. I encourage you to love God and develop a relationship with God on a daily basis, because this is the first and foremost foundation upon which you can build anything else in life. Life is full of challenges, but with God you can boldly face it all, knowing God is always by your side.

#2. Love yourself. The image you have of yourself profoundly affects your well-being. It determines whether you love yourself or not and it determines the course of your life. Of course it is easy to love yourself when you have parents who love you, but what if you don't have parents? What if your parents are not caring and loving, or even worse, abusive? What if you are growing up in a dysfunctional home like I was, without love, without approval, without acceptance? Then it is very difficult to love yourself and have confidence in who you are. It is not your fault that your mom or your dad don't love you enough, or didn't love you enough. You are beautiful inside and out, so start loving yourself today and let go. It all starts with YOU.

#3. Love people. When you love God and love yourself, then it becomes very natural to love people. Love your parents and treat them with respect. Love and encourage your friends; tell them the truth if you do not agree on something, or you don't like something they did or said. This way, loving your friends means being honest about everything with them. If you went to a party and your friend behaved inappropriately, tell him or her about it in a loving way, it will show that you care.

Loving people doesn't mean pleasing them all the time or saying "yes" to everything, it's more the opposite: you have to learn to say "no" when necessary, for the good of all. Loving people means forgiving people on a constant basis. People aren't perfect, they hurt each other. Love all people unconditionally, including strangers.

#4. Confront abuse. Abuse is the most brutal violation of human dignity and human rights, though it happens everywhere, every day. It is very sad to know that children all over the world are the most vulnerable target of abuse, and in most cases children cannot or do not know how to protect themselves. If you personally experience abuse, or you experienced it in the past and never confronted it, you have to take immediate action. You can talk to your counsellor at school, call a hot line, talk to your parent, talk to someone close who can help you and direct you to the right resources. If you don't feel safe in your home, or you don't feel safe around your friend or your boyfriend, you have to get out of that environment or that relationship. Do not be afraid and worry that you will be rejected; you have to stand for yourself and for your own good. Do not try to "justify" abuse. If you continue living in abuse, it is very dangerous, it is very wrong, and it can damage you for life. Be bold and confront abuse, knowing that in Canada you are protected by law.

#5. Develop healthy relationships. Life is all about relationships; it is about relating to people. Whether it's parents and children, teachers and students, boyfriends and girlfriends, whether it's friendship or it's you and your community, these are all relationships. Healthy relationships are like healthy food, no "junk" is acceptable. Healthy relationships are those where respect, kindness, mutual understanding, encouragement, acceptance, etc. are normal components of relating to one another. If you work from teenage years on building and nurturing healthy relationships, then your life and your future will be healthy. But it is mainly your responsibility to do that, you determine that.

#6. Develop good habits. Your greatest investment into building a successful life would be developing good habits. Good habits are not easy to form, but they are easy to live with. The earlier you become responsible for your own habits, the faster you're going to achieve whatever you set your mind to. Habits are vitally important, because habits form your character, and your character becomes a pathway to your destiny. Make a decision today, while you're still a teenager, to work on acquiring good habits for yourself. Whether it's a habit of rising early, or it's a habit of self-discipline in completing assignments promptly, or whether it's a habit of exercising three times a week, etc., these are some good habits that all successful people live by.

#7. Develop your talents. We are all born with a purpose we have to accomplish on earth. That is the reason we all have different talents. If you are not sure what your talents are, then ask yourself what you like to do. If you like volunteering in your school or in your community, then you probably have some good leadership skills and you might consider creating a business or an organization that could benefit society. If you love art, then you might consider developing your talents in performing arts, visual arts or music. If you enjoy problem solving or you're good at counselling your friends when they have difficulties, then maybe you could become a great counsellor and help people solve their life issues. Whatever talents you have, you have them with the purpose to serve people.

#8. Dream big. Let me reveal to you something profound: whatever you can imagine that you want to be one day, you will become if you set your mind to it and refuse to give up your dream. Don't dream little, dream big! Accomplishing your dream may take many years, but I can guarantee it will come to pass one day if you do not give up and if you persevere when setbacks and obstacles come your way. Be ready to set goals and work hard on achieving them. Big success comes from dreaming big dreams.

#9. Learn constantly. If you truly want to advance in life, you have to develop an attitude of constant learning. Now with the advances in information technologies you have amazing opportunities to do that. You have access to Internet everywhere you go and you have tremendous social media tools at your hands. When I was growing up the library was my favorite place to go. I developed a love for books and reading from a very young age. I loved spending time around seniors and adults and learning from them. I always was ahead of my peers. I was like that "sponge," absorbing the knowledge from everywhere I could. When I was fourteen or fifteen, I used to get compliments that I think like an adult, that I'm way ahead developmentally. I encourage you to learn and educate yourself constantly in all areas possible, and always go an extra mile.

#10. Live with passion. Finally, be dynamic, have charisma, and live your life with passion! Do not underestimate the potential you carry inside, but believe that you were born for greatness. Decide that you want to live your life to make this world a better place to live for others. Be courageous and passionate about doing what you are doing, or what you want to do. Be like that "bulldozer" and do whatever it takes to get to the place of your destination. Be an example and an inspiration for others, which is only possible to do when you live with passion!

By **Iryna Synychak**

10 TIPS BY GREG THE GADGET GUY

When Kelly approached me and asked me to give her 10 tips I could offer to teens, I was flattered but also surprised; I have little current experience with teens and it's been a long time since I was one. However, after listening to the news and reading about some of the things teens need to know, I realized that in many respects, while the times have changed, many things still stay the same.

Also, after much pondering, I thought, looking back, what were some of the things I know today that I wish I would have known or wish I could have been able to do when I was a teen. I was a quiet a shy introverted one at that, not peeking out of my shell until into my late 20's and really blossoming, if I can say that, after joining Toastmasters.

#1. Learn how to be confident in front of an audience. Whether it's in school taking on extracurricular activities or for a job interview you need to look and be comfortable. If 18 or over, join Toastmasters, if younger, find a Youth Leadership Program. They are usually free.

#2. Embrace technology but also know when it's enough. Technology is engrained in almost every part of our lives. Learn how to use it beyond facebook, Twitter and to do text messaging. If you happen to be heavily into social media, don't be doing it every waking hour. Do things face to face, take a walk and get some air.

#3. Ask for help! People are willing to help if you ask. Sometimes for various reasons, people won't offer or come to you; they're just waiting for you to make the first move. Maybe it's that they don't want to pry or make you feel needy. I found out that sometimes it's just in their nature. Just pop the question; you may be pleasantly surprised.

#4. Become fluent in another language if you can. We are a global community. It can open doors for you whether it's for a job or travel. It can also help you meet new people.

#5. Don't assume your parents don't understand. Legendary hockey player Wayne Gretzky said that you won't score on 100% of the shots you don't take. That means if you don't ask, the answer is always no. Growing up, things were tough and when it came time to take school trips I never asked my parents if I could go. As a result, I missed out on opportunities to see and learn new things. I found out later that if I had asked, my parent would have found a way (if possible) to make it happen.

#6. Find a mentor. It's amazing how many people are willing to share their experiences with you. The last rule applies here; sometimes all you have to do is ask. A mentor could be someone you admire or perhaps you want to learn a skill from for the future. Of course attitude is everything. Don't approach them as if they owe you. Be polite, be humble and put yourself out there.

#7. It's ok to be different. Looking back, my teenage years, compared to what's going on today weren't that bad. Of course it didn't seem like that back then. Bullying is a tough thing. Now I can't say that I was majorly bullied when younger but I was certainly harassed by the bigger kids. I was short; I had a cowlick so my hair stood up (of course today, messy is in) I was a geek, shy and really didn't fit in with a group.

Today, being a geek is more in vogue. Have you watched Big Bang Theory? If you are different than your peers, look at it positively. Being unique can give you a competitive advantage. It can help you stand out amongst everyone else who is the same. Think of many successful people. Perhaps there was something different about them that led them to success.

#8. Take care of your body. You may feel like you're Superman when you're young, staying up all night, going home showering then off to work or school. But as you get older, that catches up with you. Having been in a car accident when I was 17 then 6 months later had my appendix out certainly took toll on my body. While I did exercise, I didn't follow the rehabilitation as I was supposed to. Later on, when the aches and pains roll in, you look back and say, "I should have".

#9. Try it you'll like it. That's a slogan from an old Alka Seltzer commercial. We sometimes have these preconceived ideas that something is dull or lame or we might be ridiculed if we try it. Sometimes you have to sample, like at Costco where they offer free samples. You might be amazed at the results.

#10. Look at things from your parent's perspective.
Sometimes this one can be hard. When discussions or disagreements end up in a stalemate, no one wins. You want to go somewhere and they say no, while it might be hard, look at it from their perspective.

They may have grown up in a different era, different country/ culture or under different circumstances. Having different views they might be saying no, not to be difficult but rather from what they perceive. Ever watch that 70's show, or Mad Men or maybe a foreign film? In this case you might have to be the parent. Look at their situation and maybe you can find out why they might be thinking a certain way. Google it. By understanding where they are coming from, perhaps you can find a way to come to a compromise. Sometimes it could be as simple as actually acknowledging their side of the story. Maybe they are just looking for a little respect.

Of course it's easy looking back, as I'm older and perhaps a little wiser but I'm confident that out of the 10 tips presented here, you should be able to find one or two that can make what we see as often the terrible teen years a little easier.

I respect you and I understand in many cases, although not all, what you are going through. You are our future!

Greg Gazin is known to many as "The Gadget Guy", for over two decades, Greg has been a self-professed serial entrepreneur. He is a Technology Columnist, small business and technology speaker, an avid blogger www.gadgetguy.ca and podcasterwww.toastcaster.com. Greg also helps small businesses find ways to promote and market their businesses in an informative yet entertaining way.

Gadget Greg also helps consumers demystify technology and shows how it can be useful, practical and even fun. He's penned over 2,500 articles and produced content for Canoe.ca, Sun Media, Troy Media and G4TV Canada and has appeared as a Tech Expert on CITY TV's Breakfast Television and CTV NewsChannel.

Greg is the all -around "GoTo" guy. Like Linus and his blanket, Greg is rarely seen in public without his Apple MacBook Pro, multiple iPhones and 50 pounds of gadgets.

Greg is a Distinguished Toastmasters and Past District 42 Governor (Alberta & Saskatchewan). Greg credits Toastmasters and its mentors for getting him out from behind his shadow and the keyboard to in front of audiences and into situations he would never had dreamed of.

email: greg@gadgetguy.ca Twitter: @gadgetgreg

10 TIPS IN BEING A SUCCESSFUL TEAM PLAYER IN SPORTS

#1. Trust: We believe in each other.

#2. Communication: We look at each other in the eye – We tell each other the truth.

#3. Confidence: We believe in our own abilities.

#4. Commitment: We understand sacrifices are part of success – We win and we lose together.

#5. Care: We have each other's back – We leave no one behind.

#6. Respect: We respect each other and our opponents.

#7. Confront immediately: We let nothing linger.

#8. Enthusiasm: This is fun and we love it – We bring energy every day by hustling.

#9. Unselfishness: We understand our roles – Our value is not measured in playing time.

#10. Flexibility: We can handle any situation – We don't complain.

By **André Lachance**, Manager Baseball Operations
Head Coach Women's National Team, Baseball Canada
alachance@baseball.ca

10 TIPS BY ANGELA

#1. Believe in your story, the good and the not so good parts of it.

#2. Learn how your story has affected you and helped to make you who you are.

#3. Share your story with others, especially the parts about how you got through challenges and hard times.

#4. Don't judge other people. Instead ask them what their story is.

#5. When you feel adults don't understand you or get what you are dealing with, share your story with them and remember they have a story too!

#6. Keep track of your story by writing it down. Later on you will be glad you did and it helps you learn more about your story (and yourself) too!

#7. Help others to understand you and why you may act or feel a certain way by telling them your story.

#8. Don't falsify your story to be accepted by others. Your story is yours. Own it!

#9. When your story seems to be filled with stuff and people you don't like or it doesn't feel good – change it!

#10. Remember that your past story cannot be changed but you can make a better story for your future.

Anglea Schaefers, Speaker, Writer, Radio Personality, Producer & Host of Your Story Matters show. www.YourStoryMatters.net

♥ ♥ ♥ ♥ ♥

10 TIPS FROM THE IMPACT SOCIETY

A HERO is someone who uses their gifts and abilities to make a positive change in themselves and others. Who is a HERO? Everyone can be. You are a HERO.

So, how do you bring out the HERO that's inside you?

#1. Build confidence. Ask yourself two questions, what am I good at and what do I love to do? Where your answers are the same will identify your gifts & abilities. Remind yourselves of what these are often and look for opportunities to use them.

#2. Know your walls & tear them down. Sometimes there are things, thoughts, ideas and experiences that get in the way of you being able to see your gifts & abilities and act from them. Many times these walls are directly opposite to what your strengths are. For example, if you are compassionate and have been hurt, that hurt might get in the way of you being compassionate. Walls reflect false beliefs about us and that can lead to unhealthy choices.

#3. Have dignity. Dignity is treating yourself and others with respect, not allowing people's actions to negatively affect how you behave.

#4. Have character. Character is about making consistent decisions for positive change because of who you are, not your circumstances. Stop – hit pause, avoid reacting to circumstances. Think – remind yourself of who you are and what matters to you. Choose – use who you are and what you believe to choose your action.

#5. Live with honour. Respect and honour are different. Respect is earned and lost by the way people value themselves and others. Honour is something we should show ALL people by valuing and showing regard or consideration, no matter who the person is. You can choose to honour people without respecting their behavior. Honour is a choice with your actions and your voice.

#6. Choose your words wisely. The words you use to refer to yourself or others are extremely powerful. Words have the ability to build people up or tear them down. When we put negative labels on ourselves or others, our words become weapons for harming or destroying life. Pay close attention to the words you speak and write, and ask yourself if it builds or destroys?

#7. Have healthy friendships. People have a lot of influence on our decisions and actions, it is very important to have friends and family who help us make positive choices. Basement friends are people who pull and tear you down. They have their own interest in mind when it comes to you. Balcony friends are positive people that build you up. They want the best for you and encourage you in your goals & dreams. Living Room friends are people who are in the middle of the road – they hang around, neither encouraging nor discouraging you. Think about your circle of support and surround yourself with as many balcony friends as possible. If you have family that behaves as basement friends, that is difficult. However, it is your choice as to how much of that you allow to affect you. Look for other balcony friends in your life and spend as much time with them as you can. And, of course, be sure that you are a balcony friend! Choose to be smart with whom you let close to your heart.

#8. Choose contentment. Have an attitude of gratitude. Focus on what you DO have by being thankful for your relationships, your gifts & abilities and the everyday things that make your life both enjoyable and comfortable.

#9. Give back – HEROES are GIVERS. GIVERS contribute to society in a positive way whether it is helping out at home, taking care of the environment or school property or something else – they are community builders. Look for ways to use your gifts and abilities to give back to the world around you. An attitude of giving is a better way of living.

#10. Know your purpose and persevere. Build your own personal mission statement based on your gifts and abilities, your beliefs and who you wish to be in the world. This is your compass to guide you as you move forward in your journey. Know your purpose and then don't give up, no matter what.

HEROES PLEDGE:

"As a HERO, I will use my gifts & abilities to make a positive change in myself and others. I will not give up!"

Please give yourself the time and space to reflect on each of these 10 steps regularly. It is really important that you feel good about who you are so that you walk and live as the HERO that you are.

*This content is based on the HEROES experience – strength-focused, character education delivered in junior high classrooms throughout Canada by Impact Society.

Jodi Dawson | Impact Society
Vice-President, Programs & Finance www.ImpactSociety.com

10 TIPS ON SAVING FOR COLLEGE

"Getting into college is one thing. Paying for it is another." ®

As the mother of three daughters, I know firsthand how overwhelmed parents feel about paying for college. We desperately want to make our children's college dreams a reality -- we just don't want to break the bank to do it!

Paying for college has become a struggle for an increasing number of families who do not qualify for need-based aid. Merit scholarships – money awarded for college based on achievement rather than demonstrated financial need – can reduce the cost of college. Scholarships do not need to be repaid; however, they do require effort, time, and strategy.

When we could not find anyone to guide my family through the merit scholarship maze, I undertook the challenge of understanding how merit aid worked and how it could be used specifically for our family. After spending 100 hours digging through endless scholarships that did not match Rebecca's achievements, I uncovered $150,000 in merit opportunities that fit.

Three Wishes Scholarships was born from the increasing need for families to learn how to save time, reduce stress, and maximize their chances of winning merit aid so they can sleep at night knowing they have a game plan to reduce college costs.

Here are my ten tips for increasing eligibility and finding and applying for merit scholarships:

#1. Plan ahead – it's a marathon not a sprint! Create a game plan to qualify for merit scholarships when the student is in the ninth grade. How a student spends their time as a freshman will have a big impact later. Merit aid is offered for a vast array of achievements that extend well beyond academics and athletics. Encourage the student to pursue activities they enjoy and excel in. Demonstrating passion and commitment to a hobby, interest, or skill is an ideal way to lay the foundation to qualify for merit scholarships.

#2. Volunteer deep - not wide. Teens who are deeply involved in community service are well-positioned to qualify for merit scholarships. Select a few community service activities that ignite the student's passion and demonstrate leadership and commitment over an extended period of time. Quality is more important than quantity.

Community service is the great equalizer – all teens can choose to give of themselves regardless of their intellectual ability. Virtually every teen can be successful at giving back, gaining leadership skills and boosting their eligibility for merit aid.

#3. Make friends with the PSAT. While the SAT and ACT are vital to college admissions, the potential impact of the PSAT should not be ignored.

A high score on the PSAT in 11th grade can open all kinds of doors. The highest 2% of test-takers join the elite class of National Merit Finalists invited to apply for selective merit scholarships, among other perks.

Students who are prepared when they take the PSAT in 10th grade are at an advantage. Their score is a more accurate gage of how well they will do next year (when it counts) and whether tutoring or intensive practice is likely to propel their scores into National Merit range. Studying for the PSAT will not go to waste as it will prepare the student for the SAT later. -- unless, of course, the student opts to take the ACT instead.

#4. Be over-qualified and get paid to attend! Design a strategy that includes private and institutional merit scholarships. Typically smaller, private ones have the benefit of not being tied to a particular college. Organizations reward students whose achievements, community service, character, interests, activities, and goals reflect the mission of the scholarship. Grades are often not a factor. Most private merit scholarships are one-time awards.

Conversely, colleges use institutional merit scholarships to entice academically strong candidates to attend their school. These awards are typically larger than private scholarships and often cover four years (as long as the student maintains a minimum GPA and meets other requirements).

Generally, the key to winning institutional merit aid is to have a higher GPA and standardized test scores than the standard for that college. Some colleges automatically consider all admitted students for merit aid. Know the policies for the schools on the student's college list.

#5. Search early...and often! Finding the "perfect" scholarship after the deadline has passed is truly painful. Begin research in eleventh grade. Identifying scholarships early enables proper planning. With enough lead time, a student can add credentials, such as more community service hours to become qualified for a specific award.

#6. Be a detective - follow the trail to scholarships that fit! Research local and national scholarships. Seek those that match the student's various achievements, including community service, religion, hobbies, career goals, academic strengths, interests, heritage, political views, career goals and anything that is unique about the student. There is truly a scholarship for almost everything!

Read all the eligibility requirements. Some merit scholarships also have a need-based component. Be sure the student meets that criterion; otherwise stick with only merit-based scholarships.

Use scholarship search engines, internet searches, books, and newspapers to stay aware of scholarship opportunities which arise year-round. The high school guidance counselor may be helpful.

Remain on the lookout; merit scholarships are available for all levels of higher education, not just for college freshmen. New scholarships continue to arise.

There are millions of merit scholarships. The challenge is finding ones that fit.

#7. Apply smart. Be sure the student meets all the requirements of the scholarship. The goal is to spend precious time on opportunities the student has the best chance of winning. It's difficult, but be objective about the student's chance of winning a particular award.

#8. Every little bit helps. Scholarships with huge prize amounts attract more competition. Local and lesser known awards are often easier to win and the smaller prize dollars can add up. Larger prizes often require more extensive essays and research.

#9. Beat (don't meet) deadlines. Most applications are submitted online and websites can become jammed as deadlines approach. It's a shame to go to the effort of crafting a solid application only to have it thrown out for being late. Be careful of time zones when applications are due by a specific time.

Don't rush the applications. Allow a day or two to let the essay sit and review it again before submitting it. Read the entire application well in advance of the deadline to determine how much time to allow. Some require time for research or for reading an author's work before analyzing it.

Create a scholarship calendar. Enter the deadline, a "warning period" before the deadline as reminder, and when the student will work on applications. Staying organized helps keep the task more manageable.

#10. Know your audience and follow the rules. Follow scholarship directions precisely. Some require applications be submitted online, others are very specific about how to mail documents and whether or not to send supplemental materials. Do not leave any questions blank. Contact the organization for clarification. Check for typos and accuracy.

Understand how the prize money may be used and act accordingly. Some may be directed to a range of college-related expenses while others have restrictions.

Essays need to fall within the exact word or character count allowed. Take note of whether the requirements are for a certain number of words or characters. This makes a big difference!

Judges are looking for candidates whose involvements reflect the mission of their organization and the purpose of the scholarship. Applications should position the student as the candidate the judges have been hoping to find. It's not about what the student wants to share, it's about being the candidate that the judges want to support in their college dreams!

Nancy Paul founded Three Wishes Scholarships in honor of her daughters to help other college-bound families save time, reduce stress and maximize their chances of reducing the cost of college with merit scholarships. She finds $25,000-$150,000 in merit scholarship opportunities for each of her private clients. Nancy speaks, writes and conducts workshops to help families find merit scholarships that fit. She is known for being engaging, knowledgeable, and dedicated.

Passionate about the many benefits of community service for teens, Nancy speaks to groups, conducts workshops, and directs students to leverage their community service to reduce the cost of college and develop a sense of purpose. She is the author of the upcoming book, "Giving Back and Getting In: The Win-Win of Community Service for Getting into College, Paying for It & Beyond."

To contact Nancy for more personal scholarship advice, go to www.threewishes-scholarships.com or email info@threewishes-scholarships.com.

♥ ♥ ♥ ♥ ♥

10 TIPS FOR TEENAGERS

#1. Value and believe in yourself. As you grow up realize that everything you learn about yourself is influenced in large part by the people that are in your life. Friends, family, educational and government systems, social media on line, off line media such as television, magazines and books all influence the thoughts we have about ourselves as we grow up. Many of the messages you hear from your family and friends may be hurtful or unloving at times. It's not intentional.

Always know that no matter how frustrated you may get with your parents at times or how angry or upset they may seem with you in some moments, they love you no matter what. Sometimes parents allow the way they view the world to get to them and their frustration or upset has nothing to do with you at all. Don't take it personally. Understand the only opinion of yourself that matters is your opinion. You will never be able to get everyone that you meet or spend time with to see everything from your point of view, so value and believe in yourself.

#2. Forgiveness: Learn the power of forgiveness and the peace it will bring to your life. Learn from an early age that forgiveness is not about condoning the other person's behavior. Forgiveness is about understanding that the person was lashing out in the moment because they were not in control of their emotions. Forgiveness is one of the strongest forms of self-love there is. It takes courage to forgive others for things you may feel wronged you. Always know that the other person is in emotional pain when they hurt you either with their words or their actions. They were doing the best they could in the moment. An act of forgiveness could actually change a person's life in a powerful, positive and profound way. YOU could be the instrument for that positive change.

#3. Learn the strength and power in forgiving yourself when you doubt who you are, put down who you are, think badly about yourself or blame yourself. Every person in the world at some point thinks or has negative thoughts about themselves and has felt as though they are not good enough, not smart enough, not pretty enough or simply not enough for one reason or another. It's only our minds that tell us the things that are not true. Don't believe it, only believe what's in your heart. Your heart will always lead you the right way.

#4. Trust yourself. Trust yourself and listen to that 'gut' feeling when making decisions. If it feels wrong in your stomach, if your gut is telling you it's not a good idea, there's something wrong with this person and/or this situation, then trust it and follow your heart. You have all the knowledge deep within you to always know what's right for you. It takes courage to stand up for what you believe in.

Trusting yourself brings with it the freedom of choice. Understand that every single decision you make in life has a consequence. Each decision has a compound effect on the final outcome on all things in the future. It may not seem that big of a deal in the initial moment, however, take some time and decide if this decision empowers you or dis-empowers you. Is this the best decision you could make right now and how will it impact the future? It could be anything from what you eat, what you wear, who you call, what course you decide to study, what job you decide to take, what words you decide to speak or which person you decide to date. Every single decision you make creates your future outcome whether that future is in the next five minutes, five days, five weeks, months or five years. Choose those decisions wisely. Trust yourself!

#5. Build integrity into your life in all the things you do. If you say you're going to do something then do it! If you say you're going to call a friend at a certain time, or show up to go out and do something with that friend then do it! Learn to rely on yourself and show others how much they can rely on you and depend on you to keep your word. It takes strength and strong personal commitment to excel in life and your character is far more important than personality. With a strong character, which is built by integrity, the personality will develop. Integrity comes from people who walk their talk. Talk is cheap as they say. Building integrity in your life builds personal strength, certainty and reliability in who you become. If for some reason you are not able to keep your deadline or commitment then follow up and take ownership. Let the person know you're not able to keep up your commitment and reset the deadline that you will be able to keep. Become a person of integrity!

#6. Learn about money at an early age. Learn the spiritual laws of money. Realize that financial prosperity is your natural birthright and always available to you. Learn that money is an energy and not symbolic of evil or that only certain people deserve wealth and riches. Observe your parents, ask them questions about money, what their views are, find out if they think money is scarce or abundant and then make and form your own decisions based on learning about money through books, audio's, mentors, teachers, banking resources or anyone you know that appears to be doing well financially. Learn about the power of tithing through books on the spiritual laws of money. Pay yourself first, put 10% of everything you earn or receive away for yourself and know that you deserve to have money. Learn about money!

#7. Commit to reading one book a month either on self help, personal growth, business or biography of positive empowering people you admire or who have made a big impact in the world in a positive way. Commit to learning and growing by learning through others. Understand that anything in life is possible and it's not just a cliché. This lifetime is short, although in the life of a teenager it may seem long. There have been many great men and women in the world who've accomplished what seems to the average person nearly impossible. Those people are no different than you. Each of us has a mind, body, heart and spirit. With enough belief in yourself and determination to make something happen you can do anything you put your mind to. The wilder the dream seems the more likely it is that you can make it happen. Committing to reading a book a month will increase your self-confidence by increasing the skills and knowledge that you have.

#8. Create a list of 101 things you'd like to do in your life time then put it in writing. Use your imagination; make it as wild and crazy as you can. Look at your list frequently and set a deadline of when you'd like to accomplish those items. Set goals. Be among the 3% of high achievers in the world determined to make things happen. Set goals throughout your lifetime, starting in your teens. Decide what you want your life to look like along the way. Decide what you want to do in your life as you go along. Accomplishing goals in life, no matter how big or how small, are all stepping stones in building your self-confidence. As you increase your self-confidence you'll be more willing to risk bigger goals and achieve more happiness and personal success in your life.

#9. Use your manners. If you haven't already learned them, learn them, use them, respect them and be proud that you have manners. Manners are a significant form of respect for both yourself and others.

#10. Love yourself! Look in the mirror and say to yourself "I love you" ~ use your name and fill in the blank, at least once a day. Learn to like and love your body and who you are. Now that you have set your day up to like and love who you are, decide who are the five people you want to spend the most amount of time with including family and friends. These five people will have the greatest influence on your life. Family is chosen for us, but we have the choice of the friends we make. Pick them wisely and decide if you want to be like them or not. If the answer is no then respectfully move on to others who behave in the manner that feels good for you. This goes for family too. You can love and be respectful of family members, it doesn't mean you have to like who they are or how they act and treat other people. Choosing the five people you want to spend time with is a big part of how to love yourself!

BONUS TIP: Listen more than you talk. When talking with people be fully engaged. Listen to them with an open mind; be interested in what they have to say. Don't interrupt, listen respectfully and be curious about what you can learn about the person that you don't already know. Listening is an opportunity to be compassionate with other people by showing you care about them. Listening also allows you an opportunity to be forgiving, understanding and caring. Listen more than you talk!

Nancy Battye is a gifted and passionate motivational Speaker, Published Writer, Teacher, Interview and Radio Show Host. A continuous student of personal and spiritual growth, her main messages are on the topics of self-confidence, integrity, compassion and forgiveness. Nancy's program "Dancing in the Web of Life ~ Creating Community through Conversations" offers a variety of workshops for both private and corporate audiences that shifts individuals to make positive, powerful, profound change by increasing their self-esteem. To learn more contact Nancy at www.NancyBattye.com

10 SIMPLE TIPS

#1. We don't all have to look the same to be beautiful... celebrate your uniqueness.

#2. People will see you as beautiful when you see yourself as beautiful.

#3. People generally criticize others for the things they don't like about themselves.

#4. Remember, someone else's opinion is just that...their opinion...it does not have to be yours.

#5. When you walk into a new situation walk in with confidence, with the attitude you belong there, no one will question that you don't.

#6. Find a reason to smile every day and make sure you laugh out loud often.

#7. Be proud of your height, be it 4'9" or 6'2", stand tall!!

#8. Look people in the eye when you talk to them, they will listen to what you are saying.

#9. Tell yourself every day that you are fabulous! Because you are.

#10. Mistakes teach us our best lessons. You never forget when you really mess up, just make sure you remember when you did it right too.

By **Lynda Fraser.** 29 years ago (February 4, 2012) I woke up to find my youngest son sitting in the living room surrounded by flames. Without thinking about what would happen to me, I rushed into those flames to get my son. He wound up with burns to 40% of his body and spent two months in hospital. I had burns to 80% of my body and spent eight months in hospital, two years in physiotherapy and several years having reconstructive surgeries. I would not change one minute of my life because it has turned out to be an awesome adventure full of great people, lots of travel and great memories!! So today I celebrate 29 years of a full life...and look forward to what is coming next!!!

10 TIPS BY DAVID

#1. Stand for something.

#2. Volunteer your time.

#3. No it's not all about you.

#4. Live a life you want to show your children.

#5. Go to a different religious service.

#6. Read...read, and read some more.

#7. Dream high, but be grounded.

#8. Apply to a college that may be a challenge.

#9. Challenge yourself.

#10. Pick good friends.

David L McMillan is a burn survivor, Eagle Scout, father of one and married. He is also a librarian at Caldwell College, doing his doctorate in historical studies at Drew University.

10 TIPS FROM A FIREFIGHTER

#1. Have fun. Do something exciting for yourself monthly.

#2. Enjoy life. Each day is a new beginning.

#3. Make a difference. Not only in your life but in the lives of others as well.

#4. Respect. You have to show respect in order for others to respect you.

#5. Patience. Things in life may not happen when you want them too but don't give up.

#6. Faith. Your faith in God will carry you where no one else can.

#7. Believe. In yourself so others will believe in you.

#8. Responsibility. Be responsible, take ownership for what you say and do.

#9. Pride. Take pride in who you are and the things you do.

#10. Love. One another it is the greatest gift of life.

James "Rambo" Smith www.TheSingingFiremanNC.com

10 TIPS FROM 2 MOMS AND 2 TEENAGE DAUGHTERS

#1. Don't go just for the hockey boys.

#2. Stereotypes exist for a reason. Be an original.

#3. Clean your room. It will avoid fights with your parents.

#4. Take the time to look your BEST, it will make you FEEL your best.

#5. Don't change yourself to fit in, find the right group, they will fit you.

#6. Listen to music beside the top 40's, it opens your horizons.

#7. Don't cling to others. Everybody needs some space including you.

#8. Learn to play an instrument and a new language.

#9. Talk to strangers and listen to them. You might learn something new.

#10. Putting others down will NEVER give you a leg up.

By **Mariana Konsolos,** Princess Florence Handbags

www.PrincessFlorence.ca

10 TIPS FOR TEEN'S EDUCATION

(An excerpt from the "Unlock Your Potential
Study Skills Program")

How do you, as a teenager, make a one size fits all school system work for you? If you are willing to take the time to develop a personal philosophy (i.e. who do I want to become), set some goals and then learn how to have the system work FOR you instead of against – NOW you are in the driver's seat ... I know, it is all one big game!

In school and beyond, this develops the foundation:

#1. Find out what your primary and secondary learning styles are. Students need to learn according to their preferred learning style in order to retain the information.

#2. Google "free learning style assessments" and do two or three of the different tests. (Never make assumptions based on one test.) Take the average of the three. You will either be an auditory, visual or kinesthetic learner.

#3. Given your learning styles – seek out a mentor/teacher to assist in developing strategies that will work for you. We all learn differently, so just simply re-reading notes or books is not going to work for all of us. There are many different ways to retain information; find out which one works for you!

#4. Your grades will likely fall within the average grades of the five people you hang out with most in school. Choose wisely.

#5. Set goals for YOUR future in terms of where you want to be when you complete your education. You do not need to know 100% what direction you are heading in however, thinking about your future on a regular basis will lay the foundation for what is yet to come. It is OK to change your plan multiple times; it is better than having no plan at all!

#6. Begin with the end in mind. Take your end goal and work backwards in terms of milestones you need to reach until you get back to where you are now. Make sure to think BIG! You deserve a bright future, however, it will only happen by putting action steps in place to get there!

#7. Build your "road map" based on your goals. Post it where you can see it.

#8. Control your time so you can control your productivity. (Great students have 24 hours in a day. Poor students have 24 hours in a day. The magic is not in the amount of time but how productive you become with the time you have. Same goes with life in general.

#9. Use the study strategies best suited for your learning style.

#10. Review your class information in the format you work best in once a day for each subject and you will not have to cram the night before an exam comes up.

BONUS TIP:

Approach an exam as an opportunity to prove what you know. Learn to "cycle or surf" the exam so you maximize your results. What I mean by that is go through the exam and mark all the questions "easy", "medium" and "hard". This should not take you very long however, by doing so, you will most likely score higher on your exam as more often than not you will find the answers to the harder questions within the "easy " and "medium ones."

My hope is that you find these tips helpful. A lot of my private students have increased their marks significantly by using some of the above tactics. And yes, it is true. You are unique and special and one of a kind. YOU deserve to have everything that YOU can do for YOU. So go out there and create a brilliant future for yourself!

Till we meet again,

Lani Donaldson is the inspirational leader behind two highly successful companies – Beacon Literacy and Engaged Educators. Along with her business partner, Yvonne Basten, Lani continues to empower and inspire others to greater heights. Her favourite quote: " Life's a contact sport – Get a Helmet!" pretty much sums up this woman's drive. Whether in the field of business or education, Lani is a sought after speaker, consultant, educator and mentor. Her mission: To make a positive, significant difference in the lives of others, so that they may impact tomorrow in a positive way. www.LiteracyCanada.com

10 TIPS TO "STOP THE DRAMA!"

#1. Speak from the "I" – Start your sentences with the words "I think..." "I feel..." "My experience was..." No one can *make* you feel anything. You get to choose. Speaking from the "I" will allow you to own your power during a conversation.

#2. Allow yourself space to feel - Don't let a conversation run away with you. Feel your emotions and label them with feeling words before words fly out of your mouth. This will keep you from saying things you will regret.

#3. Put your internal dialogue into words – We are always interpreting how someone says something, what their body language means and what we *think* they are saying. Let them know what is going on in your head. This will allow you to verify if you are right or ask for clarification if you are mistaken.

#4. Assume the positive - Most people are not out to get you. Believe everyone has a positive or at least neutral reason for what they are doing until you have an opportunity to ask them.

#5. Never make up why someone is doing something - It is impossible to observe why. You can see what someone does and how they do it but never why. To know why they have to tell you (which means you should ask).

#6. Avoid assuming you know how someone feels. You cannot observe how someone is feeling. You can only see the external symptoms of feelings. Your interpretations of those symptoms might be wrong.

#7. Know when to call an emotional time-out and use it. When a conversation gets to the point where it is doing more damage than good, take a break. Set up time to talk about it again later. Never let a topic get pushed under the rug and 'forgotten'.

#8. Set expectations. You cannot expect someone to meet a need you never told them you have.

#9. Celebrate and remember successes. Learn from and move past disappointments.

#10. Play life brave, not afraid - trying and failing is better than doing nothing.

Secrets adapted from the Seven No-Fail Secrets to Stop The Drama! and the Nine Secrets to Great Teamwork from the book *Stop The Drama! The Ultimate Guide to Female Teams* (www.StopTheDramaNow.com) by Dr. Robyn Odegaard.

Dr. Robyn Odegaard (aka Doc Robyn) is a nationally known speaker, author and consultant. She has a doctorate in psychology and is CEO of Champion Performance Development (www.ChampPerformance.com), an organization that enables her to combine her skills in executive coaching, organizational development, and sports psychology with her love for public speaking to show her clients how they can achieve success in every aspect of their lives. Doc Robyn founded the *Stop The Drama! Campaign*, authored the book *Stop The Drama! The Ultimate Guide to Female Teams* (www.StopTheDramaNow.com), and speaks at high schools and colleges to provide students the same skills that bring success to her business clients. She is a sought after expert in leadership, teamwork, communication and conflict resolution for radio, TV and print and is passionate about sharing high performance skills proven to assist teams and individuals in achieving the most from their potential. As an avid supporter of people who strive to attain the highest level of performance in their personal and professional lives, Doc Robyn lives by the motto, "Worst case, I want to be neutral to everyone I meet. My goal is to make a positive difference."

10 TIPS TO LETTING GO OF ANGER AND BITTERNESS

#1. Feel it fully. Before you can let go of any emotion you have to feel it fully. Find yourself a safe place and some private time, tell yourself this is a time for me to express my emotion over the situation, allow the feelings to fully come to the surface and really feel the full range of your feelings. This should be a timed exercise of no more than 5- to 10-minutes allow yourself to cry, to be angry, to express frustration, do be careful not to break anything.

#2. Give yourself a rant window. Let yourself vent for a day before confronting the person who troubled you. The feelings you have trapped inside you are like poison to your heart and soul. In order to cleanse yourself of it you must be able to get the words out. Find yourself a true friend that will allow you to vent your feelings and frustrations as often as you need to and for as long as you need to. Each person is different when it comes to the time needed to process through feelings. Some may get through their emotions in a few days, some may take a few months. If it is taking a long time to process, it may be wise to consider seeking professional assistance.

#3. Remind yourself that anger hurts you more than the person who upset you, and visualize it melting away as an act of kindness to yourself. I read a quote that said "Holding onto anger is like holding a hot coal, in the end you are the one who gets burned." While it is healthy to allow frustration and anger to flow through you so that you can release it, the side effect of holding onto those feelings by forcing yourself to continue to be frustrated or angry will only hurt you in the end far more than the person who actually instigated the anger in the first place.

#4. If possible, express your anger to the person who offended you. Communicating how you feel may help you move on. If the person that helped create these negative feelings is willing to be open to sit and talk with you to process through the emotions together then this would be a very helpful exercise for the both of you. You would be able to see that the feelings may come from something other than the issue at hand. Keep in mind that the other person may be too angry themselves to talk to you, therefore sometimes it is best just to deal with the emotions on your own.

#5. Take responsibility. Many times when you're angry, you focus on what someone else did that was wrong—which essentially gives away your power. If you can't accept that you were wrong you will find it much harder, if not impossible, to process through steps one and two. If you do not accept responsibility for your thoughts, words, and actions, you run the very real risk of placing yourself into victim mode. While in the process of playing the victim you will only succeed in pushing away friends and family and find that you will hold onto your anger. Doing so will generate a lower self-esteem which will only serve to perpetuate the victim role and make it harder to heal. Always take responsibility for your own words and actions no matter the situation.

#6. Put yourself in the offender's shoes. We all make mistakes. Have you ever heard the saying "Walk a mile in their shoes?" Before you start to pass judgment on another person, take a moment to step back and try to imagine how the situation is being perceived through their eyes. Take a moment to really feel what the other person may be feeling and why they may be feeling that way. How did you come across to them, what was your body posture like, your facial expressions, what was the tone and attitude of your voice, how could they have perceived the words you said? This tip will also help you process through tip number five. Compassion dissolves anger.

#7. Throw it away; Metaphorically of course. The purpose of this exercise is to distance yourself from your problems on a psychological level. An easy way to do this is to collect a bag of rocks, pull one of the rocks out of the bag, on the rock use a marker to write the name of one of your problems/issues on the rock then out loud say "goodbye (insert the name of the problem here)" then throw the rock as hard as you can. Be careful to do this in an open area where you won't damage anything, also make sure that the area you throw the rocks is such that you cannot retrieve the rock, as this would only serve in allowing them back into your life.

#8. Use a stress ball, and express your anger physically and vocally when you use it. This exercise works in connection with tip number one, allowing you to really feel the feeling. The difference with this tip is that you are going to allow yourself another safe way to express your frustration or anger without harming yourself or others. Make a scrunched up face and grunt when you squeeze the stress ball. You may feel silly, but this allows you to actually express what you're feeling inside in a physical way.

#9. Wear a rubber band on your wrist, and gently flick it when you start obsessing on angry thoughts. This is not something new, many people will talk about doing this and the reason is because it is a very effective tool. This tip helps you to simply force your mind to reprogram your neural pathways on a real level by forcing the energy in your mind to find a new pathway to travel instead of going through the middle of the issue. This trains your mind to associate that type of persistent negativity with something unpleasant.

#10. Remind yourself these are your only three options: Remove yourself from the situation, change it, or accept it. These acts create happiness, holding onto bitterness never does. This is something that should be done every morning. You can do this by going to your bathroom mirror looking into your own eyes and reminding yourself of these three options, while looking into the mirror you should also take this moment to say positive affirmations to rewrite those negative neural pathways with stronger positive ones.

These practical and simple tips are highly effective in helping you take the steps you need to move forward with your life and release any anger or bitterness that may be holding you back. I hope one day I get to meet you and see the wonderful positive person that I know you are. Live in gratitude and happiness every day.

By **Kevin Metz** kalmkevin@gmail.com www.UBCCanada.com

10 TIPS FROM A 17-YEAR-OLD

#1. Don't do drugs do HUGS!

#2. Being a teenager is like being on a Roller coaster. It has its ups and downs, but when you get through it, life will be the way you need it to be. Be yourself.

#3. Before you do something you don't want to do, think about it and realize where it will get you in the long run. You might be taking the wrong road.

#4. Self-esteem is listening to your inner core and hearing what it says to do, filling up your self-esteem bucket.

#5. If someone can't take you for who you are then they shouldn't judge you: they won't be good friends and will only stay for the wrong reasons.

#6. Be who you want to be and do not let anyone else tell you otherwise.

#7. Getting new friends is not as hard as people say it is, all you really have to do is be yourself and if they don't like it then you do not need them.

#8. Wanting to grow up fast and get your life on the go... it's not worth it. Live your age, you will grow up sooner or later.

#9. To have respect for someone else you need to have respect for yourself first.

#10. Treat someone how you want to be treated, it shows your real personality and who you are :)

Sherisse Janvier is a graduate of Amanda Welliver's Paradigm Esteem program and she is 17-years-old.

♥ ♥ ♥ ♥ ♥

10 TIPS TO BOUNCE FORWARD

Teachers come to us in many ways and in many forms. One of my best teachers was a dog. That's right! A 90 pound Chesapeake Bay retriever named Toby who we adopted from a local rescue organization. Toby hid my belongings, chewed his way out of a fenced yard, rearranged our furniture (weekly), emptied our closets all the time and even managed to destroy six (that's right....six!) toilet tank lids. But, we loved Toby and were committed to finding a way to help him.

We learned that Toby was a dog who needed a purpose... a dog that needed a job. Toby became a therapy dog volunteering for four years at a local hospital. In many ways he became my teacher. He helped me learn not to be a perfectionist, how important it is to be persistent in your goals and stay focused on what matters, how unconditional kindness and acceptance can change the world, and how to be patient. He inspired me to write not just one book, but many books, and he also taught me to "Bounce Forward" ™.

So my tips are those that I learned from a dog... How to Bounce Forward™ (not back) in life:

#1. Patience. Sometimes what you want in life (or think you want) takes time to create, build or achieve. Be patient with yourself and with others. Sometimes in the process of being patient, better opportunities show up for you.

#2. Persistence. People often give up on their goals, just before they cross the finish line. Persist towards that which is important to you.

#3. Possibility. It doesn't always have to be perfect.... maybe it just needs to be possible (or PAWsible). Take your dream or goal, and ask yourself "what could this look like if it was super-sized?"

#4. Praise others. When you are a champion for others, they often become a champion for you. Your kind words could impact someone's life in a positive way and perhaps even more than you will ever know.

#5. Purpose. What puts a bounce in your step? What is it that you love to do? Spend time being "on purpose."

#6. Practice being your best version of you. What does your best version of you look like? Sound like? Every day focus on being your best you!

#7. Problem solve instead of problem create. When faced with a challenge, change or dilemma, look for solutions (instead of other problems), ask others for help, and think about what you DO want, not what you DON'T want.

#8. Plant seeds of forgiveness. Life happens. Sometimes you make a mistake. Sometimes others make a mistake that impacts you. Learning to forgive yourself is an important part of bouncing forward. When you are able to forgive yourself, you learn how to forgive others.

#9. Personal and professional relationships that are healthy, respectful, and safe are so important. Set boundaries in your relationships, and associate with people who lift you up instead of bring you down.

#10. Pay it Forward! You may have heard the saying Pay it Forward.... Well we call it PAWing it Forward. Toby showed kindness, unconditional love, and patience with everyone he met. Every act of kindness that **you** pay forward makes a big shift in the world...and it comes back.

Known as the Bounce Forward™ Expert, **Charmaine Hammond** helps people live inspired and resilient lives. She is a professional speaker, best-selling and award winning author of many books including *On Toby's Terms, Bounce Forward, Toby The Pet Therapy Dog & His Hospital Friends*, and co-author of *GPS Your Best Life- Charting Your Destination & Getting There In Style*. You can find out more about Charmaine, Toby, and her books at www.ontobysterms.com and www.hammondgroup.biz

♥ ♥ ♥ ♥ ♥

10 TIPS BY TRACY

I'll keep it short because who wants to listen to some old lady go on and on spouting advice, right?! ;)

#1. We control only two things in life: our choices and our attitudes. Nobody can make us do or feel a certain way without our permission.

#2. Habits (good or bad) are developed over time. Choose wisely which habits you want to live with. Chances are, they'll be around a while!

#3. Each day is full of beauty, even if you have to look a while to find it. It all depends on which filter you use to get the desired effect; kind of like posting a picture on Instagram. Same picture (life), different look (outlook).

#4. Smile, even if you don't feel like it. ESPECIALLY if you don't feel like it! Plaster that big grin on your face and then look in the mirror to see how silly you look. Just trust me on this one. It works!

#5. Your parents will always forgive you for the crazy stuff you do. Tell them. How they choose to react is up to them. At least you all know you've been honest and trustworthy.

#6. If you want to be inspired, volunteer with the poor, the sick, the disabled. They'll show you what TRUE strength is!

#7. Alone is not a terrible thing to be. When else can you have a heart to heart conversation with yourself?!

#8. Remember that, twenty years after high school, the quiet kid that everyone ignored or made fun of will almost always be the most successful person in life.

#9. Fitting in doesn't make you stand out. Forge your own trails! Be the trend-setter!

#10. Adults often don't know all the answers. Teach them well, with patience and understanding. We're often programmed with an outdated operating system and we forget to check for upgrades.

So there you have it. For what it's worth... My ten cents!

Tracy Meyn, www.TracyMeyn.com

10 TIPS FOR FORGIVENESS

HANDSOME, BEAUTIFUL AND HATRED DON'T MIX

Did you know it's impossible to be handsome, beautiful and hateful at the same time? Did you know that dark negative emotions affect the way we appear and act on the outside? In other words, our inner thoughts and attitudes are visible in our appearance and in our actions.

I met Gregg after he'd been in prison more than 20 years. One day he felt comfortable in sharing the story of what lead to his imprisonment.

Gregg was 15, intelligent, handsome, tender-hearted and very creative; but he was angry, bitter and hated the fact that his mother had remarried.

His younger siblings were sweet and innocent, and they never seemed to get into trouble like he did. It seemed like his mother was at him all the time: "Clean your room; do your homework; clear the table; pick up your clothes." He felt like she was always on his back about something. Every time he looked at his mother, hatred boiled up inside. His brow furrowed in a frown, his mouth curled in disgust and his stomach churned. Whenever he saw his step-father's gaze of disapproval his eyes immediately went to the floor, hoping to escape the pain of condemnation. He'd go to his room, slam the door and not come out for hours, not wanting to hear another command or see the disdain in his step-father's eyes.

In his room, over and over he'd rehearse the list of things his mother had said or done that hurt, made him angry or upset. As he rehearsed these sometimes small and insignificant things, they became larger and he became even angrier, bitter and filled with rage. One day he couldn't stand the pain one minute longer.

In a moment of white- hot rage, he did the unthinkable. He killed his mother, stepfather and younger siblings!

"If only someone had told me I didn't need to hang on to all that bitterness, I may not have done such a horrible thing! I didn't know how to forgive and let go of the hurt, the hate and bitterness."

Gregg's story is almost unreal, but it is true. His handsome, tender-hearted creativity were masked by the anger that over shadowed everything he did and said. We all want to be loved and accepted and we all have a longing to be seen as handsome or beautiful, but the feelings and attitudes we hold on the inside will be reflected in our appearance and our actions.

It is vital that we learn to forgive and let go of the hurtful things that happen. That doesn't mean that what happened was ok, it just means we are making a choice to not hang onto hurtful comments or events.

#1. Admit you've been hurt or that you've hurt someone else. We can only heal from those things we acknowledge. Hiding or ignoring it will only create more pain.

#2. Identify the feelings you are experiencing. The most common are anger and fear. You may also feel sad, humiliated, rejected, accused, resentful or shame.

#3. Recognize you may be "stuck" and unable or unwilling to move on from the hurtful situation. We often get stuck in anger or fear. The anger may be about something that happened or a person who hurt us. We may be worried that we can't make it through or that the hurt will happen again and again.

#4. Make a CHOICE to get "Unstuck" from the emotion that continues to resurface. If you don't know how to get unstuck, take some action: seek help, read a book, do some writing or talk with a trusted friend or counselor.

#5. Identify what you lost in the hurtful situation. A list of losses may include loss of trust, respect, reputation, friendship, relationship, a loved one, a family or marriage, a dream, physical ability or even one's self-respect.

#6. Grieve what you've lost. You may need to give yourself permission to "feel the loss or pain", and to express the sadness, disappointment and regret or other emotions. Processing loss may result in tears or angry thoughts. Verbal discussion or writing about the losses can be very helpful.

#7. Have compassion for yourself and for the one who has hurt you. Be patient and compassionate with yourself. Find a small amount of compassion for the person who hurt you. They too may be "stuck" in their own painful story, acting and reacting to their own world of pain. Compassion for the other person does not mean you're ignoring or condoning what they did, you're just realizing they may be hurting too, and hurting people often go on to hurt others.

#8. Let go of the things you cannot change. We can't change what has happened. We can only change our response. Let go of the losses and harmful emotions you are hanging on to. Burn them. Bury them. Throw them in a lake or river. Release your hold and don't pick them up again!

#9. Forgive yourself and others. Say, "I choose to no longer hold onto you or to the hurtful thing(s) that happened. I forgive you (or myself) for what has happened". Forgiveness will never excuse or erase what happened, but it will free you from the negative emotions surrounding the event.

#10. Experience the freedom and peace. Letting go of the lingering anger and resentment or the shame and guilt of the particular circumstance is like laying down a heavy burden you've struggled to carry. The heavy load is gone! It's over! What's past is past! Say, "I'm moving on!" Allow yourself to feel the release. At last the chains of bitterness have been broken. Rejoice in your new found freedom! Celebrate the feeling of peace and joy that comes over you as you realize that at last you're free!

Annette Stanwick, BScN © 2012
International Speaker, Coach, Freedom Facilitator and
Award-winning Author of Forgiveness: The Mystery and Miracle
www.annettestanwick.com

10 TIPS FROM TRACI

When I was a child, I loved ballet. I was gifted; it came naturally and easily to me. Nothing in the world could compare to the feeling of being in that place of ease, grace, and flow.

Unfortunately, a few others didn't see things in the same light. As I naturally excelled in my gift of dance, others chose to retaliate. To some, jealousy and envy can rear its ugly head and cause conflict, negative actions and negative behaviour.

Every spring we would put on a spring concert; it was our annual ballet. It was a beautiful time to step into our gifts and share them with an audience. Unfortunately, moments before going on stage, someone stole items of mine. In one case it was my costume, which was later found thrown in the trees behind the school. Another time it was my pointe shoes, later found in the toilet. I was devastated. 'Who would do this? Why would someone do this? What did I do wrong? 'These were all thoughts that raced through my mind.

From those early experiences, I developed an extreme sense of low self-worth and self-esteem. In addition, I learned not to step into my own greatness for fear of retaliation from others.

I remember going to school every day wondering if today was the day when others would like me and be nice was or if it was going to be one of those days when I wouldn't feel accepted. In the years to follow, most of the choices and experiences I lived through were based on this extreme lack of self-worth.

I focused on the 'outer shell', hoping that if I looked good THEN others would like me. I would then be good enough. I experienced many abusive and dysfunctional relationships in search of someone's love. Anyone's love. If someone loved me THEN I would also be good enough. I worked hard in order to excel in what I was good at, believing that if I did well, THEN others would love me. All the while, never feeling good enough and ultimately never finding what I was looking for. All the positive attention in the world was never enough, I was never enough.

When I reached my 40's things began to change. After living a life of fear, lack, and a constant internal struggle, I began to feel a shift; whispers would come to me, ideas, and hints. It was time to heal.

Over the following nine years I learned to follow my heart and soul. I learned to detach from a false sense of self, into a beautiful and magical way of 'being'. I shifted from fearing myself and others, into loving and respecting myself and others. The fear was gone. Love remained.

You are a divine being, a soul who has arrived on this earth with a purpose. What is that purpose? It is to be YOU. You bring something to this world that no-one before you ever has, and no-one after you ever will. You cannot be duplicated. You are a true masterpiece!

My words of wisdom for you are:

#1. Surround yourself with positive and joyful people. You will lift each other higher and attract more of the same.

#2. Always know there are people who love you dearly. Be smart about your choices. Be good, be safe, be careful ... and have fun!

#3. Nothing lights up a room more than your joyful smile.

#4. Your youth and energy bring joy to others.

#5. The good, bad, and ugly are all learnings. Embrace them. Learn to love your journey.

#6. Every choice has value. When faced with decisions, ask yourself 'How do I want things to be?'

#7. Follow your gut feeling. It is there for your greater good. It will always lead you in the right direction.

#8. Love yourself, you are worthy of all the unconditional love this world has to offer.

#9. Step into your greatness. Let your light shine.

#10. You are a miracle. You have infinite value. You are a masterpiece.

Traci Sparling is the go to Self-Care Coach for women who want to embody their Sassy, Sexy and Soulful selves to the fullest. Through trial and error, love and heartbreak, joy and disappointment, Traci has truly lived many lives within her 50 years.

As an entrepreneur, single mom and grandmother, Traci has experienced firsthand the many challenges women face in living one's passion through the principles of self-care, self-love and self-respect.

While millions share Traci's life experience in silence, she chooses to expose them. Showing women of all ages, races and physical abilities that they too can conquer anything life puts before them, all while gracefully embracing the deeper learnings of each individual experience.

Through her tremendous strength, courage, and uncompromising faith and self-love, Traci is a true symbol that we can embrace the life we love and not have to choose between our favorite high heels and our yoga mat! www.TraciSparling.com

10 TIPS TO USING FACEBOOK EFFECTIVELY

Facebook was created to connect the world. It makes it easier for us to stay connected and know what is going on with those people who are important to us. It also allows us to reach out and connect with people we might not know.

Facebook is more than just a way to stay connected. Facebook is a window into the character and values of each individual and for today's youth that responsibility needs to be considered seriously. With an increase in cyber bullying and teenage suicide there is more at stake than just a Facebook status update. Along with university and job applications around the corner, your online reputation is more important than you might think.

Facebook does not govern behavior. There is no moderator that comes along and whispers in your ear "That post might not be a good idea if someone is considering hiring you" or "What you just wrote is hurtful and you should apologize." Each person is in complete control of what they communicate and even if you think something is gone because you pressed the "x" button, the damage may already be done.

#1. Does it pass the mom test? The next time you press the submit button on a post, ask yourself, "What would mom say?" If it is something you would be embarrassed to show your mom, rethink what you are about to post. This is the NUMBER one tip you should consider every time you update Facebook. WWMS?

#2. Is that photo really okay? There are millions of photos uploaded to Facebook daily. Mobile phones have allowed us to share life experiences instantly with the click of a button. Some of the types of photos you should really think about before posting are: Nude or almost nude photos, drunken party pictures, or party pictures that show drugs.

Some may suggest this is common sense behavior but I see these things on Facebook all the time. Young girls standing in front of a mirror barely dressed, snapping a picture of their new womanly body. I also see drunken party pictures that show you doing things you would not have done had you been sober.

The problem with doing this is, later on when you are trying to get a job, someone is going to look at those photos. The question you should be asking yourself is, "Would I bring these photos to the most important job interview of my life?" If not – don't post them.

You might be thinking "Yabbut my profile is private; no one can see that stuff." If you have friends, your profile is not completely private. You don't know who your friends know, and how easily hiring managers access Facebook photos when it comes to doing a reference check. In some cases, your Facebook profile is checked out prior to you being called in for an interview. And if someone else shares a photo of you and tags you, their privacy settings might be set to public making it that much easier for people to peak into your Facebook world.

#3. Is that language appropriate? The words you use matter and often just like in email, we interpret tone and meaning in the words we read. When your language is filled with f-bombs and other colorful words you are once again making an impression to the world.

This time it may not just be a hiring manager looking at your profile. It might be the teacher in charge of making the cut on a team or deciding on the leading role in a play and they need to decide if your online behavior is an asset or a liability to them. If you cannot use judgment online – what might you be like on the team? Choose your words carefully. Not only when it comes to profanity but when it comes to proper spelling and grammar.

#4. Am I engaging in wall to wall fighting? You have probably seen this happen to someone; you might have done it or had it happen to you too. Truth: wall to wall fighting is petty and dumb.

You might think you look cool and courageous but what you are really doing is alienating yourself from your friends because none of them want to "get into it" with you on Facebook for fear of the Facebook Fight. Once again, you have and always will have an audience. The reputation that you are building is sticky, it is not easy to shed.

#5. Am I judging or bullying and could I regret this? It's easy to hide behind a computer screen and type mean things. It is much harder to say those same words when you are face to face, belly to belly, eye to eye with another person.

In real life, you can see the emotion and hurt on someone's face and often know when enough is enough. On Facebook it's easy to be tough and mean spirited. And don't think people don't understand when you speak in code and use initials and made up words to make a point.

We all see it and know what is happening. The really big problem is kids are killing themselves over the pressure of how they are being treated online.

Do you really want to push someone to even think about suicide because you have been so mean and nasty to them? Have you considered what happens to you should that happen? Be the nicer person. Look out for others when you see them being picked on and offer encouragement and support. Don't be that person everyone is intimidated and afraid of.

#6. Is my opinion expressed correctly? We all have opinions and we love to share them on Facebook. Sometimes the things we share might be a bit too open and should be discussed with your parents or BFF, not on Facebook.

Be conscious of what you say and how you are perceived and ask yourself, is this really my opinion or am I just looking for attention? Would you want to be on the local news with your parents defending that opinion or is it just a whim and something you thought would be funny? Your opinions, expressed publicly, cause others to form opinions about you and your character. Are you expressing the ones that cause you to be perceived the way you want to be perceived?

#7. Do I know my privacy options? Log out of Facebook and then Google your name plus Facebook. See how others can view your profile and determine if your privacy is set up the way you would like it to be.

You can configure your privacy settings so all anyone else can see is your profile picture and timeline cover photo. Spend some time understanding the control you have and make sure your cell phone number is private so you don't end up with texts from strangers.

#8. Block mean people relentlessly. If someone is bothering you on Facebook block them. You do not have to be friends with anyone. You can block them if they are upsetting you in any way. It is YOUR Facebook and you should not let others upset you by feeling pressured to keep them as friends.

If someone is harassing and mean – tell your parents. There are laws around cyber bullying and speaking up is often all you need to do in order to make it stop. If you don't want to involve your parents for some reason – block them, easy to do.

#9. Guard and change your password frequently. Use a password with numbers and letters that only you can figure out and don't share it with your BFF. This is one of the easiest ways to get your account hacked and your reputation ruined.

When someone else has access to your Facebook, they can pretend they are you and do things that have a negative impact on your reputation. Sometimes it can be hard to get people to believe it wasn't actually you who did it.

#10. Remember to always log out. When you use Facebook on a public computer, always log out and clear history if you can. If you use Facebook on your mobile phone, be sure to have a password on your mobile phone so if you lose your phone, people cannot access your private information. Sounds simple enough but phones are lost all the time and this is how people get access to your Facebook and your personal pictures. Keep it private, put a lock on it!

My final thought - All of your activity on Facebook is open to perception. Everything you do creates your online reputation. The good news is you are 100% in control of everything you do and with some careful thought put into what you post you can have a reputation that opens doors to job interviews, has teachers raving about you and a background you can feel proud of.

Lisa Larter helps entrepreneurs, authors, small businesses and corporations build relationships with their customers through social media so they can drive traffic and increase sales. Often, she is the strategist who helps them figure it all out. You could say she is a serial entrepreneur with hard-hitting impact. She is known for her no-nonsense approach to helping business owners and executives drive results through solid strategic planning, social media, and customer experiences.

She coaches clients to maximize sales and grow their business using social media, relationships, systems and technology. By utilizing best practices, her clients master how to immediately implement a plan to maximize their brand, increase sales and exponentially grow the platform from which their business operates. www.LisaLarter.com

10 TIPS ON MAKING A GOOD IMPRESSION

#1. Be on time. There's nothing more disrespectful than being late for meetings, appointments, or dates. Being late says "Your time means nothing to me." Being on time, every single time, says "You are important to me."

#2. Look them in the eye. The most basic form of meaningful human contact is to simply look someone in the eyes. That doesn't mean stare or never look away. Eye to eye contact is a great way to connect.

#3. Handshakes still count. Especially with adults, your handshake is a big part of your first impression. The best handshake is firm, without being too much of a squeeze.

#4. Dress appropriately. Whether it's a job interview, meeting a new teacher, or going on a date, just use common sense and wear clothing that makes sense. If you want to make a statement about who you are, with what you wear, that's fine. Just think it through.

#5. Ask questions. Make it about them before you make it about you. Ask a question or two early on to demonstrate that you are interested in the other person. By the way, you can't fake being interested. Either you are or you aren't, and if you aren't, you won't make much of an impression.

#6. Don't dominate the conversation. Let everyone else talk as much as you are talking. Some people are so in love with the sound of their own voice that they simply shut everyone else down.

#7. Know what's going on in the world. Read a little bit of everything. The other person has interests, and if you can join them in informed conversation about their interests, you definitely make a positive impression.

#8. Find personal interests in common. If you see something that indicates to you what the other person is interested in, like a t-shirt from a particular school, strike up a conversation about it. Create common bonds with common interests.

#9. Spread your attention around. If you're with a group, don't focus on one person to the exclusion of everyone else. Spend time and attention on everyone.

#10. Make a great final impression. If you've had a good time, say so. If the other person has done something for you, say thank you. Leave them thinking, "I like that person."

Joe Calloway is a performance coach and advisor who helps great companies get even better. He helps organizations focus on what is truly important, inspires constant improvement, and motivates people to immediate action. Joe has been a business author, coach, and speaker for 30 years and his client list reads like an international Who's Who in business, ranging from companies like Coca Cola and IBM to Saks Fifth Avenue and American Express.

Joe is the author of four ground-breaking business books including *Becoming A Category of One: How Extraordinary Companies Transcend Commodity And Defy Comparison*, which received rave reviews from The New York Times, Retailing Today, Publishers Weekly and many others.

Joe is a guest lecturer at the Scarlett Leadership Institute, and has served on the faculty of the Center for Professional Development at Belmont University. Joe is a popular speaker for business meetings and events, and he also works with clients to help them achieve specific results and improvements in exclusive 90 day advisory programs. www.JoeCalloway.com

10 TIPS FROM A MATCHMAKER

#1. Love yourself. The teenage years can be tough since hormones and the ego are in charge. In our younger years it's all about fitting in, what's cool, how we look and how others perceive us. As we get older, we come into our own and value ourselves more for our individuality. If you can work on that now, and raise your self- esteem, you will glide through life with grace and ease, instead of flying by the seat of your pants trying to please everyone else.

#2. Learn how to save money. When we are young, we feel like we have all the time in the world and we can be reckless and everything will work out in the end. But guess what? Time flies, and fast! If you can get a handle on saving for the future, you will be way ahead of those airheads that will end up in credit card debt barely scraping by on their salary from some fast food joint, while you are writing them postcards from your holiday in Paris while strolling through flea markets finding treasures for your beautiful home on the lake.

#3. Save the drinking for later. I know, you feel all grown up already and chomping at the bit to start doing grown up things. But, if you suddenly find yourself in the middle of an episode of "Mad Men," know that the next stop could be juvi hall or rehab and then you won't be able to enjoy that occasional martini or glass of chardonnay in Paris when you are 21 ..... ever... without relapsing and ending up in a ditch somewhere behind a bowling alley.

#4. Be a bookworm. Books are cool. You can travel the world within the pages of a book. A book will keep you company when you are lonely, a book will give you knowledge, make you laugh and cry. Books rule!

#5. Nurture your creativity. Life is sweet when you can escape the pressures of life to go paint a picture, write a poem, play an instrument, or knit a scarf. Let your passion shine through and share your gifts with the world. Justin Bieber posted videos on youtube of himself singing and the rest is history.

#6. Eat your veggies. Guess what? Veggies DO taste good. In our society, lazy people have tried to make it cool to eat crap. Be an original and respect your body, it is an amazing machine made of stardust. It deserves the best fuel and plenty of water. Processed food full of chemicals and fat will make you fat and stupid.

#7. Keep an open heart. Bullying seems to be at an all-time high. I was bullied as a child and nothing feels worse than to dread going to school. Before thinking of putting another person down or hurting their feelings, put yourself in their shoes. How would you feel?

#8. Don't let a breakup break you. With hormones raging, a break up can seem like the end of the world. Trust me, you WILL find love again. Enjoy the fun times you spend with the opposite sex, but know that everything is exaggerated at this tender age. Find solace with your friends, family and your creativity. Find a new hobby, a new passion and throw yourself into it.

#9. Learn a new language. Being bi-lingual is super cool, and it helps keep your brain fit. Remember, when you are in Paris shopping at flea markets with the money you saved instead of buying that tenth video game or hundred dollar sneakers, you can converse with the locals in francais.

#10. Be an original. When I was a kid, I had bright red hair. BRIGHT red. The only people who appreciated it were old ladies and my parents. So of course kids called me names. When I came home crying to my mother, "mom, Stacey called me carrot top!" My mother said, "she's just jealous because she has mousey brown hair." I realized that was true. Redheads are only 2 to 3 percent of the world population. I was indeed unique and special. I felt SO lucky that I didn't have plain old brown hair. Whatever is different about you is your gift. Treasure it.

Marla Martenson is a professional matchmaker, life coach and speaker. Marla is the author of two relationship advice books. *Excuse Me, Your Soul Mate Is Waiting* and *Good Date, Bad Date* and two memoirs, *Diary of a Beverly Hills Matchmaker* and *Hearts On The Line*.

She has appeared on countless radio and TV shows including the Today Show, WGN Chicago Morning News, San Diego Living, Urban Rush and Better TV. Marla lives in Los Angeles with her husband, composer, Adolfo Jon Alexi. You can find out more about Marla at www.MarlaMartenson.com

♥ ♥ ♥ ♥ ♥

TEN TIPS FROM RENEE

#1. Stand up for yourself, politely.

#2. Bullying is BS. There is always someone more powerful.

#3. Books are as precious as people. Treat them well.

#4. Volunteer! The feeling that you get, is like no other!

#5. Mix colours, you don't need to be matchy matchy.

#6. Get over stereo types, I did, and I made a best friend!

#7. If you're stressed to the max, TALK to Someone. You would be surprised how much better you'll feel.

#8. Tell the truth.

#9. Having the trust of others is a priceless gift! Help people learn; to trust you.

#10. Learn to dance. You'll find out why.

Renee HolBrook is the proud mother of two young adult children. She's been in the business of communicating for over 20 years; and is the CEO of her own company, Expertly Speaking. Renee helps people find the right words, to get their message across with impact. No matter what the business or personal need is, she'll get the words right out of your mouth. www.ExpertlySpeaking.com

10 TIPS FOR TEENAGERS FROM LISA

Life is full of options and recommendations. So many people in your life will have an opinion about the way you should be and what you should or should not do in various circumstances. Sometimes it can seem complicated to choose what to do and what is right for us. Sometimes it can be a challenge to avoid comparing yourself to others, and focus on being the most amazing and authentic you that you can be! There are 10 things you can choose to do to focus on your possibilities, your purpose and your potential as you make decisions each day.

#1. Choose to make time in your life to spend time doing what makes you happy. What do you love to do? Life gets busy & time can fly by. Find time for what you enjoy so that you live your life fully with purpose.

#2. Choose a career that is right for you. Think carefully about what you want to do for a career and take time to research your options. Choose something that will make you happy, using natural skills you love to use. This will bring you much more joy and success than choosing a career because it is what you think others want you to do. It is OK to develop new interests, change your mind and try something different along the way.

#3. Continue to set realistic and challenging goals. Commit to working hard toward what is important to you each day and your determination will produce progress.

#4. Be willing to continue learning and trying new things and more opportunities will open up for you. Find positive, successful mentors to help guide you to accomplish great things!

#5. Keep your focus on enthusiastically achieving your goals. Mistakes will happen along the way, learn from them and keep going. Achievements take time. Focus on what you CAN do and choose to stay positive.

#6. Surround yourself with people in all areas of your life who respect you, value you, encourage you and please do the same for them.

#7. Be kind and remember to help others along the way, and you can have an amazing day every day! It feels fantastic to put a smile on someone's face. You can also volunteer and help your community or special charities of interest.

#8. Finish today, and each day, with what you are grateful for. Tomorrow is another day with new adventures and possibilities.

#9. You are the best person to be who you are! Trust yourself and be true to the most exceptional you that you can be. Your unique combination of qualities makes you awesome.

#10. This is your life. Choose to love yourself always and take conscious responsibility for creating an amazing life every day.

Known as the 'Reframing Expert', **Lisa Litwinski** helps people to choose their way to higher levels of success and fulfillment. She works with people to 'Increase Your Deserve Level' at work and in life, and helps organizations to engage healthy, collaborative teams. Lisa has trained thousands and coached hundreds on their value, impact and capacity to create positive results. She is a Professional Speaker, Team-Building Facilitative-Trainer and the Creator of *Today, I Choose*™ daily inspirational cards for intentional growth and results. You can find out more about Lisa, her products and services at www.litpathlearning.com or www.litpathlearning.com/products

"You Deserve to Choose to be True to Yourself Each & Every Day." ~ Lisa Litwinski

10 QUOTES FOR TEENAGERS

I am presenting my list by way of quotations that guide my daily thoughts and actions. I hope they can guide and motivate you as well. An additional way to use these motivational tips is to read and learn more about the person quoted.

#1. *"Act as if what you do makes a difference. It does"* ~ William James

#2. *"I am not what happened to me; I am what I choose to become."* ~ Carl Gustav Jung

#3. *"It is no use walking anywhere to preach unless our walking is our preaching."* ~ Francis of Assisi

#4. *"Here is the test to find whether your mission on earth is finished. If you're alive, it isn't."* ~ Johan Sebastian Bach

#5. *"Ask not what the world needs. Ask what makes you come alive ... then go do it. Because what the world needs is people who have come alive."* ~ Howard Thurman

#6. *"You can have everything in life that you want if you just give enough other people what they want."* ~ Zig Ziglar

#7. *"You don't have to see the whole staircase, just take the first step"* ~ Martin Luther King

#8. *"People are made to be loved and things are made to be used; there is much chaos in this world because things are being loved and people are being used."* ~ Unknown

#9. *"It's never too late to be what you might have been."* ~ George Eliot

#10. *"Your life is your message."* ~ Eknath Easwaren

And three more for good measure:

"Remembering that you are going to die is the best way I know to avoid the trap of thinking that you have something to lose - you are already naked...there is no reason not to follow your heart" ~ Steve Jobs

"We all must all suffer one of two pains: the pain of discipline or the pain of regret. The difference is discipline weighs ounces while regret weighs tons." ~ Jim Rohn

"What if you woke up today with only the things you thanked God for yesterday?" ~ **Unknown**

Malcolm Dayton has been a licensed counselor and certified coach for more than twenty-five years. Due to multiple sclerosis and immune disorder, he closed his private practice and brought his work online. Malcolm specializes in working with the heart-centered (but, technically-challenged) solopreneur by way of:

FULLIVING™ Optimal Performance for the Solopreneur (http://fulliving.com), and *Enlightened eBusiness Creations* (http://enlightenedEbusiness.com) for online branding, website and mobile design & development, and social media marketing. MalcolmDayton@EnlightenedEbusiness.com

Simply Focused Photography
780-217-8088

Celebrating the baby boomer woman

The
Fabulous@50
Martini

Every good martini should have flavour, sparkle and something to make
your lips pucker. Ingredients: Plenty of fabulous women 40-60.Vibrant
website with blogs, a marketplace and a free newsletter.
Diamond membership with gifts and benefits. Be Fabulous!
Magazine, with stories on fashion, food, travel, sex,
finances for the baby boomer women.
Fabulous@50 Experience & Martini
Party - a tradeshow with a twist.
Put all the ingredients into
a mixing glass filled
with happiness,
stir for 30
seconds.
Strain
into an
abun-
dantly
chilled
martini
glass,
add a
dash
of fun,
and
gar-
nish
with
inspi-
ra-
tion,
grati-
tude, and a splash
of love and kindness.

www.fabulousat50.com

259

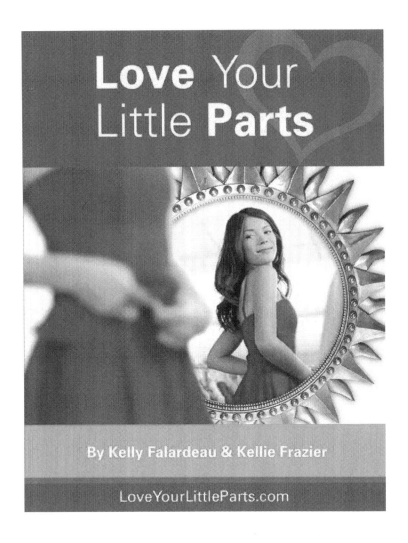

Love Your Little Parts

By Kelly Falardeau & Kellie Frazier

LoveYourLittleParts.com

Kelly Falardeau and Kellie Frazier collaborated to create an amazing program for women to learn how to create their own self-worth.

**For more information, go to
www.LoveYourLittleParts.com**

To order Kelly's books:

"No Risk No Rewards" or *"Self-Esteem Doesn't Come in a Bottle"*, go to: www.KellyFalardeau.com or search on Amazon.com

ABOUT KELLY

Kelly Falardeau is an author, entrepreneur and a motivational speaker and now a recipient of the Queen Elizabeth II Diamond Jubilee medal.

Friends, family and those who have worked with Kelly all say that Kelly doesn't let fear stop her – when she wants to achieve something, she just does it. They also say that the fact that Kelly is a burn survivor since she was two-years old is so motivating because she does not let circumstances dictate her success.

At 21, she was nominated and won the position of President of the Alberta Burn Rehabilitation Society. As a kid, she also won the 4-H Most Improved Member award plus various public speaking awards and even the fastest senior typist award in high school.

Kelly has been featured on TV in Canada such as Global TV Edmonton and Calgary, CTS TV, CTV TV, Breakfast TV, Access TV, CBC, A-Channel and CFRN. She has also appeared as a guest on a various radio shows too. Articles have been written about her in the Edmonton Woman Magazine, Edmonton Examiner, Edmonton Journal, Edmonton Sun, Pioneer Balloons Balloon Magazine and she also won the MOM Executive Officer award from the Mom Magazine.

Kelly was chosen amongst thousands to present her business to the Dragons for the Dragons' Den television series plus won the "Fierce Woman of the Year 2010" award. Kelly was selected out of 1500-women to compete in the Every Woman model search competition, sponsored by Fashion Has No Borders. She faced her fear of being judged by her appearance and walked the runway and won the Peoples' Choice award.

She is a sought-after international speaker because of her ability to engage others. She is able to move audience's emotions and make them see how a bad situation can become a great one. She will have you crying, laughing and dancing in your chairs as she shares her many stories about '*No Risks, No Rewards*' or going from '*Near Death to Success*' or '*Self Esteem Doesn't Come in a Bottle.*'

To book Kelly for your next event visit her website at: www.KellyFalardeau.com

Made in the USA
Lexington, KY
20 November 2012